New Casebooks

POETRY

WILLIAM BLAKE Edited by David Punter
CHAUCER Edited by Valerie Allen and Aries Axiotis
COLERIDGE, KEATS AND SHELLEY Edited by Peter J. Kitson
JOHN DONNE Edited by Andrew Mousley
SEAMUS HEANEY Edited by Michael Allen
PHILIP LARKIN Edited by Stephen Regan
DYLAN THOMAS Edited by John Goodby and Chris Wigginton
VICTORIAN WOMEN POETS Edited by Joseph Bristow
WORDSWORTH Edited by John Williams
PARADISE LOST Edited by William Zunder

NOVELS AND PROSE

AUSTEN: *Emma* Edited by David Monaghan
AUSTEN: *Mansfield Park* and *Persuasion* Edited by Judy Simons
AUSTEN: *Sense and Sensibility* and *Pride and Prejudice* Edited by Robert Clark
CHARLOTTE BRONTË: *Jane Eyre* Edited by Heather Glen
CHARLOTTE BRONTË: *Villette* Edited by Pauline Nestor
EMILY BRONTË: *Wuthering Heights* Edited by Patsy Stoneman
ANGELA CARTER Edited by Alison Easton
WILKIE COLLINS Edited by Lyn Pykett
JOSEPH CONRAD Edited by Elaine Jordan
DICKENS: *Bleak House* Edited by Jeremy Tambling
DICKENS: *David Copperfield* and *Hard Times* Edited by John Peck
DICKENS: *Great Expectations* Edited by Roger Sell
ELIOT: *The Mill on the Floss* and *Silas Marner* Edited by Nahem Yousaf and Andrew Maunder
ELIOT: *Middlemarch* Edited by John Peck
E.M. FORSTER Edited by Jeremy Tambling
HARDY: *Jude the Obscure* Edited by Penny Boumelha
HARDY: *The Mayor of Casterbridge* Edited by Julian Wolfreys
HARDY: *Tess of the D'Urbervilles* Edited by Peter Widdowson
JAMES: *Turn of the Screw* and *What Maisie Knew* Edited by Neil Cornwell and Maggie Malone
JOYCE: *Dubliners* Edited by Andrew Thacker
JOYCE: *Ulyssess* Edited by Rainer Emig
LAWRENCE: *The Rainbow* and *Women in Love* Edited by Gary Day and Libby Di Niro
LAWRENCE: *Sons and Lovers* Edited by Rick Rylance
TONI MORRISON Edited by Linden Peach
GEORGE ORWELL Edited by Bryan Loughrey and Graham Holderness
SHELLEY: *Frankenstein* Edited by Fred Botting
STOKER: *Dracula* Edited by Glennis Byron
WOOLF: *Mrs Dalloway* and *To the Lighthouse* Edited by Su Reid

(continued overleaf)

DRAMA

BECKETT: *Waiting for Godot* and *Endgame* Edited by Steven Connor
APHRA BEHN Edited by Janet Todd
REVENGE TRAGEDY Edited by Stevie Simkin
SHAKESPEARE: *Antony and Cleopatra* Edited by John Drakakis
SHAKESPEARE: *Hamlet* Edited by Martin Coyle
SHAKESPEARE: *Julius Caesar* Edited by Richard Wilson
SHAKESPEARE: *King Lear* Edited by Kiernan Ryan
SHAKESPEARE: *Macbeth* Edited by Alan Sinfield
SHAKESPEARE: *The Merchant of Venice* Edited by Martin Coyle
SHAKESPEARE: *A Midsummer Night's Dream* Edited by Richard Dutton
SHAKESPEARE: *Much Ado About Nothing* and *The Taming of the Shrew*
  Edited by Marion Wynne-Davies
SHAKESPEARE: *Romeo and Juliet* Edited by R. S. White
SHAKESPEARE: *The Tempest* Edited by R. S. White
SHAKESPEARE: *Twelfth Night* Edited by R. S. White
SHAKESPEARE, FEMINISM AND GENDER: Edited by Kate Chedgzoy
SHAKESPEARE ON FILM Edited by Robert Shaughnessy
SHAKESPEARE IN PERFORMANCE Edited by Robert Shaughnessy
SHAKESPEARE'S HISTORY PLAYS Edited by Graham Holderness
SHAKESPEARE'S PROBLEM PLAYS Edited by Simon Barker
SHAKESPEARE'S ROMANCES Edited by Alison Thorne
SHAKESPEARE'S TRAGEDIES Edited by Susan Zimmerman
JOHN WEBSTER: *The Duchess of Malfi* Edited by Dympna Callaghan

GENERAL THEMES

FEMINIST THEATRE AND THEORY Edited by Helene Keyssar
POST-COLONIAL LITERATURES Edited by Michael Parker and Roger Starkey

New Casebooks Series
Series Standing Order
ISBN 0–333–71702–3 hardcover
ISBN 0–333–69345–0 paperback
(outside North America only)

You can receive future titles in this series as they are published by placing a standing order. Please contact your bookseller or, in case of difficulty, write to us at the address below with your name and address, the title of the series and the ISBN quoted above.

Customer Services Department, Macmillan Distribution Ltd
Houndmills, Basingstoke, Hampshire RG21 6XS, England

New Casebooks

DRACULA

BRAM STOKER

EDITED BY GLENNIS BYRON

palgrave
macmillan

First Published 1999

Published by
PALGRAVE MACMILLAN
Houndmills, Basingstoke, Hampshire RG21 6XS and
175 Fifth Avenue, New York, N.Y. 10010
Companies and representatives throughout the world

PALGRAVE MACMILLAN is the global academic imprint of the Palgrave
Macmillan division of St. Martin's Press, LLC and of Palgrave Macmillan Ltd.
Macmillan® is a registered trademark in the United States, United Kingdom
and other countries. Palgrave is a registered trademark in the European
Union and other countries.

ISBN-10: 0–333–71615-9 hardback
ISBN-13: 978-0-333-71615-1 hardback
ISBN-10: 0–333–71616–7 paperback
ISBN-13: 978-0-333-71616-8 paperback

This book is printed on paper suitable for recycling and made from fully
managed and sustained forest sources. Logging, pulping and manufacturing
processes are expected to conform to the environmental regulations of the
country of origin.

A catalogue record for this book is available from the British Library.

First published in the United States of America 1999 by
ST. MARTIN'S PRESS, LLC.,
Scholarly and Reference Division,
175 Fifth Avenue, New York, N.Y. 10010

ISBN 0-312-21828-1

Typeset by EXPO Holdings, Malaysia

Transferred to digital printing 2003

Printed in Great Britain by the MPG Books Group, Bodmin and King's Lynn

Contents

.

Acknowledgements

The editor and publishers wish to thank the following for permission to use copyright material:

Stephen D. Arata, for 'The Occidental Tourist: *Dracula* and the Anxiety of Reverse Colonization', *Victorian Studies,* 33:4 (1990), 621–45, by permission of the Trustees of Indiana University; Nina Auerbach for material from *Our Vampires, Ourselves* (1995), Ch. 2, pp. 63–85, by permission of the University of Chicago Press; Elisabeth Bronfen, for material from *Over Her Dead Body: Death, Feminity and the Aesthetic* (1992), pp. 313–22, by permission of Manchester University Press; Christopher Craft, for '"Kiss Me with Those Red Lips": Gender and Inversion in Bram Stoker's *Dracula',* *Representations,* 8 (1984), 107–12, 116–30. Copyright © 1984 by the Regents of the University of California, by permission of the University of California Press on behalf of the Society for the Study of Social Problems; David Glover, for material from *Vampires, Mummies, and Liberals: Bram Stoker and the Politics of Popular Fiction* (1996), pp. 136–51. Copyright © 1996 Duke University Press, by permission of Duke University Press; Judith Halberstam, for material from *Skin Shows: Gothic Horror and the Technology of Monsters* (1995), pp. 86–106. Copyright © 1995 Duke University Press by permission of Duke University Press; Franco Moretti, for material from *Signs Taken for Wonders: Essays in the Sociology of Literary Forms* (1983), Ch. 3, pp. 83–5, 90–8, by permission of Verso; Rebecca A. Pope, for 'Writing and Biting in *Dracula',* *LIT,* 1 (1990), 199–216, by permission of Gordon and Breach Science Publishers; David Punter, for material from *The Literature of Terror: A History of Gothic Fictions from 1765 to the Present Day* (1980) Longman, Ch. 9, pp. 256–63, by permission of Addison Wesley Longman; Phyllis Roth, for 'Suddenly Sexual Women in Bram

Stoker's *Dracula'*, *Literature and Psychology*, 27:3 (1977), 113–21, by permission of the author.

Every effort has been made to trace the copyright holders but if any have been inadvertently overlooked the publishers will be pleased to make the necessary arrangement at the first opportunity.

General Editors' Preface

The purpose of this series of New Casebooks is to reveal some of the ways in which contemporary criticism has changed our understanding of commonly studied texts and writers and, indeed, of the nature of criticism itself. Central to the series is a concern with modern critical theory and its effect on current approaches to the study of literature. Each New Casebook editor has been asked to select a sequence of essays which will introduce the reader to the new critical approaches to the text or texts being discussed in the volume and also illuminate the rich interchange between critical theory and critical practice that characterises so much current writing about literature.

In this focus on modern critical thinking and practice New Casebooks aim not only to inform but also to stimulate, with volumes seeking to reflect both the controversy and the excitement of current criticism. Because much of this criticism is difficult and often employs an unfamiliar critical language, editors have been asked to give the reader as much help as they feel is appropriate, but without simplifying the essays or the issues they raise. Again, editors have been asked to supply a list of further reading which will enable readers to follow up issues raised by the essays in the volume.

The project of New Casebooks, then, is to bring together in an illuminating way those critics who best illustrate the ways in which contemporary criticism has established new methods of analysing texts and who have reinvigorated the important debate about how we 'read' literature. The hope is, of course, that New Casebooks will not only open up this debate to a wider audience, but will also encourage students to extend their own ideas, and think afresh about their responses to the texts they are studying.

John Peck and Martin Coyle
University of Wales, Cardiff

Introduction

GLENNIS BYRON

The vampire has many powers, but in one respect is not completely free. 'He cannot', as Van Helsing explains, 'go where he lists; he who is not of nature has yet to obey some of nature's laws – why we know not. He may not enter anywhere at first, unless there be someone of the household who bid him to come.'[1] *Dracula*, now over 100 years old and never out of print since its publication in 1897, has always been given free rein over the popular imagination, and our fascination with Stoker's King Vampire today shows little sign of waning. Film-makers and writers continually resurrect the count, infusing him with fresh blood, producing and reproducing new variations that simultaneously feed and create a seemingly insatiable public appetite. No other monster has endured, and proliferated, in quite the same way – even if we now seem to prefer interviewing, rather than staking, our vampires.

It is only over the last 25 years, however, that *Dracula* has begun to attract much serious critical attention. During the early twentieth century, discussions of the Gothic, the genre with which *Dracula* is most closely identified, were found mainly in historical surveys of the novel; here it would be relegated to the realm of 'popular fiction', fascinating – a curiosity – but peripheral to the main line of development traced through the 'realist' novel. The subsequent shift in values and perspectives implicit in new theoretical developments, however, has challenged traditional notions of the canon, expanded the horizons of critical study, and moved previously marginalised works into the critical arena.[2] The vampire, finally, has been invited into the classroom.

GOTHIC TRANSGRESSIONS

With the late-nineteenth-century publication of such novels as Robert Louis Stevenson's *Dr Jekyll and Mr Hyde* (1886), Oscar Wilde's *The Picture of Dorian Gray* (1891), and Bram Stoker's *Dracula* (1897), the Gothic figures of the double and the vampire re-emerged to establish themselves in their most enduring form as potent literary myths. A time when boundaries were crumbling, the empire in decline, the comfortable middle-class family and its values threatened by forces from both within and without, it is not so surprising that, as David Punter observes in *The Literature of Terror*, the Victorian *fin de siècle* saw 'a burst of symbolic energy as powerful as that of the original Gothic'.[3] The Gothic exposes and explores the desires, anxieties, and fears that both society and the individual, in their striving to maintain stability, attempt to suppress; it is interested in the exploration of what is forbidden, in the dissolution of certainties, categories; above all, it is associated with transgression. Not only do the texts themselves, in crossing the boundaries of the 'real', transgress, but transgression is a central focus of the Gothic plot: all barriers are broken down, all secret spaces penetrated.

Dracula clearly belongs to the Gothic in its association with the disruption and transgression of both social and psychic limits and boundaries. The count himself, confounding all categories, can be seen as the ultimate embodiment of transgression: as shapeshifter he has no stable fixed identity; as 'vampire' he straddles the boundaries between life and death; as 'undead' he is both absent and present. He is, indeed, as many first time readers of *Dracula* are surprised to find, quite literally as absent as he is present. Although central to the initial episode in Transylvania, he all but disappears after arriving in London and then finally emerges again back in Transylvania only to be destroyed. For much of the novel he is little more than a troubling telepathic presence in Mina Harker's mind, causing conflict even within, to use Van Helsing's words, this 'sweet, sweet, good, good woman' (p. 308). In the context of transgression, this is particularly appropriate: while the vampire himself embodies transgression, he is, even more importantly, also the catalyst which releases subversive disruptive desire in others. When Arthur Holmwood says of Lucy, 'There is something preying on my dear girl's mind' (p. 109), he unconsciously puts his finger on the real nature of the threat posed by Dracula: it is more than just bodies that he penetrates and disturbs.

It is this experience of transgression which accounts for the various Gothic effects found in *Dracula*: for the pleasure and for the anxiety and horror which inform the responses of the characters and vicariously, perhaps, the readers. Pleasure is produced by the freedom from constraints consequent upon transgression, from the release of energies and desires normally repressed in the interest of both social and mental stability. David Punter (essay 1) has shown how Lucy, attempting to describe her vague memories of an encounter with Dracula while sleepwalking, expresses the joy attendant upon the liberation from the conventional self in a series of images of the unconscious: the leaping fish, the howling dogs, and the sense of sinking into deep green waters; she experiences previously unrecognised sensations that can only be expressed in terms of contradictions, as something 'very sweet and very bitter' (p. 98). Jonathan Harker, who retains more conscious awareness as he yields to the forbidden delights of the three female vampires, knows he is doing something wrong. 'I felt in my heart a wicked, burning desire that they would kiss me with those red lips', he later confesses to his diary, and then adds: 'It is not good to note this down, lest some day it should meet Mina's eyes and cause her pain; but it is the truth' (p. 37). In 'a languorous ecstasy' (p. 38) he nevertheless succumbs to the 'wickedness'. As the fair girl 'went on her knees and bent over me, fairly gloating' and her churning mouth goes 'lower and lower', Harker waits in 'an agony of delightful anticipation' (p. 38) for the moment of penetration. A number of the essays in this collection comment on the wide range of taboos being broken, boundaries transgressed, in this passage; perhaps the least of the 'wickednesses' is that, as Stephen King trenchantly observes, 'In the England of 1897, a girl who "went on her knees" was not the sort of girl you brought home to meet your mother.'[4]

Transgression, as Fred Botting suggests and the characters' responses confirm, is 'ambivalent in its aims and effects'; it produces not only pleasure but simultaneously anxiety and fear by projecting 'an uncontrollable and overwhelming power which threatens not only the loss of sanity, honour, property or social standing but the very order which supports and is regulated by the coherence of those terms'.[5] What is specifically at stake in *Dracula* is the undermining and blurring of all the psychic and social categories upon which the security and comfort of the middle-class Victorian world depend. And so Lucy, when her conscious self regains control, is 'full of vague fear' (p. 108), while for Harker, even as he yields, the experience is not only thrilling but also repulsive, the breath of the woman both honey-sweet and bitterly offensive. The encounter causes him to question his sanity, and hoping 'that I may not go mad, if, indeed, I be not mad already', feeling 'as though my own brain was unhinged' (p. 36), he turns to record his experience in the diary which offers him the seeming fixity of the text, an opportunity to reaffirm his sense of a stable identity: 'accurate' recording is called upon to re-establish threatened categories.

Even more than fear and anxiety, transgression produces horror. Julia Kristeva speculates that in our culture what causes abjection (horror or revulsion) is 'not lack of cleanliness or health ... but what disturbs identity, system, order. What does not respect borders, positions, rules.'[6] Consider the reactions of the men when Dracula forces Mina to feed from an open wound in his breast. Here the mother figure is being nurtured, not nurturing. Here the pure woman seems to have been surprised in a 'perverse' sexual act. This is, at least, certainly suggested by the space opened up when Mina breaks off her description of how he 'pressed my mouth to the wound, so that I must either suffocate or swallow some of the –' (p. 288). As an anonymous commentator dryly observes, 'Name your bodily fluid'.[7] Most transgressive of all, perhaps, is Mina's shocking admission: 'strangely enough, I did not want to hinder him' (p. 287). The men react with horror to the disruption of categories, the confusion of boundaries, the undermining of all the middle-class values they hold so dear, and part of the horror is directed at Mina, for her apparent complicity, for the momentary lapse which allows the emergence of her own transgressive desires.[8] No matter how sweet and how good they declare her to be, Mina must be punished and is branded with the sacred wafer, the red mark on her forehead functioning as a visible sign of transgression.

Gothic is consequently implicated not only in the transgression of limits, but also in the reconstitution of limits. Giving in to boundless freedom prompts fear and horror as well as pleasure: the vampire must be destroyed, boundaries reconfirmed, Mina returned to her proper role as nurturing mother, full of 'sweetness and loving care' (p. 378). Both social and psychic order must be restored. The most widely discussed scene in Stoker's novel brutally enacts this reconstitution of boundaries. Once a barely repressed sensuality is released, the vamped Lucy becomes flagrantly carnal, sexually aggressive, a voluptuous, seductive, wanton 'nightmare of Lucy' (p. 214). This metamorphosis is reversed only when she is forcibly reminded of who holds the power to penetrate by her fiancé Arthur: egged on by his watching friends, he repeatedly pounds in the 'mercy-bearing stake', and the writhing, quivering body beneath him is released from the grip of desire to become again 'Lucy as we had seen her in her life, with her face of unequalled sweetness and purity' (p. 216). The violent climax releases 'holy calm', and the watching men smugly congratulate themselves, empathising with Arthur's ordeal: 'It had indeed been an awful strain on him' (p. 216). As Philip Martin notes, 'Male strength is thus set against the usurping female power'.[9] Although all female vampires are returned to conventional passivity by staking, it is notable that Dracula himself is destroyed not with symbolic penetration by the men, which would involve further transgression, but with a symbolic castration: he dies like a man.

As Christopher Craft (essay 6) observes, then, the movement found in *Dracula*, as in so many other Gothic texts, is that each 'first invites or admits a monster, then entertains and is entertained by monstrosity for some extended duration, until in its closing pages it expels or repudiates the monster and all the disruption that he/she/it brings'.[10] The ultimate restitution of conservative social order is, however, problematised. The boundary between good and evil, sanity and insanity, purity and corruption remains difficult to fix, and Gothic always questions the possibility of such clear distinctions; in place of clear-cut structural oppositions there is, Fred Botting writes, 'a play of ambivalence, a dynamic of limit and transgression that both restores and contests boundaries'.[11] The fundamentally oppositional terms depend upon each other; it is their ambivalent relationship that allows limits to be defined, or as Van Helsing puts it, 'it is not the least of its terrors that this evil thing is rooted deep in all good' (p. 241). The threatening other has not been destroyed, simply repressed once more. The degree to which *Dracula*, or indeed any Gothic text, restores and preserves ideology and the degree to which the monster remains a site of cultural resistance is difficult to fix.

THE FRAMEWORK OF THE DEBATE

While most of the critics represented in this collection agree in seeing Dracula as a transgressive force, the psychological or social significance they attach to him and the actual nature of the pleasures and anxieties he produces vary greatly, and one of the major debates in *Dracula* criticism has involved the specific nature of the threatening other which is both the embodiment and agent of transgression. David Punter (essay 1) identifies many of the basic issues with which the text engages and sets out the framework for most future debate about *Dracula* by indicating the two most fruitful avenues of interpretation. From a Freudian perspective, Dracula is the endless desire of the unconscious for gratification, while Van Helsing is those aspects of the ego which serve to repress this tendency towards disruptive self-fulfilment in the interests of maintaining social and psychological stability. From a Marxist perspective, Dracula is the final aristocrat, the tyrant seeking to preserve the survival of his house, while the vampire hunters embody the bourgeois family with all the solid, reasonable, and moral values of middle-class Victorian society. The two earliest essays reproduced in this collection, those of Phyllis A. Roth (essay 2) and Franco Moretti (essay 3), are the most influential interpretations, from, respectively, the Freudian and Marxist perspectives, to emerge from the initial critical reassessment of *Dracula* in the late 1970s.

Published one year after the term 'psychoanalysis' was introduced, *Dracula* engages with many of the current debates in the field of what was then more usually called 'mental physiology', the study of the workings of the mind. Seward, for example, studies madness and is concerned with the workings of the unconscious, drawing twice upon the term 'unconscious cerebration' then recently popularised by W. B. Carpenter in *Principles of Mental Physiology* (1874). The theory of 'unconscious cerebration' suggested that delayed or stalled impressions could become lost to 'conscious memory' and then later 'express themselves in *involuntary muscular movements*'.[12] As David Glover notes, 'there is no theory of repression at work in this psychology, but what is evident is a shift toward a heteronomous model of mental life in which the hidden levels or dimensions of the mind can hold surprising consequences for our conscious selves.'[13] The importance of dreams, somnambulism, hypnotism, and 'unconscious cerebration' to *Dracula* demonstrate that Stoker was as interested as Carpenter in the hidden dimensions of the mind.

The investigation of hysteria and the practice of hypnotism were a growing part of the movement away from a more materialist science. Van Helsing practises hypnosis and both he and Seward are familiar with Charcot, who used hypnotism in his treatment of hysterical symptoms in women at the Salpêtrière in the 1870s, pointing forward to Freud and Breuer's *Studies in Hysteria*, which appeared two years before *Dracula* was published. Stoker's characters – even the men – are repeatedly associated with reactions identified as 'hysterical'. In the notorious King Laugh scene, Van Helsing himself gives way 'to a regular fit of hysterics' (p. 174) when he responds to Lucy's burial with uncontrollable laughter; male hysteria, however, is normalised, acceptable as a spontaneous means of obtaining relief from strain, and always soon followed by a return to calm. Lucy herself is more the true hysteric. Women were always considered more neurally susceptible to strain and consequently more liable to hysteria. As Thomas Laycock, author of *Treatise on the Nervous Diseases of Women* (1840), observes in his later study of *Mind and Brain*, 'Woman, as compared with man, is of the nervous temperament. Her nervous system is therefore more easily acted upon by all impressions, and more liable to all diseases of excitement.'[14]

As Laycock's argument suggests, there was some reluctance to move completely away from a materialist explanation of behaviour, and this reluctance is also articulated in *Dracula*. The constant desire to find some 'functional cause' for Lucy's condition indicates an unwillingness to accept that 'it must be something mental' (p. 111). And while Dracula's ultimate defeat is in large part due to Van Helsing placing Mina into the hypnotic trance which allows her to connect with and track him, there is an equal reliance upon the more materialist science of physiognomy. On one level, then, there is an attempt to move away from the shadowy arena of the mind, and the attempt is understandable: the hypnotic trance involves a discomfiting fluidity, an undermining of the fixity of identity; physiognomy in contrast seems to offer a more reassuring way of locating and fixing lines of difference. The text nevertheless continues to subvert the validity of this 'science'; categories continually break down as the sleeping Lucy, 'with her face of unequalled sweetness and purity' (pp. 216–17), awakens to snarl and seduce, while the count, supposedly identifiable as a criminal type according to the classifications of Nordau and Lombroso, can still pass unnoticed amongst the crowds of Piccadilly. Lines of difference are not so easily stabilised. The unreliability of the material points forward to a necessary engagement with the fluidity of the unconscious.

Like Gothic fiction generally, *Dracula* is concerned with unconscious desires, with the release of what has been psychically repressed, and so, from the start, has inevitably been amenable to psychoanalytical readings, particularly those which focus on sexuality.

Although it has been suggested that all monsters can represent the terrifying form of sexual desire released from social and psychical repression, the bite and the blood, among other things, make the vampire myth a particularly resonant form of violent sexual fantasy. The earliest readings of *Dracula* were Freudian and, like much early Freudian criticism, tended to universalise the desires and fears that were identified. Drawing upon Freud's claim that 'morbid dread always signifies repressed sexual wishes', and noting that in 'the unconscious mind blood is commonly an equivalent for semen', Ernest Jones observes in *On the Nightmare* (1929) that the vampire superstition 'yields plain indications of most kinds of sexual perversions, and that the belief assumes various forms according as this or that perversion is more prominent.'[15] Noting the fixation on the oral and the merging of cruelty and greed with a possessive kind of love, early Freudian critics see the world of Dracula as the unconscious world of infantile sexuality and the text as giving free play to those desires unacceptable to society which the adult human must repress.

In 'The Psychoanalysis of Ghost Stories', Maurice Richardson, who memorably dubs *Dracula* a 'kind of incestuous, necrophilous, oral-anal-sadistic all-in wrestling match',[16] reads the text as a revelation of Stoker's own repressed anxieties and a 'quite blatant demonstration of the Oedipus complex' with Dracula as a 'father-figure of huge potency'.[17] For critics like Richardson, the key Freudian text was *Totem and Taboo*, the core fantasy of *Dracula* the struggle of the sons with the father for control of the women. Psychoanalysing the text of *Dracula* originally involved psychoanalysing the author, usually paying particular attention to Stoker's fixation with Henry Irving. In 'The Monster in the Bedroom', Christopher Bentley further argues that nothing in Stoker's work or life suggests he would have been aware of the sexual content of his book. In addition to the powerful constraints upon any author of the time, 'for many writers, including Stoker himself, an even stronger reason for avoiding sexual matters was a personal reticence amounting to repression'. What is consciously repressed 'appears in a covert and perverted form through the novel'.[18] Bentley then goes on to elucidate these perversions – and with some gusto. His article, as Stephanie Dematrakopoulos wryly observes, 'is, in fact, more titillating than the novel itself'.[19]

A crucial turning point in psychoanalytical readings of *Dracula* came with Phyllis Roth's 'Suddenly Sexual Women' (essay 2). Roth identifies the core fantasy as not oedipal but pre-oedipal, the central anxiety of the novel as the fear not of the father, but of the devouring mother, the figure represented by both women. Lucy, more sexual and therefore more threatening, must be destroyed; however, in order to assuage the anxiety caused by matricide, when the story is told again, Mina, less sexually threatening, more accepting, is saved. In identifying a horrific hostility towards women in the text, Roth established the basis for much further debate about representations of gender and sexuality.

In the excerpt from 'Dialectic of Fear' reproduced in this collection, Franco Moretti (essay 3) provides an example of the other avenue of interpretation suggested by David Punter. In contrast to Punter, however, who reads Dracula as 'the final aristocrat',[20] and the anxieties of the text as the anxieties of the middle class concerning the aristocracy they have displaced, Moretti argues that Dracula actually lacks all the qualities and values of the aristocrat and is rather 'a true monopolist'.[21] Moretti grounds his analysis in one of the many vampire analogies used by Marx, that 'Capital is dead labour which, vampire-like, lives only by sucking living labour, and lives the more, the more labour it sucks'.[22] Dracula is identified as an aristocrat only because the excessive form of capitalism he represents must be seen by a Victorian bourgeoisie, identifying itself with free trade and free competition, as foreign and feudal, something out of which their more advanced economy has emerged; they cannot recognise that 'competition itself can generate monopoly in new forms',[23] that Dracula may be their future rather than their past.

In Signs Taken For Wonders, the book from which this essay is taken, Moretti aims to analyse the way in which literature, and particularly popular fiction like Dracula, functions to effect the reader's consent to the dominant ideologies of society. While Roth sees the reader, like the male characters, identifying with the aggression projected onto the vampire, and the text as transgressive, for Moretti Dracula is ultimately conservative, prohibitive, 'professing to save the individual, it in fact annuls him';[24] thinking for oneself is nothing more than a danger the text strives to exorcise. In Moretti's reading of Dracula, the reader identifies with the narrators, their fear becomes the reader's fear, and it functions to reinforce and revalidate the ideological values threatened by the monster. 'The restoration of a logical order coincides with unconscious and irrational adherence to a system of values beyond dispute'; the reader ends 'coming contentedly to terms with a social body' which is in fact 'based on irrationality and menace'.[25]

DESTABILISING THE TEXT

Most subsequent criticism has been unwilling to accept that the text is quite as stable as the readings of Roth and Moretti might suggest. Poststructuralist theorists have found shifts and breaks within the text, and unmasked various internal contradictions and inconsistencies. Later materialist critics have questioned whether ideology is ultimately as coherent or even as persuasive as Moretti's reading would indicate, whether culture is quite so determined by the nature of the economic base, and whether the reader's opportunities for identification are as reduced as Moretti suggests when he argues that the reader is frightened into 'consenting' to the reinstatement of the ideological values initially threatened. Roth's identification of the narrative's hostility towards women has similarly been questioned, initiating a prolonged debate over whether *Dracula* should be read as misogynist or feminist, and whether Stoker was supporting or challenging the conventional Victorian middle-class view of women. It seems unlikely that this is a debate which will be resolved. While the women may eventually be violently returned to their 'proper' passive place in society and sexual threat dissolved into a sentimental vision of maternity, many feminist critics have noted that the text nevertheless also seems to celebrate the freedom and energy the women experience in being vamped and to offer a sympathetic reading of the limitations placed upon women by a society that so rigidly delimited gender roles.[26] When Van Helsing attempts to restrict Mina's participation in the hunt for Dracula, claiming there is 'no part for a woman ... her heart may fail her in so much and so many horrors' (p. 235), we can see how Mina, as woman, is being constructed through language to redefine masculine power and autonomy and to reassure that power of its illusory reality. But setting up woman as Otherness in order to guarantee the system is to set up not only difference to the norm of that order, but also excess of the order, that which exceeds signification, and this is also where Dracula is positioned. The men stop informing Mina of their activities, leaving her feeling frustrated, helpless, in the dark; this is an error: in the dark is exactly where the vampire is most likely to find her.

In a later Lacanian reading, Elisabeth Bronfen (essay 4), like Roth, focuses on the two women, but for Bronfen the theme of sexuality is advanced in *Dracula* to veil yet another concern: vampire lore becomes a trope for western attitudes towards death. And while

Bronfen, like Roth, traces a movement from disorder to a reinstatement of stability, she nevertheless suggests that such stability is ultimately undermined. The vampire, an undead body, disseminates an uncanny state of living-death with each bite. The responses to that death, she argues, can be divided in Lacanian terms into hysteric and obsessional discourse. Hysteric discourse, usually encoded as feminine, is associated with a celebration of duplicity and a fluid relation to the unconscious. This, Bronfen argues, is embodied in both Lucy and Mina after they are attacked, as they hover between life and death, conscious and unconscious states. Obsessional discourse, usually encoded masculine, is embodied in the vampire hunters. Aiming to fix the disruption of the symbolic by the semiotic, they strive to erect clear divisions in order to repress the void of death which is, in Lacanian terms, the end of the motivating principle in life, the end of desire. Their mission to stake the vampire becomes a trope for the fixing of the fluid ambivalent body to a stable signifier.

While both women oscillate between the conscious and unconscious self, Mina, who is from the start more rational, more clearly on the side of the symbolic, of the paternal law, resists the call of death; Lucy, who as her somnambulism reveals is troubled and restless even before Dracula's arrival, responds immediately to desire, to the call of the Other. She must be destroyed, the living and dead separated, and a canny image of difference reinstated. Mina, who participates in transcribing events, in turning the fluidity and horror of unconscious desires and dreams into supposedly semantically stable documentation, survives. The obsessional discourse of the vampire hunters is nevertheless ultimately undermined, Bronfen suggests. Not only does the entire text function to excite the imagination, drawing the reader into the realms of the Other, but the 'real', the authentic, continue to elude fixity in the mass of typewriting collected in which 'there is hardly one authentic document' (p. 378). The movement from sexuality in the Freudian readings to death in Bronfen's Lacanian analysis leads us ultimately, then, to a concern with textuality.

TEXTUAL ANXIETIES

In his foreword to the 1988 collection of essays on *Dracula* – Margaret Carter's *Dracula: The Vampire and the Critics* – William Veeder suggested that one of the new directions *Dracula* criticism might take would be towards a closer textual analysis, leading towards a clearer understanding of genre, the production of narrative, and the novel's preoccupation with textuality. For a long time, critics tended to avoid such subjects, considering, as Veeder observes, that Stoker was 'less an artist than an automatic writer'.[27] Complaints about Stoker's writing began with the first reviews. It is 'wanting in the constructive art as well as in the higher literary sense',[28] complained one anonymous reviewer of *Dracula*, and for a long time this set the tone for critical responses to the text. Even when Oxford University Press announced that *Dracula* was to be the one-hundredth title in its World Classics Series in 1983, the Press rather uneasily suggested that many of the other authors in the series, Dickens, James, Tolstoy, and the like, would 'no doubt turn over in their graves'.[29] A. N. Wilson did little to dispel this sense of uneasiness in his introduction as he attempted to justify *Dracula* as a 'classic', apologetically noting that indeed no one 'in their right mind would think of Stoker as "a great writer"' or Dracula as 'a great work of literature'.[30]

David Punter (essay 1), however, had already argued in 1980 that *Dracula* was indeed 'a well-written and formally inventive sensation novel',[31] and such critics as Carol Senf in '*Dracula*: The Unseen Face in the Mirror' (1979) and David Seed in 'The Narrative Method of *Dracula*' (1985) are among the many critics who have demonstrated just how careful a craftsman Stoker was. The anxious sense that *Dracula* is not a work of 'literature' nevertheless seems strangely persistent, continuing to underwrite many assessments of the novel. Even Maud Ellmann, whose essay replaces that of Wilson in the new Oxford edition, begins her introduction with the concession that it is, indeed, 'a creaky novel' written by a 'cack-handed narrator', even if this does 'nothing to diminish the fascination of the story', and she defends *Dracula* with the claim that 'For generations of readers who have found it un-put-downable, the novel wouldn't be so good if it weren't so very bad'.[32]

While there now seems little reason for critical anxiety over the status of the novel as literature, there is, nevertheless, certainly a textual anxiety in *Dracula* about its own status as writing. The story begins with a prefatory statement which claims that they have put together the papers

> so that a history almost at variance with the possibilities of latter-day belief may stand forth as simple fact. There is throughout no statement of past things wherein memory may err, for all the records

chosen are exactly contemporary, given from the standpoints and within the range of knowledge of those who made them.

The story ends, however, with Jonathan's note that 'in all the mass of material of which the record is composed, there is hardly one authentic document! nothing but a mass of type-writing, ... We could hardly ask anyone, even did we wish to, to accept these proofs of so wild a story' (p. 378). Whether this is factual, truthful, authentic, or simply a wild story is impossible to determine. The mass of typewriting that is collected in order to authorise the story as 'truth' is, ultimately, what undermines it. This anxiety over 'authenticity' suggested in Elisabeth Bronfen's essay has been further explored in various readings of *Dracula* which focus on its narrative production. In 'Writing and Biting in *Dracula*', Rebecca A. Pope (essay 5) suggests the text invites a Bakhtinian analysis. To demonstrate how the text plays out the tensions of the historical moment, she focuses upon the relations between gender and textuality, and Mina's role as the maker of texts. Pope's Bakhtinian reading uncovers conflicting ideologies, subversive voices which erupt to challenge traditional patriarchal structures in much the same way as Kristeva's notion of the semiotic, a violent force which disrupts the symbolic, or Lacan's reading of the 'real', that which is beyond semiotic, imaginary or symbolic categories. Mina's appropriation of textuality as a strategy of resistance may come to an end as she is finally reinscribed in terms of the traditional gender code as mother and homemaker, but her 'textual work' remains to subvert unities and hierarchies, and the 'polyphony of voices' is never subsumed into one transcendent authoritative voice. Pope's Bakhtinian framework is as suspicious as Bronfen's Lacanian analysis of finding any 'closure'.

VICTORIAN DIS-EASE: OTHERS AND OTHERING

Pope's attention to the specific moment of production is part of a more general move towards placing the novel in its historical context. As David Punter originally noted, Dracula is one of the most important expressions of *both* the social and psychological dilemmas of the late nineteenth century; what makes the text so distinctive is Stoker's location of psychological fears specifically within late Victorian society. While readings such as those offered by Roth and Bronfen have contributed immensely to our understanding of the psychic anxieties articulated by the text,[33] the most significant re-evaluation of *Dracula* was prompted by the movement during the seventies towards a concern with the historical, social, and political conditions and consequences of the production and interpretation of texts. New historicist readings in particular, juxtaposing *Dracula* with contemporary non-literary texts, emphasised its status as a peculiarly Victorian novel, engaging with many of the social anxieties of the day. One of the ways in which many of the critical essays reproduced in this collection are linked is in their concern with identifying the historically specific nature both of the threatening other and of the anxieties that this generates.

Perhaps most influential in directing attention to these anxieties has been Christopher Craft's seminal essay '"Kiss Me with Those Red Lips": Gender and Inversion in Bram Stoker's *Dracula*' (essay 6). Many readings of the disruption of gender roles in the novel focused upon the fear of aggressive female sexuality, the threat of the New Woman and her rejection of conventional feminine roles. Craft, however, beginning his reading with the scene of Harker's temptation, shows how it is also Jonathan's feminine passivity that engages with the anxieties of the time. This was not only the age of the New Woman, but also the time when society became more aware of homosexuality, when what was termed 'sexual inversion' first entered discourse in such texts as Symonds's *A Problem in Greek Ethics* (1883) and Ellis's *Sexual Inversion*, published but immediately suppressed in 1897, the year in which *Dracula* first appeared. For Craft, the fearful confusion of gender categories is embodied in the actual vampire mouth, the soft inviting orifice which delivers only a piercing bone. What is always threatened but never finally represented by the text is 'that Dracula will seduce, penetrate, drain another male' and 'this desire finds evasive fulfilment in an important series of heterosexual displacements'. *Dracula*, then, represents displaced homosexual desire. 'Men touching women touch each other', Craft observes, 'and desire discovers itself to be more fluid than the Crew of Light would consciously allow.'[34]

For queer and lesbian theory, which aims to break down barriers, merge categories, and elicit previously unthinkable transformations, the vampire has become a significant site of resistance. Richard Dyer offers a general reading of the manner in which the link between 'queerness' and vampirism is historically and culturally constructed. Significantly, with queer theory, the anxieties that pervade vampire fiction seem to dissolve; there is, he argues, an identification with the *vampire*, rather than a 'self-oppressive' siding with those characters who must expose and destroy what is threatening and 'queer'.[35] Vampiric activity is a source of pleasure; recognition offers identity. In this context, as Ken Gelder interestingly notes, the perspective of those 'for whom the vampire is that foreign Thing which produces "anxiety" when it comes close to us ... flatly reproduces the homophobic paranoia of Victorian vampire fiction's "paternal figures"'.[36]

The breakdown of traditional gender roles, the confusion of masculine and feminine, was seen by many Victorians as only one indication of a more general threat of cultural decay and corruption, of a more widespread degeneration of society. The discourse of degeneration spanned many fields, and the source of the supposed threat accordingly varied. As David Glover suggests, the various theories might be seen 'as a set of overlapping hypotheses competing with each other to define the true dimensions of the culture's crisis, its sources and parameters'.[37] The discourse of degeneration influences *Dracula* in many ways; Stoker even makes specific reference to two of the key figures in the debate: the criminologist Cesare Lombroso, who used phrenology to argue that habitual criminals were throwbacks to primitive races, and the doctor and journalist Max Nordau, whose *Degeneration* extended Lombroso's arguments and further attacked many contemporary writers, including Wilde and Ibsen, claiming artistic degeneration through excessive emotionality. According to Stephen Arata (essay 7), *Dracula* enacts late Victorian society's most important and pervasive narrative of decline: the narrative of reverse colonisation. The expansion of empire resulted in the subsequent entry of a wide range of peoples from different cultures, prompting a fear of racial degeneration, threatening the stability of identity. Dracula's plans for colonisation are quite clear: 'Your girls that you all love are mine already', he tells the vampire hunters, 'and through them you and others shall yet be mine – my creatures, to do my bidding and to be my jackals when I want to feed' (p. 306).

While many critics have contested earlier psychoanalytical readings, insisting on the need to restore Dracula to his historical context, others have focused on exploring the ways in which our historically specific readings of the text are actually generated. Nina Auerbach (essay 8) engages with such a position when she argues that we need to go beyond placing *Dracula* in the context of the late nineteenth century, that the nature of the threatening other can be best identified by seeing *Dracula* in the context of our own twentieth century. First, however, Auerbach considers earlier vampires to suggest that, by contrast, Dracula appears strikingly respectable. Arguing against the accepted notion that Dracula is both the embodiment of and catalyst for transgression, she claims that instead of blurring boundaries, he is obsessed with hierarchies, emphasising divisions, bound by endless rules and regulations. His life is highly regulated, and he is ultimately shown 'adhering to more taboos than he breaks'.[38] Here is 'vampire propriety'. The women he infects become similarly taboo bound. Lucy, for example, becomes far more virtuous in 'undeath' than in life; transformed from horrid flirt to dutiful wife, she finally directs her attention more properly only to her fiancé.

For Auerbach, Dracula also breaks with the tradition of earlier vampires, those who cultivated an insidious intimacy with their victims, by remaining aloof, alien, cold, and impersonal. In this sense, he becomes the embodiment not of the past, but of the future, a 'harbinger of a world to come, a world that is our own'. Dracula 'is the twentieth century he still haunts'.[39] The threatening other is us. This, she suggests, accounts for the way we have appropriated and transformed Stoker's creation. Unwilling to confront a disturbing reflection of ourselves, we transform an impersonal monster driven only by the desire for power and possession into the hero of romance.

Judith Halberstam's poststructuralist reading (essay 9) is less concerned with identifying the other than with identifying the actual process of othering. Like many critics, she connects Stoker's Dracula with the late-nineteenth-century construction of the monstrous Jew. Halberstam does not, however, draw upon the figure of the Jew in order to suggest the specific nature of the threatening other; this, indeed, she would see as reductive. Rather, Halberstam connects the myth of the vampire with late-nineteenth-century anti-semitic discourse to show their corresponding abilities to 'condense many monstrous traits into one body',[40] to make an argument about the very production of monstrosity. Wary of psychoanalytic readings that produce identity primarily as sexuality, Halberstam argues that monstrosity is never unitary, but always an aggregate of race, class, and gender, always condensing many monstrous traits into one body. As all threats, all fears about race, class, gender, sexuality, and empire, were embodied in the monster Jew produced by nineteenth-century anti-semitic discourse, so all threats, all fears, are embodied in Dracula. In projecting this multiplicity of others, Stoker's text, rather than simply constructing the other, subversively reveals the process of othering at work. Creating the monster, the narrative simultaneously draws attention to its constructed nature and reveals mechanisms of monster production. As Foucault argues, it is through discourse that the play of power is conducted in western societies; language is one of the material manifestations of the ways in which power is distributed on both the personal and the social level. Halberstam's analysis of these discursive conditions allows us to see just how the Other is constructed and positioned as both alien and inferior. Equally importantly, however, by demonstrating how subjectivities are *always* constructed, how all identities are positioned in language, *Dracula* ultimately also 'denaturalises in turn the humanness of its enemies'.[41] Their supposedly superior 'humanity' is, like the vampire's 'otherness', simply the product of an ongoing struggle in the discursive construction and reconstruction of power.

DRACULAS TODAY

'This was the being I was helping to transfer to London, where, perhaps for centuries to come, he might, amongst its teeming millions, satiate his lust for blood, and create a new and ever widening circle of semi-demons to batten on the helpless' (p. 51). The proliferation of vampires in the twentieth century would suggest that, in one sense, Dracula has indeed achieved what Jonathan Harker feared. The vampire has developed into a full-scale industry. In addition to the numerous rewritings of *Dracula* in both film and literature, consumer demand is met in increasingly inventive and profitable ways. Vampire sites run riot on the internet, offering copious amounts of information … and a plethora of products. Tours of key 'Transylvanian' sites can be obtained on CD. For a few thousand dollars one becomes the proud owner of a life-like wax Lestat doll – doubtlessly not to be kept too close to the fire. Vampire devotees with enough money to spend no longer need to be satisfied with ridiculous plastic teeth – a dentist can be found more than willing to fit them with some impressive 'real' fangs. While technology is appropriated in Stoker's text in the struggle to destroy the vampire, now it is simply used to sell him. He has been turned into moral philosopher, social rebel, and, above all, into the seductive lead in a sentimental romance. Our vampires are, above all, our lovers; they must offer great sex – an expectation unforgettably imaged in the heaving horde of Hammer bosoms – but also tenderness and love.

In recent times, the vampire has been most notoriously reconstructed as tender lover in Francis Ford Coppola's *Bram Stoker's Dracula*, the vampiric state of undeath appropriated to prove that, as the trailer to the film proclaimed, 'Love Never Dies'. Such reconstructions, however, pervade numerous twentieth-century vampire narratives, including Whitley Strieber's *The Hunger*, where it is never quite clear whether Miriam hungers most for blood or companionship; Todd Grimson's *Stainless*, where the love relationship between the vampire Justine and Keith, 'the human who looks after her',[42] blends Shakespeare with Stoker to concoct a tragic Romeo and Juliet for a postmodern age; and even vampire porn films like Jamie Gillis's *Dracula Exotica*, where the influence of true love turns Dracula from bat into dove.

Kathleen Spencer has noted that while the worlds of the seminal Gothic fictions of the late eighteenth century are 'traditionally distanced somewhat from the world of their audience, set back in time and "away" in space', late-nineteenth-century Gothic fictions like *Dracula* insist 'on the modernity of the setting – not on the distance between the world of the text and the world of the reader, but on their *identity*'.[43] If we were now to search for some general point that might distinguish late-nineteenth-century Gothic from that of the late twentieth century, we might suggest that the identity upon which we now insist is between the monster and ourselves. The 'most distinctive feature of the modern vampire myth' as David Glover (essay 10) observes, is 'the tormented humanisation of the nosferatu, which reverses the emphasis on the monstrous in texts like the original *Dracula* and brings them closer to us.' While in Stoker the primary psychological conflict is the struggle within the victims between their 'good and demonic selves', now 'it is the vampire itself who is torn between conflicting forces'.[44] This is forcefully confirmed by our two reigning queens of Gothic fiction: Anne Rice, whose vampires are sensitive aesthetes, agonising over moral questions, and Poppy Z. Brite, who despite producing some of the most coldly manic horrors of our *fin de siècle* in *Lost Souls*, focuses mainly on the adolescent conflict over identity caused by Nothing's gradual discovery of his true vampiric nature, a conflict so easily identified with by her readers. Vampires, these new writers seem to say, are us.

This treatment of the vampire, as David Glover demonstrates through his analysis of Francis Ford Coppola's *Bram Stoker's Dracula* and Dan Simmons's *Children of the Night*, seems to move towards a new humanism, a new myth that 'holds out the promise of a transcendence of petty historical and ethnic differences, subsuming them into a new liberal cosmopolitanism, a universalistic identity in which everyone can find their place'.[45] There is, as Todd Grimson's *Stainless* suggests, the myth of differences being dissolved, the hope that 'this chasm between oneself and all *others* can be momentarily bandaged, the wound can be healed'.[46] But this new myth, Glover argues, should not be too easily accepted, not without, at least, a recognition of what lies behind the construction of all such myths of transnational communities. The new humanist ideal can only be achieved by purging the marks of the beast from Coppola's vampire, by destroying the 'decadent' bulk of the *strigoi* in Simmons's *Children of the Night*. Such purging is 'of a piece with one of the cornerstones of racist doctrine'. Such myths are constructed by the ideological operation of separation: 'the sifting of an ideal humanity from the detritus of history, safeguarding it from an animal or tribal or degenerate past'.[47] Before we heal the chasm we must identify the separating boundaries, before we humanise we must identify what is inhuman. If, as Judith Halberstam suggests, Bram Stoker's *Dracula* denaturalises the human, then with our twentieth-century vampires we seem to want to 'humanise' the 'unnatural', apparently forgetting not just the instability of all such structural oppositions, but also the essentially conservative and separatist ideology that underwrites their construction.

NOTES

1. Bram Stoker, *Dracula*, ed. Maud Ellmann (Oxford, 1996), p. 220. All further references to the novel will be given in parentheses in the text.

2. See the Introduction to Fred Botting, *Gothic* (London, 1996).

3. David Punter, *The Literature of Terror: A History of Gothic Fictions from 1765 to the Present Day* (London, 1980), p. 239.

4. Stephen King, *Danse Macabre* (New York, 1981), p. 65.

5. Botting, *Gothic*, p. 7.

6. Julia Kristeva, *Powers of Horror: An Essay on Abjection* (New York, 1982), p. 4.

7. 'Passnotes', *The Guardian* (16 June 1997), p. 3.

8. In this context it is notable that, for Kristeva, abjection is additionally what emerges from unconscious responses to the pre-oedipal mother (*Powers of Horror*, p. 13).

9. Philip Martin, 'The Vampire in the Looking-Glass: Reflection and Projection in Bram Stoker's *Dracula*', in *Nineteenth-Century Suspense: From Poe to Conan Doyle*, ed. Clive Bloom et al. (Basingtoke, 1988), p. 84.

10. See p. 94 below.

11. Botting, *Gothic*, p. 9.

12. William B. Carpenter, *Principles of Mental Physiology* (London, 1874), p. 524.

13. David Glover, *Vampires, Mummies, and Liberals. Bram Stoker and the Politics of Popular Fiction* (Durham, NC, 1996), p. 77.

14. Thomas Laycock, *Mind and Brain*, 2 vols (Edinburgh, 1860), Vol. 2, p. 317.

15. Ernest Jones, *On the Nightmare* (New York, 1951), pp. 106, 98.

16. Maurice Richardson, 'The Psychoanalysis of Ghost Stories', *The Twentieth Century*, 166 (1959), 427.

17. Ibid., 427.

18. C. F. Bentley, 'The Monster in the Bedroom', *Literature and Psychology*, 22 (1972), 28.

19. Stephanie Demetrakopoulos, 'Feminism, Sex Role Exchanges, and Other Subliminal Fantasies in Bram Stoker's *Dracula*', *Frontiers*, 2:3 (1977), 105.

20. See below, p. 23.

21. See below, p. 47. Burton Hatlen, conversely, identifies Dracula with the lower classes and the threat of a revolutionary attack upon the privileged. See Burton Hatlen, 'The Return of the Repressed/Oppressed in Bram Stoker's *Dracula*', *Minnesota Review*, 15 (1980), 80–97.

22. Quoted in Moretti; see p. 45 below.

23. See p. 47 below.

24. *Signs Taken For Wonders. Essays in the Sociology of Literary Forms*, trans. Susan Fischer, David Forgacs, and David Miller (London, 1983), p. 107.

25. Ibid., pp. 107, 108.

26. For an excellent discussion, see Carol A. Senf, 'Dracula: Stoker's Response to the New Woman', *Victorian Studies*, 26:1 (1982), 33–49.

27. William Veeder, 'Foreword', in *Dracula: The Vampire and the Critics*, ed. Margaret L. Carter (Ann Arbor, MI, 1988), p. xiv.

28. *The Athenaeum* (26 June 1897), p. 835.

29. See James Twitchell, *Dreadful Pleasures: An Anatomy of Modern Horror* (Oxford, 1985), p. 127.

30. A. N. Wilson, intro., *Dracula* (Oxford, 1983), p. xiv.

31. See p. 22 below.

32. Maud Ellmann, intro., *Dracula* (Oxford, 1996), pp. vii–viii.

33. Bronfen does, in fact, consider the interrelationship between historical reality and cultural representation in other chapters of *Over Her Dead Body*, but the focus of her argument generally remains on the psychological.

34. See pp. 96, 115 below.

35. Richard Dyer, 'Children of the Night: Vampirism as Homosexuality, Homosexuality as Vampirism', in Susannah Radstone (ed.), *Sweet Dreams: Sexuality, Gender, and Popular Fiction* (London, 1988), p. 59.

36. Ken Gelder, *Reading the Vampire* (London, 1994), p. 64.

37. David Glover, *Vampires, Mummies, and Liberals*, p. 67.

38. Nine Auerbach, *Our Vampires, Ourselves* (Chicago, 1995), p. 85.

39. See pp. 146, 145 below.

40. See p. 174 below.

41. See p. 192 below.

42. Todd Grimson, *Stainless* (London, 1996), p. 1.

43. Kathleen L. Spencer, 'Purity and Danger: *Dracula*, the Urban Gothic, and the Late Victorian Degeneracy Crisis', *ELH*, 59:1 (1992), 200.

44. See pp. 210, 211 below.

45. See p. 212 below.

46. Grimson, *Stainless*, p. 198.

47. See pp. 213, 212 below.

1

Dracula and Taboo

DAVID PUNTER

Bram Stoker's greatly underrated *Dracula* is not only a well-written and formally inventive sensation novel but also one of the most important expressions of the social and psychological dilemmas of the late nineteenth century. For obvious reasons, the intellectual content of *Dracula* has not been taken seriously; yet it deserves to be, less because of any distinction in Stoker's own attitudes and perceptions than as a powerful record of social pressures and anxieties. It has always been a difficult book to place, largely because if one accepts the conventional view of the expiry of Gothic before the middle of the nineteenth century *Dracula* becomes a kind of sport; but in fact it belongs securely with *Jekyll and Hyde*, *Dorian Gray* and *The Island of Dr Moreau*, while transcending all of them in its development of a symbolic structure in which to carry and deal with contradictions. The use of the term 'myth' to describe a work of written literature is open to abuse, but if there is any modern work which fits the term adequately, it is *Dracula*, if on the grounds of reception alone.

At the heart of *Dracula* (if the pun may be forgiven) is blood. The vampire thrives on the blood of others, and the whole effort of Van Helsing and his colleagues is to fight this one-way flow of blood, by transfusion and any other possible means. 'The vampire live on', says Van Helsing in his broken English, 'and cannot die by mere passing of the time; he can flourish when that he can fatten on the blood of the living. Even more, we have seen amongst us that he can even grow younger; that his vital faculties grow strenuous, and seem as though they refresh themselves when his special pabulum is plenty. But he cannot flourish without this diet; he eat not as others' (p. 245). Here, as elsewhere in *Dracula*, is a religious inversion, brought out the more strongly by the biblical tone of Van Helsing's discourse: the blood is the life. Stoker is well aware of the rich possibilities for ambiguity and bitter humour in this central motif. When Van Helsing recounts the ship's captain's response to his vampire passenger, there is a vertiginous interplay of conventional swear-words and deeper ironic significance: Dracula

> give much talk to captain as to how and where his box is to be place; but the captain like it not and swear at him in many tongues, and tell him that if he like he can come and see where it shall be. But he say 'no'; that he come not yet, for that he have much to do. Whereupon the captain tell him that he had better be quick [*sic*] – with blood – for that his ship will leave the place – of blood – before the turn of the tide – with blood.
>
> (pp. 322–3)

But the blood which gives Dracula his life is, as usual in vampire legendry, not merely literal. Dracula the individual needs blood, but Dracula is not merely an individual; he is, as he tells Harker, a dynasty, a 'house', the proud descendant and bearer of a long aristocratic tradition. He recites to Harker a catalogue of the gallant feats of his ancestors, ending thus:

> when, after the battle of Mohács, we threw off the Hungarian yoke, we of the Dracula blood were amongst their leaders, for our spirit would not brook that we were not free. Ah, young sir, the Szekelys – and the Dracula as their heart's blood, their brains, and their swords – can boast a record that mushroom growths like the Hapsburgs and the Romanoffs can never reach. The warlike days are over. Blood is too precious a thing in these days of dishonourable peace; and the glories of the great races are as a tale that is told.
>
> (pp. 38–9)

The long historical progression of the bourgeoisie's attempts to understand the significance of noble 'blood' reaches a point of apotheosis in *Dracula*, for Dracula is the final aristocrat; he has rarefied his needs, and the needs of his house and line, to the point where he has no longer any need of any exchange-system or life-support except blood. All other material connections with the 'dishonourable' bourgeois world have been severed: the aristocrat has paid the tragic price of social supersession, yet his doom perforce involves others.

Cheated of his right of actual dominion, his power is exerted in mere survival: his relationship to the world is the culmination of tyranny, yet it is justified in that it is not his own survival that he seeks but the survival of the house, and thus, of course, the survival of the dead. Stoker brings out the ambiguity in the legends very well when Dracula tells Harker his history:

> In his speaking of things and people, and especially of battles, he spoke as if he had been present at them all. This he afterwards explained by saying that to a 'boyar' the pride of his house and name is his own pride, that their glory is his glory, that their fate is his fate. Whenever he spoke of his house he always said, 'we', and spoke almost in the plural, like a king speaking.
>
> (p. 37)

It is impossible to tell whether what is at stake is Dracula's personal longevity or his total identification with his line.

And if one looks again at the old legends themselves, what emerges as very obvious is that they were partly invented to explain the problem of the connection between aristocracy and immortality. To the peasantry of central Europe, it may well have seemed that the feudal lord *was* immortal: the actual inhabitant of the castle upon the mountain might change, but that might not even be known. What would have been known was that there was always a lord; that by some possibly miraculous means life and title persisted, at the expense, of course, of peasant blood, in the literal sense of blood shed in battle and in cruelty. Dracula can no longer survive on blood of this kind; he needs alternative sources of nourishment to suit his socially attenuated existence. The dominion of the sword is replaced by the more naked yet more subtle dominion of the tooth; as the nobleman's real powers disappear, he becomes invested with semi-supernatural abilities, exercised by night rather than in the broad day of legendary feudal conflict.

But thus far *Dracula* is merely another variant on the vampire legendry which we have already seen in John Polidori's 'The Vampyre' (1819), another modification of pre-bourgeois fears of tyrannical violence imaged in terms of the primal fear of blood-sucking. What makes *Dracula* distinctive is Stoker's location of this set of symbols within late Victorian society. Over against the 'house' which Dracula represents Stoker places the bourgeois family, seen around the moment of maximum bonding, on the eve of marriage. *Dracula* is a dramatised conflict of social forces and attitudes: opposite

the strength of the vampire we are shown the strength of bourgeois
marital relations and sentimental love, as in Mina's letter to Lucy
after her marriage to Harker.

> Well, my dear, what could I say? I could only tell him that I was the
> happiest woman in all the wide world, and that I had nothing to give
> him except myself, my life, and my trust, and that with these went my
> love, and duty for all the days of my life. And, my dear, when he
> kissed me, and drew me to him with his poor weak hands, it was like
> a very solemn pledge between us ...
>   Lucy dear, do you know why I tell you all this? It is not only because
> it is all sweet to me, but because you have been, and are, very dear to
> me. It was my privilege to be your friend and guide when you came
> from the schoolroom to prepare for the world of life. I want you to see
> now, and with the eyes of a very happy wife, whither duty has led me;
> so that in your own married life you too may be all happy as I am.
>
> (p. 115)

The list of structural oppositions is long. Dracula stands for lineage,
the principal group of characters for family; Dracula for the wild-
ness of night, they for the security of day; Dracula for unintelligible
and bitter passion, they for the sweet and reasonable emotions;
Dracula for the physical and erotic, they for repressed and eth-
erealised love. And at the kernel of this structure is embedded the
further opposition between Dracula and his arch-enemy Van
Helsing, who is imported to put a stiffening of science and reason
into the 'team':

> He is seemingly arbitrary man, but this because he knows what he is
> talking about better than any one else. He is a philosopher and a
> metaphysician, and one of the most advanced scientists of his day;
> and he has, I believe, an absolutely open mind. This, with an iron
> nerve, a temper of the ice-brook, an indomitable resolution, self-
> command, and toleration exalted from virtues to blessings, and the
> kindliest and truest heart that beats – these form his equipment for
> the noble work that he is doing for mankind – work both in theory
> and practice, for his views are as wide as his all-embracing sympathy.
>
> (p. 121)

Van Helsing is a superman, and therefore combines in himself a
number of contradictory qualities, but the emphasis in his character
is on order, neatness, reserve, in Freudian terms on those aspects of
the ego which serve the purpose of quashing the tendency towards
chaos and libidinal fulfilment which would otherwise disrupt social

and psychological organisation. Dracula's is the passion which never dies, the endless desire of the unconscious for gratification, which has to be repressed – particularly on the eve of marriage, of course – in order to maintain stable ideology. He is 'un-dead' because desire never dies; gratification merely moves desire on to further objects. There is, for Dracula as for the unconscious, no final satisfaction, for his very nature is desire.

Towards these structures the text manifests a socially revealing ambivalence. One of the aspects of decadence was the supremacy of the moment of attraction in the continual dialectic of attraction and repulsion which characterised the relation between the dominant middle class and its 'un-dead' predecessor. From the bourgeois point of view, Dracula is, like Schedoni, Frankenstein and Dorian Gray, a manic individualist; from his own point of view, which is not absent in the text, he is the bearer of the promise of true union, union which transcends death. From the bourgeois point of view, Dracula stands for sexual perversion and sadism; but we also know that what his victims experience at the moment of consummation is joy, unhealthy perhaps but of a power unknown in conventional relationships. Dracula exists and exerts power through right immemorial; Van Helsing and his associates defeat him in the appropriate fashion, through hard work and diligent application, the weapons of a class which derives its existence from labour. Lest some of this seem fanciful, we can cite some of Stoker's dream symbolism:

> I didn't quite dream; but it all seemed to be real. I only wanted to be here in this spot – I don't know why, for I was afraid of something – I don't know what. I remember, though I supposed I was asleep, passing through the streets and over the bridge. A fish leaped as I went by, and I leaned over to look at it, and I heard a lot of dogs howling – the whole town seemed as if it must be full of dogs all howling at once – as I went up the steps. Then I had a vague memory of something long and dark with red eyes, just as we saw in the sunset, and something very sweet and very bitter all around me at once; and then I seemed sinking into deep green water, and there was a singing in my ears, as I have heard there is to drowning men; and then everything seemed passing away from me; my soul seemed to go out from my body and float about the air. I seem to remember that once the West Lighthouse was right under me, and then there was a sort of agonising feeling, as if I were in an earthquake, and I came back and found you shaking my body. I saw you do it before I felt you.

(p. 108)

This reads almost like a case study in emotional ambivalence. Beginning by establishing that there is a difficulty in assessing Dracula's reality *vis-à-vis* the world's, Lucy then goes on to demonstrate that Dracula represents the 'un-known', that which is not available to consciousness, and to illustrate this with a succession of images of the unconscious: the leaping fish, emerging from psychic depths like Coleridge's fountain, the howling dogs, symbol of yearning and wordless need, and the 'something long and dark with red eyes', which is Dracula but also prefigures the phallic connotations of the lighthouse. She sinks into the primal fluid of the unconscious, assailed by sensations which she can only describe as contradictory, 'sweet' and 'bitter', and her soul and body separate as she abandons responsibility for her situation. Dracula, the unconscious, takes the sins of the world on his shoulders because his existence, and the acquiescence of his victims, demonstrate the limitations of the moral will. Lucy, of course, can only experience the consummation of the lighthouse and the earthquake while in this trance-like state, and then translates her experience back into 'safe' terms, 'you shaking my body'. She sees Mina before she feels her because she is sinking into the liberation which her conventional self denies: every time Dracula strikes it becomes harder for his victim to return to normality.

The myth in *Dracula*, more clearly even than in other versions of the vampire legends, is an inversion of Christianity, and particularly of Pauline Christianity, in that Dracula promises – and gives – the real resurrection of the body, but disunited from soul. Stoker's attitude to this is of course shocked, but then Stoker appears from the text to be almost traumatised by a specific sexual fear, a fear of the so-called 'New Woman' and the reversal of sexual roles which her emergence implies. Mina is afraid that 'some of the "New Women" writers will some day start an idea that men and women should be allowed to see each other asleep before proposing or accepting. But I suppose the New Woman won't condescend in future to accept; she will do the proposing herself. And a nice job she will make of it, too! There's some consolation in that' (p. 100). Behind the smugness lies disturbance; it is ironic, but with an irony familiar in the Gothic from Radcliffe on, that precisely the authorial conservatism of *Dracula* makes its rendition of the threats to comfortable Victorian sexual and familial life pointed and perceptive. A crucial scene occurs when Arthur visits Lucy, who is failing fast. When he first sees her, she 'looked her best, with all the soft lines matching the angelic beauty of her eyes'. But as she sinks into sleep, this model of feminity and passivity begins to change:

> Her breathing grew stertorous, the mouth opened, and the pale gums, drawn back, made the teeth look longer and sharper than ever. In a sort of sleep-waking, vague, unconscious way she opened her eyes, which were now dull and hard at once, and said in a soft, voluptuous voice, such as I had never heard from her lips: –
> 'Arthur! Oh, my love, I am so glad you have come! Kiss me!'
>
> (pp. 167–8)

Upon which Van Helsing, whose role is to protect against this kind of overt passion and reversal of roles, comes between them. And this scene is prefigured by the 'key-note' scene where Harker is menaced in Dracula's castle by the three female vampires:

> All three had brilliant white teeth that shone like pearls against the ruby of their voluptuous lips. There was something about them that made me uneasy, some longing and at the same time some deadly fear. I felt in my heart a wicked, burning desire that they would kiss me with those red lips. It is not good to note this down; lest some day it should meet Mina's eyes and cause her pain; but it is the truth.
>
> (p. 46)

It is hard to summarise *Dracula*, for it is such a wide-ranging book, but in general it is fair to say that its power derives from its dealings with taboo. Where taboo sets up certain bounding lines and divisions which enable society to function without disruption, Dracula blurs those lines. He blurs the line between man and beast, thus echoing the fears of degeneracy in Stevenson, Wilde and Wells; he blurs the line between man and God by daring to partake of immortal life and by practising a corrupt but superhuman form of love; and he blurs the line between man and woman by demonstrating the existence of female passion. In his figure are delineated so many primitive fears: he is a shape-changer, a merger of species, the harbinger of ethnic collapse. His 'disciple' Renfield regards him as a god; and his satanic aspects are all the more interesting if we remember that his real-life ancestor gained his reputation for cruelty because of his assiduity in defending the Christian faith against the marauding Turk.

Where Moreau constitutes an ambiguous and accidental threat to empire from without, destroying genetic and racial barriers which are essential to smooth government, Dracula threatens it from

within, attacking the whole concept of morality by preying upon
and liberating aspects of the personality which are not under moral
control, and colonising on his own behalf by infection in a savage
and quite unintentional parody of imperialism. The ironic refrain of
Wilde's *Ballad of Reading Gaol* (1898), the perception that you
always kill the thing you love, that only love allows the proximity
which can lead to real damage, is given a savage new twist by
Stoker, in whose text one can see the traces of the illimitable desire
which turns love into possession and demands incorporation of the
love-object. Dracula is the logical culmination of the Victorian and
Gothic hero, the hero in whom power and attraction are bent to
the service of Thanatos, and for whom the price of immortality is
the death of the soul.

From David Punter, *The Literature of Terror: A History of Gothic
Fictions from 1765 to the Present Day* (London, 1996), Vol. 2,
pp. 15–22.

NOTES

[Primarily Freudian, but tempered by Marxist criticism, David Punter's
wide-ranging survey in *The Literature of Terror* argues against seeing Gothic
fiction as a mode of escapism, and was instrumental in establishing the
Gothic as an important representation of deep-rooted social and psychological fears. The reading of *Dracula* reprinted here is taken from a chapter
entitled 'Gothic and Decadence'. The decadent Gothic novels of the late
1880s and 1890s, Punter argues, are linked by an interest in the problem of
degeneration, and this inevitably leads to a central concern with the question of what it means to be 'human'. The power of *Dracula*, he suggests,
derives from its dealings with taboo: taboo sets up boundaries that enable
society to function smoothly, boundaries, for example, between man and
beast, man and woman, man and God; Dracula blurs these boundaries,
echoing society's fears of degeneration. In Freudian terms, he is the 'endless
desire of the unconscious for gratification'. In Marxist terms, he is the 'final
aristocrat' set against the bourgeois late Victorian family. Focusing upon
the text as an expression of both psychic and social anxieties, Punter's essay
effectively demonstrates that psychoanalytic readings do not necessarily pre-
clude historicism. All quotations from Stoker's *Dracula* in this essay are
taken from the 1965 Signet edition. Ed.]

2

Suddenly Sexual Women in Bram Stoker's *Dracula*

PHYLLIS A. ROTH

Criticism of Bram Stoker's *Dracula*, though not extensive, yet not insubstantial, points primarily in a single direction: the few articles published perceive *Dracula* as the consistent success it has been because, in the words of Royce MacGillivray, 'Such a myth lives not merely because it has been skilfully marketed by entrepreneurs [primarily the movie industry] but because it expresses something that large numbers of readers feel to be true about their own lives.'[1] In other words, *Dracula* successfully manages a fantasy which is congruent with a fundamental fantasy shared by many others. Several of the interpretations of *Dracula* either explicitly or implicitly indicate that this 'core fantasy'[2] derives from the Oedipus complex – indeed, Maurice Richardson calls *Dracula* 'a quite blatant demonstration of the Oedipus complex ... a kind of incestuous, necrophilous, oral-anal-sadistic all-in wrestling match'[3] and this reading would seem to be valid.

Nevertheless, the Oedipus complex and the critics' use of it does not go far enough in explaining the novel: in explaining what I see to be the primary focus of the fantasy content and in explaining what allows Stoker and, vicariously, his readers, to act out what are essentially threatening, even horrifying wishes which must engage the most polarised of ambivalences. I propose, in the following, to summarise the interpretations to date, to indicate the pre-Oedipal focus of the fantasies, specifically the child's relation with and hostility toward the mother, and to indicate how the novel's fantasies are managed in such a way as to transform horror into pleasure. Moreover, I would emphasise that for both the Victorians and twentieth-century readers, much of the novel's great appeal derives from its hostility toward female sexuality. In 'Fictional Convention and Sex in *Dracula*', Carrol Fry observes that the female vampires are equivalent to the fallen women of eighteenth- and nineteenth-century fiction.[4]

The facile and stereotypical dichtomy between the dark woman and the fair, the fallen and the idealised, is obvious in *Dracula*. Indeed, among the more gratuitous passages in the novel are those in which the 'New Woman' who is sexually aggressive is verbally assaulted. Mina Harker remarks that such a woman, whom she holds in contempt, 'will do the proposing herself'.[5] Additionally, we must compare Van Helsing's hope 'that there are good women still left to make life happy' (p. 207) with Mina's assertion that 'the world seems full of good men – even if there *are* monsters in it' (p. 250). A remarkable contrast![6]

Perhaps nowhere is the dichotomy of sensual and sexless woman more dramatic than it is in *Dracula* and nowhere is the suddenly sexual woman more violently and self-righteously persecuted than in Stoker's 'thriller'.

The equation of vampirism with sexuality is well established in the criticism. Richardson refers to Freud's observation that 'morbid dread always signifies repressed sexual wishes'.[7] We must agree that *Dracula* is permeated by 'morbid dread'. However, another tone interrupts the dread of impending doom throughout the novel; that note is one of lustful anticipation, certainly anticipation of catching and destroying forever the master vampire, Count Dracula, but additionally, lustful anticipation of a consummation one can only describe as sexual. One thinks, for example, of the candle's 'sperm' which 'dropped in white patches' on Lucy's coffin as Van Helsing opens it for the first time (p. 220). Together the critics have enumerated the most striking instances of this tone and its attendant imagery, but to recall: first, the scene in which Jonathan Harker searches the Castle Dracula, in a state of fascinated and morbid dread, for proof of his host's nature. Harker meets with three vampire women (whose relation to Dracula is incestuous[8]) whose appeal is described almost pornographically:

> All three had brilliant white teeth that shone like pearls against the ruby of their voluptuous lips. There was something about them that made me uneasy, some longing and at the same time deadly fear. I

felt in my heart a wicked, burning desire that they would kiss me with those red lips.

The three debate who has the right to feast on Jonathan first, but they conclude, 'He is young and strong; there are kisses for us all' (p. 47). While this discussion takes place, Jonathan is 'in an agony of delightful anticipation' (p. 48). At the very end of the novel, Van Helsing falls prey to the same attempted seduction by, and the same ambivalence toward, the three vampires.

Two more scenes of relatively explicit and uninhibited sexuality mark the novel about one-half, then two-thirds, through. First the scene in which Lucy Westenra is laid to her final rest by her fiancé, Arthur Holmwood, later Lord Godalming, which is worth quoting from at length:

> Arthur placed the point [of the stake] over the heart, and as I looked I could see its dint in the white flesh. Then he struck with all his might.
> The thing in the coffin writhed; and a hideous, blood-curdling screech came from the opened red lips. The body shook and quivered and twisted in wild contortions; the sharp white teeth champed together till the lips were cut, and the mouth was smeared with a crimson foam. But Arthur never faltered. He looked like a figure of Thor as his untrembling arm rose and fell, driving deeper and deeper the mercy-bearing stake, whilst the blood from the pierced heart welled and spurted up around it.
>
> (p. 241)

Such a description needs no comment here, though we will return to it in another context. Finally, the scene which Joseph Bierman has described quite correctly as a 'primal scene in oral terms',[9] the scene in which Dracula slits open his breast and forces Mina Harker to drink his blood:

> With his left hand he held both Mrs Harker's hands, keeping them away with her arms at full tension; his right hand gripped her by the back of the neck, forcing her face down on his bosom. Her white nightdress was smeared with blood, and a thin stream trickled down the man's bare chest which was shown by his torn-open dress. The attitude of the two had a terrible resemblance to a child forcing a kitten's nose into a saucer of milk to compel it to drink.
>
> (p. 313)

Two major points are to be made here, in addition to marking the clearly erotic nature of the descriptions. These are, in the main, the only sexual scenes and descriptions in the novel; and, not only are the scenes heterosexual,[10] they are incestuous, especially when taken together, as we shall see.

To consider the first point, only relations with vampires are sexualised in this novel; indeed, a deliberate attempt is made to make sexuality seem unthinkable in 'normal relations' between the sexes. All the close relationships, including those between Lucy and her three suitors and Mina and her husband, are spiritualised beyond credibility. Only when Lucy becomes a vampire is she allowed to be 'voluptuous', yet she must have been so long before, judging from her effect on men and from Mina's descriptions of her. (Mina, herself, never suffers the fate of voluptuousness before or after being bitten, for reasons which will become apparent later.) Clearly, then, vampirism is associated not only with death, immortality and orality; it is equivalent to sexuality.[11]

Moreover, in psychoanalytic terms, the vampirism is a disguise for greatly desired and equally strongly feared fantasies. These fantasies, as stated, have encouraged critics to point to the Oedipus complex at the centre of the novel. Dracula, for example, is seen as the 'father-figure of huge potency'.[12] Royce MacGillivray remarks that:

> Dracula even aspires to be, in a sense, the father of the band that is pursuing him. Because he intends, as he tells them, to turn them all into vampires, he will be their creator and therefore 'father'.[13]

The major focus of the novel, in this analysis, is the battle of the sons against the father to release the desired woman, the mother, she whom it is felt originally belonged to the son till the father seduced her away. Richardson comments:

> the set-up reminds one rather of the primal horde as pictured somewhat fantastically perhaps by Freud in *Totem and Taboo*, with the brothers banding together against the father who has tried to keep all the females to himself.[14]

The Oedipal rivalry is not, however, merely a matter of the Van Helsing group, in which, as Richardson says, 'Van Helsing represents the good father figure',[15] pitted against the Big Daddy, Dracula. Rather, from the novel's beginning, a marked rivalry among the men is evident. This rivalry is defended against by the constant, almost obsessive, assertion of the value of friendship and *agape* among members of the Van Helsing group. Specifically, the defence of overcompensation is employed, most often by Van Helsing in his assertions of esteem for Dr Seward and his friends. The others, too, repeat expressions of mutual affection *ad nauseum*: they clearly protest too much. Perhaps this is most obviously symbolised, and unintentionally exposed, by the blood transfusions from Arthur, Seward, Quincey Morris, and Van Helsing to Lucy Westenra. The great friendship among rivals for Lucy's hand lacks credibility and is especially strained when Van Helsing makes it clear that the transfusions (merely the reverse of the vampire's bloodletting) are in their nature sexual; others have recognised, too, that Van Helsing's warning to Seward not to tell Arthur that anyone else has given Lucy blood, indicates the sexual nature of the operation.[16] Furthermore, Arthur himself feels that, as a result of having given Lucy his blood, they are in effect married. Thus, the friendships of the novel mask a deep-seated rivalry and hostility.

Dracula does then appear to enact the Oedipal rivalry among sons and between the son and the father for the affections of the mother. The fantasy of parricide and its acting out is obviously satisfying. According to Holland, such a threatening wish-fulfilment can be rewarding when properly defended against or associated with other pleasurable fantasies. Among the other fantasies are those of life after death, the triumph of 'good over evil', mere man over superhuman forces, and the rational West over the mysterious East.[17] Most likely not frightening and certainly intellectualised, these simplistic abstractions provide a diversion from more threatening material and assure the fantast that God's in his heaven; all's right with the world. On the surface, this is the moral of the end of the novel: Dracula is safely reduced to ashes. Mina is cleansed, the 'boys' are triumphant. Were this all the theme of interest the novel presented, however, it would be neither so popular with Victorians and their successors nor worthy of scholarly concern.

Up to now my discussion has been taken from the point of view of reader identification with those who are doing battle against the evil in this world, against Count Dracula. On the surface of it, this is where one's sympathies lie in reading the novel and it is this level of analysis which has been explored by previous critics. However, what is far more significant in the interrelation of fantasy and defence is the duplication of characters and structure which betrays an identification with Dracula and a fantasy of matricide underlying the more obvious parricidal wishes.

As observed, the split between the sexual vampire family and the asexual Van Helsing group is not at all clear-cut: Jonathan, Van Helsing, Seward and Holmwood are all overwhelmingly attracted to the vampires, to sexuality. Fearing this, they employ two defences, projection[18] and denial: it is not we who want the vampires, it is they who want us (to eat us, to seduce us, to kill us). Despite the projections, we should recall that almost all the on-stage killing is done by the 'good guys': that of Lucy, the vampire women, and Dracula. The projection of the wish to kill onto the vampires wears thinnest perhaps when Dr Seward, contemplating the condition of Lucy, asserts that 'had she then to be killed I could have done it with savage delight' (p. 236). Even earlier, when Dr Seward is rejected by Lucy, he longs for a cause with which to distract himself from the pain of rejection: 'Oh, Lucy, Lucy, I cannot be angry with you. ... If I only could have as strong a cause as my poor mad friend there [significantly, he refers to Renfield] – a good, unselfish cause to make me work – that would be indeed happiness' (p. 84). Seward's wish is immediately fulfilled by Lucy's vampirism and the subsequent need to destroy her. Obviously, the acting out of such murderous impulses is threatening: in addition to the defences mentioned above, the use of religion not only to exorcise the evil but to justify the murders is striking. In other words, Christianity is on our side, we *must* be right. In this connection, it is helpful to mention Wasson's observation[19] of the significance of the name 'Lord Godalming' (the point is repeated). Additional justification is provided by the murdered themselves: the peace into which they subside is to be read as a thank you note. Correlated with the religious defence is one described by Freud in *Totem and Taboo* in which the violator of the taboo can avert disaster by Lady Macbeth-like compulsive rituals and renunciations.[20] The repeated use of the Host, the complicated ritual of the slaying of the vampires, and the ostensible, though not necessarily conscious, renunciation of sexuality are the penance paid by those in *Dracula* who violate the taboos against incest and the murder of parents.

Since we now see that Dracula acts out the repressed fantasies of the others, since those others wish to do what he can do, we have no difficulty in recognising an identification with the aggressor on the part of characters and reader alike. It is important, then, to see what it is that Dracula is after.

The novel tells of two major episodes, the seduction of Lucy and of Mina, to which the experience of Harker at Castle Dracula provides a preface, a hero, one whose narrative encloses the others and with whom, therefore, one might readily identify. This, however, is a defence against the central identification of the novel with Dracula and his attacks on the women. It is relevant in this context to observe how spontaneous and ultimately trivial Dracula's interest in Harker is. When Harker arrives at Castle Dracula, his host makes a lunge for him, but only after Harker has cut his finger and is bleeding. Dracula manages to control himself and we hear no more about his interest in Harker's blood until the scene with the vampire women when he says, 'This man belongs to me!' (p. 49) and, again a little later, 'have patience. Tonight is mine. To-morrow night is yours!' (p. 61) After this we hear no more of Dracula's interest in Jonathan: indeed, when Dracula arrives in England, he never again goes after Jonathan. For his part, Jonathan appears far more concerned about the vampire women than about Dracula – they are more horrible and fascinating to him. Indeed, Harker is relieved to be saved from the women by Dracula. Moreover, the novel focuses on the Lucy and Mina episodes from which, at first, the Jonathan episodes may seem disconnected; actually, they are not, but we can only see why after we understand what is going on in the rest of the novel.

In accepting the notion of identification with the aggressor in *Dracula*, as I believe we must, what we accept is an understanding of the reader's identification with the aggressor's victimisation of women. Dracula's desire is for the destruction of Lucy and Mina and what this means is obvious when we recall that his attacks on these two closest of friends seem incredibly coincidental on the narrative level. Only on a deeper level is there no coincidence at all: the level on which one recognises that Lucy and Mina are essentially the same figure: the mother. Dracula is, in fact, the same story told twice with different outcomes. In the former, the mother is more desirable, more sexual, more threatening and must be destroyed. And the physical descriptions of Lucy reflect this greater ambivalence: early in the story, when Lucy is not yet completely vampirised, Dr Seward describes her hair 'in its usual sunny ripples' (p. 180); later, when the men watch her return to her tomb, Lucy is described as 'a dark-haired woman' (p. 235). The conventional fair/dark split, symbolic of respective moral casts, seems to be unconscious here, reflecting the ambivalence aroused by the sexualised female. Not only is Lucy the more sexualised figure, she is the more rejecting figure, rejecting two of the three 'sons' in the novel. This section of the book ends with her destruction, not by Dracula but by the man whom she was to marry. The novel could not end here, though; the story had to be told again to assuage the anxiety occasioned by matricide. This time, the mother is much less sexually threatening and is ultimately saved. Moreover, Mina is never described physically and is the opposite of rejecting: all the men become her sons, symbolised by the naming of her actual son after them all. What remains constant is the attempt to destroy the mother. What changes is the way the fantasies are managed. To speak of the novel in terms of the child's ambivalence toward the mother is not just to speak psychoanalytically. We need only recall that Lucy, as 'bloofer lady', as well as the other vampire women, prey on children. In the case of Lucy, the children are as attracted to her as threatened by her.

I have already described the evidence that the Van Helsing men themselves desire to do away with Lucy. Perhaps the story needed to be retold because the desire was too close to the surface to be satisfying; certainly, the reader would not be satisfied had the novel ended with Arthur's murder of Lucy. What is perhaps not so clear is that the desire to destroy Mina is equally strong. Let us look first at the defences against this desire. I have already mentioned the great professions of affection for Mina made by most of the male characters. Mina indeed acts and is treated as both the saint and the mother (ironically, this is particularly clear when she comforts Arthur for the loss of Lucy). She is all good, all pure, all true. When, however, she is seduced away from the straight and narrow by Dracula, she is 'unclean', tainted and stained with a mark on her forehead immediately occasioned by Van Helsing's touching her forehead with the Host. Van Helsing's hostility toward Mina is further revealed when he cruelly reminds her of her 'intercourse' with Dracula: "'Do you forget", he said, with actually a smile, "that last night be banqueted heavily and will sleep late?"' (p. 328). This hostility is so obvious that the other men are shocked. Nevertheless, the 'sons', moreover, and the reader as well, identify with Dracula's attack on Mina; indeed, the men cause it, as indicated by the events which transpire when all the characters are at Seward's hospital-asylum. The members of the brotherhood go out at night to seek out Dracula's lairs, and they leave Mina undefended at the hospital. They claim that this ensures her safety; in fact, it ensures the reverse. Furthermore, this is the real purpose in leaving Mina out of the plans and in the hospital. They have clear indications in Renfield's warnings of what is to happen to her and they all, especially her husband, observe that she is not well and seems to be getting weaker. That they could rationalise these signs away while looking for and finding them everywhere else further indicates that they are avoiding seeing what they want to ignore; in other words, they want Dracula to get her. This is not to deny that they also want to save Mina; it is simply to claim that the ambivalence toward the mother is fully realised in the novel.

We can now return to that ambivalence and, I believe, with the understanding of the significance of the mother figure, comprehend the precise perspective of the novel. Several critics have correctly emphasised the regression to both orality and anality[21] in *Dracula*. Certainly, the sexuality is perceived in oral terms. The primal scene already discussed makes abundantly clear that intercourse is perceived in terms of nursing. As C. F. Bentley sees it:

> Stoker is describing a symbolic act of enforced fellation, where blood is again a substitute for semen, and where a chaste female suffers a violation that is essentially sexual. Of particular interest in the ... passage is the striking image of 'a child forcing a kitten's nose into a saucer of milk to compel it to drink', suggesting an element of regressive infantilism in the vampire superstition.[22]

The scene referred to is, in several senses, the climax of the novel; it is the most explicit view of the act of vampirism and is, therefore, all the more significant as an expression of the nature of sexual intercourse as the novel depicts it. In it, the woman is doing the sucking. Bierman comments that 'The reader by this point in the novel has become used to Dracula doing the sucking, but not to Dracula being sucked and specifically at the breast.'[23] While it is true that the reader may most often think of Dracula as the active partner, the fact is that the scenes of vampire sexuality are described from the male perspective, with the females as the active assailants.[24] Only the acts of phallic aggression, the killings, involve the males in active roles. *Dracula*, then, dramatises the child's view of intercourse insofar as it is seen as a wounding and a killing. But the primary preoccupation, as attested to by the primal scene, is with the role of the female in the act. Thus, it is not surprising that the central anxiety of the novel is the fear of the devouring woman and, in documenting this, we will find that all the pieces of the novel fall into place, most especially the Jonathan Harker prologue.

As mentioned, Harker's desire and primary anxiety is not with Dracula but with the female vampires. In his initial and aborted seduction by them, he describes his ambivalence. Interestingly, Harker seeks out this episode by violating the Count's (father's) injunction to remain in his room: 'let me warn you with all seriousness, that should you leave these rooms you will not by any chance go to sleep in any other part of the castle' (p. 42). This, of course, is what Harker promptly does. When Dracula breaks in and discovers Harker with the vampire women, he acts like both a jealous husband and an irate father: 'His eyes were positively blazing. The red light in them was lurid ... "How dare you touch him, any of you?"' (pp. 48–9). Jonathan's role as child here is reinforced by the fact that, when Dracula takes him away from the women, he gives them a child as substitute. But most interesting is Jonathan's perspective as he awaits, in a state of erotic arousal, the embraces of the vampire women, especially the fair one: 'The other was fair as fair can be, with great wavy masses of golden hair and eyes like pale sapphires. I seemed somehow to know her face and to know it in connection with some dreamy fear, but I could not recollect at the moment how or where' (p. 47). As far as we know, Jonathan never recollects, but we should be able to understand that the face is that of the mother (almost archetypally presented), she whom he desires yet fears, the temptress-seductress, Medusa. Moreover, this golden girl reappears in the early description of Lucy.

At the end of the following chapter, Jonathan exclaims, 'I am alone in the castle with those awful women. Faugh! Mina is a woman, and there is nought in common.' Clearly, however, there is. Mina at the breast of Count Dracula is identical to the vampire women whose desire is to draw out of the male the fluid necessary for life. That this is viewed as an act of castration is clear from Jonathan's conclusion: 'At least God's mercy is better than that of these monsters, and the precipice is steep and high. At its foot a man may sleep – as a man. Good-bye, all! Mina!' (p. 4; emphasis mine).

The threatening Oedipal fantasy, the regression to a primary oral obsession, the attraction and destruction of the vampires of Dracula are, then, interrelated and interdependent. What they spell out is a fusion of the memory of nursing at the mother's breast with a primal scene fantasy which results in the conviction that the sexually desirable woman will annihilate if she is not first destroyed. The fantasy of incest and matricide evokes the mythic image of the vagina dentata evident in so many folk tales[25] in which the mouth and the vagina are identified with one another by the primitive mind and pose the threat of castration to all men until the teeth are extracted by the hero. The conclusion of Dracula, the 'salvation' of

Mina, is equivalent to such an 'extraction': Mina will not remain the *vagina dentata* to threaten them all.

Central to the structure and unconscious theme of *Dracula* is, then, primarily the desire to destroy the threatening mother, she who threatens by being desirable. Otto Rank best explains why it is Dracula whom the novel seems to portray as the threat when he says, in a study which is pertinent to ours:

> through the displacement of anxiety on to the father, the renunci-
> ation of the mother, necessary for the sake of life, is assured. For this
> feared father prevents the return to the mother and thereby the re-
> leasing of the much more painful primary anxiety, which is related to
> the mother's genitals as the place of birth and later transferred to
> objects taking the place of the genitals [such as the mouth].[26]

Finally, the novel has it both ways: Dracula is destroyed[27] and Van Helsing saved; Lucy is destroyed and Mina saved. The novel ends on a rather ironic note, given our understanding here, as Harker concludes with a quote from the good father, Van Helsing:

> 'We want no proofs; we ask none to believe us! This boy will some
> day know what a brave and gallant woman his mother is. Already he
> knows her sweetness and loving care; later on he will understand how
> some men so loved her, that they did dare so much for her sake.'

(p. 416)

From *Literature and Psychology*, 27:3 (1977), 113–21.

NOTES

[Phyllis A. Roth's early Freudian reading of *Dracula* argues against the pre-vious criticism which identified the core fantasy of the text as emerging from the Oedipal complex and the efforts of the vampire hunters to destroy Dracula as the battle of the sons against the father for the affections of the mother. Instead, Roth argues that the hostility towards the sexualised woman so prevalent in *Dracula* suggests that the driving fantasy may actu-ally be pre-Oedipal, and the primary desire is the desire to destroy the threatening mother. The pleasure of the text, she suggests, derives from the manner in which Stoker allows the reader to act out these horrific desires which must be repressed, forced out of conscious awareness into the realm of the unconscious, by the adult. Roth's reading steps towards suggesting the importance of historical context and in particular the emerging hostility towards the 'New Woman' in late Victorian society. Additionally, by moving towards a more feminist reading, Roth sets the stage for many of the most illuminating readings of gender issues in *Dracula* that have emerged in the last twenty years. Ed.]

1. Royce MacGillivray, '*Dracula*: Bram Stoker's Spoiled Masterpiece', *Queen's Quarterly*, 79 (1972), 518.

2. See Norman N. Holland, *The Dynamics of Literary Response* (New York, 1975).

3. Maurice Richardson, 'The Psychoanalysis of Ghost Stories', *Twentieth Century*, 166 (December 1959), 427.

4. Carol Frye, 'Fictional Conventions and Sexuality in *Dracula*', *Victorian Newsletter*, 42 (1972).

5. Bram Stoker, *Dracula* (New York, 1974), pp. 103–4. All subsequent references will be to this Dell edition and will appear parenthetically.

6. While it is not my concern in this paper to deal biographically with *Dracula*, the Harry Ludlam biography (a book which is admittedly anti-psychological in orientation despite its provocative title, *A Biography of Dracula: The Life Story of Bram Stoker*) includes some suggestive comments about Bram Stoker's relationship with his mother. Ludlam remarks an ambivalence toward women on the part of Charlotte Stoker who, on the one hand, decried the situation of poor Irish girls in the workhouse which was 'the very hot-bed of vice' and advocated respectability through emigration for the girls and, on the the other, 'declared often that she "did not care tuppence" for her daughters'. Too, Charlotte told her son Irish folk tales of banshee horrors and a true story of 'the horrors she had suffered as a child in Sligo during the great cholera outbreak that claimed many thousand of victims in Ireland alone, and which provoked the most dreadful cruelties' (New York, 1962), p. 14.

7. Richardson, 'The Psychoanalysis of Ghost Stories', 419.

8. C. F. Bentley, 'The Monster in the Bedroom: Sexual Symbolism in Bram Stoker's *Dracula*', *Literature and Psychology*, 22:1 (1972), 29.

9. Joseph S. Bierman, '*Dracula*: Prolonged Childhood Illness and the Oral Triad', *American Imago*, 29 (Summer 1972), 194.

10. Bentley, 'The Monster in the Bedroom', 27.

11. See Tsvetan Todorov, *The Fantastic*, trans. Richard Howard (Cleveland, OH, 1973), pp. 136–9.

12. Richardson, 'The Psychoanalysis of Ghost Stories', 427.

13. MacGillivray, '*Dracula*: Bram Stoker's Spoiled Masterpiece', 522.

14. Richardson, 'The Psychoanalysis of Ghost Stories', 28. The Oedipal fantasy of the destruction of the father is reinforced by a number of

additional, and actually gratuitous, paternal deaths in the novel. See also MacGillivray, 'Dracula: Bram Stoker's Spoiled Masterpiece', 523.

15. Richardson, 'The Psychoanalysis of Ghost Stories', 428.

16. See, for instance, Richardson, 'The Psychoanalysis of Ghost Stories', 427.

17. Richard Wasson, 'The Politics of Dracula', English Literature in Transition, 9 (1966), 24–7.

18. Sigmund Freud, Totem and Taboo, trans. James Strachey, in The Standard Edition of the Complete Psychological Works of Sigmund Freud, Vol. 13: 1913–14 (London, 1962), pp. 60–3.

19. Richard Wasson, 'The Politics of Dracula', 26.

20. Sigmund Freud, Totem and Taboo, pp. 37ff.

21. Bentley, 'The Monster in the Bedroom', 29–30; MacGillivray 'Dracula: Bram Stoker's Spoiled Masterpiece', 522.

22. Bentley, 'The Monster in the Bedroom', 30.

23. Bierman, 'Dracula: Prolonged Childhood Illness and the Oral Triad', 194. Bierman's analysis is concerned to demonstrate that 'Dracula mirrors Stoker's early childhood' and is a highly speculative but fascinating study. The emphasis is on Stoker's rivalry with his brothers but it provides, albeit indirectly, further evidence of hostility towards the rejecting mother.

24. Ludlam cites one of the actors in the original stage production of Dracula as indicating that the adaptation was so successful that 'Disturbances in the circle or stalls as people felt faint and had to be taken out were not uncommon – and they were perfectly genuine, not a publicity stunt. Strangely enough, they were generally men' (A Biography of Dracula: The Life Story of Bram Stoker [New York, 1962], p. 165).

25. See, for instance, Wolfgang Lederer, MD, The Fear of Women (New York, 1968), especially the chapter entitled 'A Snapping of Teeth'.

26. Otto Rank, The Trauma of Birth (New York, 1973), p. 73.

27. When discussing this paper with a class, two of my students argued that Dracula is not, in fact, destroyed at the novel's conclusion. They maintained that his last look is one of triumph and that his heart is not staked but pierced by a mere bowie knife. Their suggestion that, at least, the men do not follow the elaborate procedures to ensure the destruction of Dracula that they religiously observe with regard to that of the women, is certainly of value here, whether or not one agrees that Dracula still stalks the land. My thanks to Lucinda Donnelly and Barbara Kotacka for these observations.

3

Dracula and Capitalism

FRANCO MORETTI

TOWARDS A SOCIOLOGY OF THE MODERN MONSTER

The fear of bourgeois civilisation is summed up in two names: Frankenstein and Dracula. The monster and the vampire are born together, one night in 1816, in the drawing room of the Villa Chapuis near Geneva, out of a society game among friends to while away a rainy summer. Born in the full spate of the industrial revolution, they rise again together in the critical years at the end of the nineteenth century, under the names of Hyde and Dracula. In the twentieth century they conquer the cinema: after the First World War, in German Expressionism; after the 1929 crisis, with the big RKO productions in America; then in 1956–57, Peter Cushing and Christopher Lee, directed by Terence Fisher, again, triumphantly, incarnate this twin-faced nightmare.

Frankenstein and Dracula lead parallel lives. They are two indivisible, because complementary, figures; the two horrible faces of a single society, its *extremes*: the disfigured wretch and the ruthless proprietor. The worker and capital: 'the whole of society must split into the two classes of *property owners* and propertyless *workers*.'[1] That 'must', which for Marx is a scientific prediction of the future (and the guarantee of a future reordering of society) is a forewarning of the end for nineteenth-century bourgeois culture. The literature of terror is born precisely *out of the terror of a split society*, and out of the desire to heal it. It is for just this reason that Dracula and Frankenstein, with rare exceptions, do not appear together. The threat would be too great: and this literature, having produced

43

terror, must also erase it and restore peace. It must restore the broken equilibrium, giving the illusion of being able to stop history: because the monster expresses the anxiety that the future will be monstrous. His antagonist – the enemy of the monster – will always be, by contrast, a representative of the present, a distillation of complacent nineteenth-century mediocrity: nationalistic, stupid, superstitious, philistine, impotent, self-satisfied. But this does not show through. Fascinated by the horror of the monster, the public accepts the vices of its destroyer without a murmur,[2] just as it accepts his literary depiction, the jaded and repetitive typology which regains its strength and its virginity on contact with the unknown. The monster, then, serves to displace the antagonisms and horrors evidenced *within* society *outside* society itself. In *Frankenstein* the struggle will be between a 'race of devils' and the 'species of man'. Whoever dares to fight the monster automatically becomes the representative of the species, of the whole of society. The monster, the utterly unknown, serves to reconstruct a universality, a social cohesion which – in itself – would no longer carry conviction.

Frankenstein's monster and Dracula the vampire are, unlike previous monsters, dynamic, *totalising* monsters. This is what makes them frightening. Before, things were different. Sade's malefactors agree to operate on the margins of society, hidden away in their towers. Justine is their victim because she rejects the modern world, the world of the city, of exchange, of her reduction to a commodity. She thus gives herself over to the old horror of the feudal world, the will of the individual master. Moreover, in Sade the evil has a 'natural' limit which cannot be overstepped: the gratification of the master's desire. Once he is satiated, the torture ceases too. Dracula, on the other hand, is an ascetic of terror: in him is celebrated the victory 'of the desire for *possession* over that of *enjoyment*';[3] and possession as such, indifferent to consumption, is by its very nature insatiable and unlimited. Polidori's vampire is still a petty feudal lord forced to travel round Europe strangling young ladies for the miserable purpose of *surviving*. Time is against him, against his conservative desires. Stoker's Dracula, by contrast, is a rational entrepreneur who invests his gold to expand his dominion: to conquer the City of London. And already Frankenstein's monster sows devastation over the whole world, from the Alps to Scotland, from Eastern Europe to the Pole. By comparison, the gigantic ghost of *The Castle of Otranto* looks like a dwarf. He is confined to a single place; he can appear once only; he is merely a relic of the past. Once order is re-established he is silent for ever. The modern monsters, however, threaten to live for ever, and to conquer the world. For this reason they must be killed.[4] [...]

DRACULA

Count Dracula is an aristocrat only in manner of speaking. Jonathan Harker – the London estate agent who stays in his castle, and whose diary opens Stoker's novel – observes with astonishment that Dracula lacks precisely what makes a man 'noble': servants. Dracula stoops to driving the carriage, cooking the meals, making the beds, cleaning the castle. The Count has read Adam Smith: he knows that servants are unproductive workers who diminish the income of the person who keeps them. Dracula also lacks the aristocrat's conspicuous consumption: he does not eat, he does not drink, he does not make love, he does not like showy clothes, he does not go to the theatre and he does not go hunting, he does not hold receptions and does not build stately homes. Not even his violence has pleasure as its goal. Dracula (unlike Vlad the Impaler, the historical Dracula, and all other vampires before him) does not *like* spilling blood: he *needs* blood. He sucks just as much as is necessary and never wastes a drop. His ultimate aim is not to destroy the lives of others according to whim, to waste them, but to *use* them.[5] Dracula, in other words, is a saver, an ascetic, an upholder of the Protestant ethic. And in fact he has no body, or rather, he has no shadow. His body admittedly exists, but it is 'incorporeal' – 'sensibly supersensible' as Marx wrote of the commodity, 'impossible as a physical fact', as Mary Shelley defines the monster in the first lines of her preface. In fact it is impossible, 'physically', to estrange a man from himself, to de-humanise him. But alienated labour, as a *social* relation, makes it possible. So too there really exists a social product which has no body, which has exchange-value but no use-value. This product, we know, is money.[6] And when Harker explores the castle, he finds just one thing: 'a great heap of gold ... – gold of all kinds, Roman, and British, and Austrian, and Hungarian, and Greek and Turkish money, covered with a film of dust, as though it had lain long in the ground' (p. 47). The money that had been buried comes back to life, becomes capital and embarks on the conquest of the world: this and none other is the story of Dracula the vampire.

'Capital is dead labour which, vampire-like, lives only by sucking living labour, and lives the more, the more labour it sucks.'[7] Marx's analogy unravels the vampire metaphor. As everyone knows, the

vampire is dead and yet not dead: he is an Un-Dead, a 'dead' person
who yet manages to live thanks to the blood he sucks from the living.
Their strength becomes *his* strength.[8] The *stronger* the vampire
becomes, the *weaker* the living become: 'the capitalist gets rich, not,
like the miser, in proportion to his personal labour and restricted
consumption, but at the same rate as he squeezes out labour-power
from others, and compels the worker to renounce all the enjoyments
of life.'[9] Like capital, Dracula is impelled towards a continuous
growth, an unlimited expansion of his domain: accumulation is inherent in his nature. 'This', Harker exclaims, 'was the being I was
helping to transfer to London, where, perhaps for centuries to come,
he might, amongst its teeming millions, satiate his lust for blood, and
create a *new and ever widening* circle of semi-demons to batten on
the helpless' (p. 51; my italics). 'And so the circle goes on *ever
widening*' (p. 214), Van Helsing says later on; and Seward describes
Dracula as 'the father or furtherer of a *new* order of beings' (p. 302;
my italics). All Dracula's actions really have as their final goal the
creation of this 'new order of beings' which finds its most fertile soil,
logically enough, in England. And finally, just as the capitalist is
'capital personified' and must subordinate his private existence to the
abstract and incessant movement of accumulation, so Dracula is not
impelled by the *desire* for power but by the *curse* of power, by an
obligation he cannot escape. 'When they (the Un-Dead) become
such', Van Helsing explains, 'there comes with the change the curse
of immortality; they cannot die, but must go on age after age adding
new victims and multiplying the evils of the world' (p. 214). It is
remarked later of the vampire that he 'can do all these things, *yet he
is not free*' (p. 239; my italics). His curse compels him to make ever
more victims, just as the capitalist is compelled to accumulate. His
nature forces him to struggle to be unlimited, to subjugate *the whole
of society*. For this reason, one cannot 'coexist' with the vampire.
One must either succumb to him or kill him, thereby freeing the
world of his presence and him of his curse. When the knife plunges
into Dracula's heart, in the moment before his dissolution, 'there was
in the face a look of peace, such as I would never have imagined
might have rested there' (p. 377). There flashes forth here the idea,
to which we shall return, of the *purification* of capital.

If the vampire is a metaphor for capital, then Stoker's vampire, who
is of 1897, must be the capital of 1897. The capital which, after lying
'buried' for twenty long years of recession, rises again to set out on the
irreversible road of concentration and monopoly. And Dracula is a

true monopolist: solitary and despotic, he will not brook competition. Like monopoly capital, his ambition is to subjugate the last vestiges of the liberal era and destroy all forms of economic independence. He no longer restricts himself to incorporating (in a literal sense) the physical and moral strength of his victims. He intends to make them his *for ever*. Hence the horror, for the bourgeois mind. One is bound to Dracula, as to the devil, for *life*, no longer 'for a fixed period', as the classic bourgeois contract stipulated with the intention of maintaining the freedom of the contracting parties. The vampire, like monopoly, destroys the hope that one's independence can one day be brought back. He threatens the idea of individual liberty. For this reason the nineteenth-century bourgeois is able to imagine monopoly only in the guise of Count Dracula, the aristocrat, the figure of the past, the relic of distant lands and dark ages. Because the nineteenth-century bourgeois believes in free trade, and he knows that in order to become established, free competition had to destroy the tyranny of feudal monopoly. For him, then, monopoly and free competition are irreconcilable concepts. Monopoly is the *past* of competition, the middle ages. He cannot believe it can be its *future*, that competition itself can *generate* monopoly in new forms. And yet 'modern monopoly is ... the true synthesis ... the negation of feudal monopoly insofar as it implies the system of competition, and the negation of competition insofar as it is monopoly.'[10]

Dracula is thus at once the final product of the bourgeois century and its negation. In Stoker's novel only this second aspect – the negative and destructive one – appears. There are very good reasons for this. In Britain at the end of the nineteenth century, monopolistic concentration was far less developed (for various economic and political reasons) than in the other advanced capitalist societies. Monopoly could thus be perceived as something extraneous to British history: as a *foreign threat*. This is why Dracula is not British, while his antagonists (with one exception, as we shall see, and with the addition of Van Helsing, born in that other classic homeland of free trade, Holland) are British through and through. Nationalism – the defence to the death of British civilisation – has a central role in *Dracula*. The idea of the nation is central because it is collective: it coordinates individual energies and enables them to resist the threat. For while Dracula threatens the freedom of the individual, the latter alone lacks the power to resist or defeat him. Indeed the followers of pure economic individualism, those who pursue their own profit, are, without knowing it, the vampire's best allies.[11] Individualism is not the weapon with which Dracula can be beaten. Other things are needed – in effect two: money and religion. These are considered as a single whole, which must not be separated: in other words, money at the service of religion and vice versa. The money of Dracula's enemies is money that *refuses to become capital*, that wants not to obey the profane economic laws of capitalism but to be used *to do good*. Towards the end of the novel, Mina Harker thinks of her friends' financial commitment: 'it made me think of the wonderful power of money! What can it not do when it is properly applied; and what might it do when basely used!' (p. 356). This is the point: money should be used according to justice. Money must not have its end *in itself*, in its continuous accumulation. It must have, rather, a *moral*, anti-economic end to the point where colossal expenditures and losses can be calmly accepted. This idea of money is, for the capitalist, something inadmissible. But it is also the great ideological lie of Victorian capitalism, a capitalism which is ashamed of itself and which hides factories and stations beneath cumbrous Gothic superstructures; which prolongs and extols aristocratic models of life; which exalts the holiness of the family as the latter begins secretly to break up. Dracula's enemies are precisely the exponents of *this* capitalism. They are the militant version of Dickens's benefactors. They find their fulfilment in religious superstition, whereas the vampire is paralysed by it. And yet the crucifixes, holy wafers, garlic, magic flowers, and so on, are not important for their *intrinsic* religious meaning but for a subtler reason. Their true function consists in setting impassable limits to the vampire's activity. They prevent him from entering this or that house, conquering this or that person, carrying out this or that metamorphosis. But setting limits to the vampire-capital means attacking his very raison d'être: he must by his nature be able to expand without limit, to destroy every restraint upon his action. Religious superstition imposes the same limits on Dracula that Victorian capitalism declares itself to accept spontaneously. But Dracula – who is capital that is not ashamed of itself, true to its own nature, an end in itself – cannot survive in these conditions. And so this symbol of a cruel historical development falls victim to a handful of whited sepulchres, a bunch of fanatics who want to arrest the course of history. It is they who are the relics of the dark ages.

At the end of *Dracula* the vampire's defeat is complete. Dracula and his lovers are destroyed, Mina Harker is saved at the last moment. Only one cloud darkens the happy ending. In killing Dracula, Quincy P. Morris, the American who has been helping his British friends to save their nation, dies too, almost by accident. The occurrence seems inexplicable, extraneous to the logic of the narrative, yet it fits perfectly into Stoker's sociological design. The American, Morris, *must* die, because Morris is a vampire. From his first appearance he is shrouded in mystery (a friendly sort of mystery, it is true – but isn't Count Dracula himself likeable, at the beginning?). 'He is such a nice fellow, an American from Texas, and he looks so young and so fresh [he *looks*: like Dracula, who looks it but isn't] that it seems almost impossible that he has been to so many places and has had such adventures' (p. 57). What places? What adventures? Where does all his money come from? What does Mr Morris do? Where does he live? Nobody knows any of this. But nobody suspects. Nobody suspects even when Lucy dies – and then turns into a vampire – immediately after receiving a blood transfusion from Morris. Nobody suspects when Morris, shortly afterwards, tells the story of his mare, sucked dry of blood in the Pampas (like Dracula, Morris has been round the world) by 'one of those big bats that they call vampires' (p. 151). It is the first time that the name 'vampire' is mentioned in the novel: but there is no reaction. And there is no reaction a few lines further on when Morris, 'coming close to me, ... spoke in a fierce half-whisper: "What took it [the blood] out?"' (p. 151). But Dr Seward shakes his head; he hasn't the slightest idea. And Morris, reassured, promises to help. Nobody, finally, suspects when, in the course of the meeting to plan the vampire hunt, Morris leaves the room to take a shot – missing, naturally – at the big bat on the window-ledge listening to the preparations; or when, after Dracula bursts into the household, Morris hides among the trees, the only effect of which is that he loses sight of Dracula and invites the others to call off the hunt for the night. This is pretty well all Morris does in *Dracula*. He would be a totally superfluous character if, unlike the others, he were not characterised by this mysterious connivance with the world of the vampires. So long as things go well for Dracula, Morris acts like an accomplice. As soon as there is a reversal of fortunes, he turns into his staunchest enemy. Morris enters into competition with Dracula; he would like to replace him in the conquest of the Old World. He does not succeed in the novel but he will succeed, in 'real' history, a few years afterwards.

While it is interesting to understand that Morris is connected with the vampires – because America will end up by subjugating Britain in reality and Britain is, albeit unconsciously, afraid of it – the decisive thing is to understand why Stoker does *not* portray him as a vampire. The answer lies in the bourgeois conception of monopoly described earlier. For Stoker, monopoly *must* be feudal, oriental, tyrannical. It cannot be the product of that very society he wants to defend. And Morris, naturally, is by contrast a product of Western civilisation, just as America is a rib of Britain and American capitalism a consequence of British capitalism. To make Morris a vampire would mean accusing capitalism directly: or rather accusing Britain, admitting that it is Britain herself that has given birth to the monster. This cannot be. For the good of Britain, then, Morris must be sacrificed. But Britain must be kept out of a crime whose legitimacy she cannot recognise. He will be killed by the chance knife-thrust of a gypsy (whom the British will allow to escape unpunished). And at the moment when Morris dies, and the threat disappears, old England grants its blessing to this excessively pushy and unscrupulous financier, and raises him to the dignity of a Bengal Lancer: 'And, to our bitter grief, with a smile and in silence, he died, a gallant gentleman' (p. 378; the sentence significantly abounds in the clichés of heroic-imperial English literature). These, it should be noted, are the *last* words of the novel, whose true ending does not lie – as is clear by now – in the death of the Romanian count, but in the killing of the American financier.[12]

One of the most striking aspects of *Dracula* – as of *Frankenstein* before it – is its system of narrative senders. To begin with, there is the fact that in this network of letters, diaries, notes, telegrams, notices, phonograph recordings and articles, the narrative function proper, namely the description and ordering of events, is reserved for the British alone. We never have access to Van Helsing's point of view, or to Morris's, and still less to Dracula's. The string of events exists only in the form and with the meaning stamped upon it by British Victorian culture. It is those cultural categories, those moral values, those forms of expression that are endangered by the vampire: it is those same categories, forms and values that reassert themselves and emerge triumphant. It is a victory of convention over exception, of the present over the possible future, of standard British English over any kind of linguistic transgression. In *Dracula* we have, transparently, the perfect and immutable English of the narrators on the one hand, and Morris's American 'dialect', Dracula's schoolbook English and Van Helsing's bloomers on the other. As Dracula is a danger because he constitutes an unforeseen variation from the British cultural code, so the maximum threat on the plane of content coincides with the maximum efficiency and dislocation of the English language. Half way through the novel, when Dracula seems to be in control of the situation, the frequency of Van Helsing's speeches increases enormously, and his perverse English dominates the stage. It becomes dominant because although the English language possesses the word 'vampire', it is unable to ascribe a meaning to it, in the same way that British society considers 'capitalist monopoly' a meaningless expression. Van Helsing has to explain, in his approximate and mangled English, what a vampire is. Only then, when these notions have been translated into the linguistic and cultural code of the English, and the code has been reorganised and reinforced, can the narrative return to its previous fluidity, the hunt begin and victory appear secure.[13] It is entirely logical that the last sentence should be, as we saw, a veritable procession of literary English.

In *Dracula* there is no omniscient narrator, only individual and mutually separate points of view. The first-person account is a clear expression of the desire to keep hold of one's individuality, which the vampire threatens to subjugate. Yet so long as the conflict is one between human 'individualism' and vampirical 'totalisation', things do not go at all well for the humans. Just as a system of perfect competition cannot do other than give way to monopoly, so a handful of isolated individuals cannot oppose the concentrated force of the vampire. It is a problem we have already witnessed on the plane of content: here it re-emerges on the plane of narrative forms. The individuality of the narration must be preserved and at the same time its negative aspect – the doubt, importance, ignorance and even mutual distrust and hostility of the protagonists – must be eliminated.[14] Stoker's solution is brilliant. It is to collate, to make a systematic integration of the different points of view. In the second half of *Dracula*, that of the hunt (which begins, it should be noted, only *after* the collation), it is more accurate to speak of a 'collective' narrator than of different narrators. There are no longer, as there were at the beginning, *different* versions of a single episode, a procedure which expressed the uncertainty and error of the individual account. The narrative now expresses the *general* point of view, the official version of events. Even the style loses its initial idiosyncrasies, be they professional or individual, and is amalgamated into Standard British English. This collation is, in other words, the Victorian compromise in the field of narrative technique. It unifies the different interests and cultural paradigms of the dominant class (law, commerce, the land, science) under the banner of the common good. It restores the narrative equilibrium, giving this dark episode a form and a meaning which are finally clear, communicable and universal.

From Franco Moretti, *Signs Taken For Wonders: Essays in the Sociology of Literary Forms* (London, 1983), pp. 83–5, 90–8.

NOTES

[This extract comes from the chapter on *Dracula* and *Frankenstein* called 'Dialectic of Fear' in *Signs Taken For Wonders*, a book in which Moretti practises what he calls 'a sociology of symbolic forms' (p. 19). Moretti's analysis of *Dracula*, first published as an essay in 1978, is divided into two discrete strands; while his reading of vampirism as expressing the child's ambivalent relation to its mother is concerned with psychosexual repression, his more influential Marxist reading, reproduced here, moves the focus away from sexuality to class and economic concerns and, although still dealing with history in a fairly generalised manner, promotes a movement towards a more materialist and historicist reading of the text. Moretti explores the ways in which literary forms persuade us to give our consent to the dominant ideology. He consequently argues against the common notion that horror is transgressive or subversive and instead sees it as conservative and prohibitive, 'training' us into a 'compromise' with reality, into accepting a social order based on irrationality and menace. Later materialist critics would probably question the stability of ideology that appears implicit in Moretti's reading, finding moments of resistance, and would see the reader's position as less constrained, as negotiated rather than prescribed. All quotations from Stoker's *Dracula* are taken from the 1996 Oxford edition; page references have been added by the editor. Ed.]

1. Karl Marx, 'Economic and Philosophical Manuscripts' (1844), in *Early Writings* (Harmondsworth, 1975), p. 322.

2. The 'classic' detective novel has a similar function. The crime casts suspicion over all the characters: their actions become equivocal, their ideals questionable, their aims mysterious. But once the culprit is found, the suspicion immediately evaporates and everyone is rehabilitated. 'A murderer has to be indicted because that is the only way to provide the rest of the cast with an acquittal wholly satisfying to reason. But the psychological purpose of the story is summed up in that acquittal. The detective myth exists not to provoke or endorse guilt but to dissipate it. The solution pronounces the general absolution.' Brigid Brophy, 'Detective Fiction: A Modern Myth', *Hudson Review*, 1 (1965), 29. General absolution is nothing other than the instinctive approval of the general laws of society which proclaim their goodness and justice in the presence of the individual transgression, the exceptional criminal 'case'.

3. Marx, 'Economic and Philosophical Manuscripts'.

4. In Fisher's films, the vitality of the monster and the vampire is completely lost. They never begin with an offensive by the monster (who

would be quite happy to stay at home), but with an error or an act of stupidity by 'man'. The invitation is transparently to refrain from wandering, to leave things as they are. The monster is no longer frightening in himself but because his zone of influence has been violated, because men have not kept to the agreement. It is a *welfare state* sort of terror, proper to an era of peaceful coexistence.

5. Harker himself is forced to recognise this clear-headed bourgeois rationality in Dracula, after the latter has saved him from the purely destructive desire of his lovers: 'surely it is maddening to think that of all the foul things that lurk in this hateful place the Count is the least dreadful to me: that to him alone I can look for safety, even though this be only whilst I can *serve his purpose*' (my italics). So *un*-cruel is Dracula that, once he has made use of Harker, he lets him go free without having harmed a hair on his head.

6. Before Dracula there had been another literary character who had lost his shadow: Peter Schlemihl. He had exchanged it for a purse full of money. But he soon realises that money can only give him one thing: more money, still more money, all the money he wants (the purse is bottomless). But *only* money. The only desire Peter can satisfy is thus the abstract and immaterial desire for money. His mutilated and unnatural body denies him access to tangible, material, corporeal desires. So great a scandal is it that once the girl he loves (and who loves him) finds out, she refuses to marry him. Peter runs away in desperation: he can no longer love. (Just like Dracula: '"You yourself have never loved; you never love!" ... Then the Count turned ... and said in a soft whisper: – "Yes, I too can love; you yourselves can tell it from the past. Is it not so?"') Chamisso's story is a fable (*The Marvellous Story of Peter Schlemihl*); published in 1813, the same period as *Frankenstein*, it too revolves around the conflict between the spread of capitalism (Peter) and feudal social structures (Mina and her village). As in *Frankenstein*, capitalism appears in it as a fortuitous episode, involving just one individual and lasting only a short time. But the underlying intuition has an extraordinary power; it stands on a par with the punishment of Midas, for whom gold prevented consumption.

7. Karl Marx, *Capital*, Vol. 1 (Harmondsworth, 1976), p. 342.

8. '... the Un-Dead are strong. [Dracula] have (*sic*) always the strength in his head of twenty men; even we four who gave our strength to Miss Lucy it also is all to him' (p. 183). One cannot help recalling the words of Mephistopheles analysed by Marx: 'Six stallions, say, I can afford, / Is not their strength my property? / I tear along, a sporting lord, / As if their legs belonged to me' (quoted in Marx, 'Economic and Philosophical Manuscripts', p. 376).

9. Marx, *Capital*, p. 741.

10. Karl Marx, 'The Property of Philosophy' (1847), in Marx and Engels, *Collected Works*, Vol. 6 (London, 1976), p. 195.

11. This is the case with all the minor characters in the novel. These (the stevedores and lawyers, sailors and estate agents, porters and accountants) are always more than satisfied with their dealings with Dracula, for the simple reason that Dracula pays well and in cash, or even facilitates the work. Dracula is one of them: an excellent master for wage-earners, an excellent partner for big businessmen. They understand one another so well, they are so useful to each other, that Dracula never behaves like a vampire with them: he does not need to suck their blood, he can buy it.

12. The finishing touch is Jonathan Harker's short 'Note', written seven years after the events have ended. Harker informs the reader that he and Mina have christened their son 'Quincey', and that 'His mother holds, I know, the secret belief that some of our brave friend's spirit has passed into him' (p. 336). The American outsider Morris is 'recycled' within the triumphant Victorian family, not without being made to undergo a final tacit humiliation (which would delight a linguist): his name – Quincy, as appears from the signature of the only note in his own handwriting – is transformed, by the addition of an 'e' into the much more English Quincey.

13. In Stoker's novel the function of Van Helsing describes a parabola: absent at the beginning, dominant at the centre, removed to the margins of the action at the end. His aid is indeed irreplaceable, but once she has obtained it, Britain can settle matters herself; it is indicative that he is only a spectator at the killing of Dracula. In this, yet again, Fisher's *Dracula* betrays the ideological intention of the original: the great final duel between Dracula and Van Helsing belongs to a very different system of oppositions from Stoker's, where there prevails the conflict between Good and Evil, Light and Darkness, Frugality and Luxury, Reason and Superstition. See David Pirie, *A Heritage of Horror: The English Gothic Cinema 1947–1972* (London, 1973), pp. 51ff.

14. The story of Lucy illuminates the interrelationship of the characters. In the opening chapters, no fewer than three of the main characters (Seward, Holmwood and Morris) enter into competition for her hand. In other words, Lucy objectively turns these men into *rivals*, she divides them, and this makes things easier for Dracula who, making them by contrast be friends again, prepares her downfall. The moral is that, when faced with the vampire, one must curb all individual appetites and interests. Poor Lucy, who acts solely on her desires and impulses (she is a woman who *chooses* her own husband, without mentioning it to her mother!) is first killed by Dracula and then, for safety's sake, run through the heart by her fiancé on what, going by the calendar, should have been their wedding night (and the whole episode, as we shall see, oozes sexual meanings).

4

Hysteric and Obsessional Discourse: Responding to Death in *Dracula*

ELISABETH BRONFEN

Much has been written about the theme of sexuality in *Dracula*, about masculine homoeroticism, the exchange of women's bodies among men, perverse sexual practices connected with sucking and the fear of female sexuality.[1] Yet vampire lore also serves as a central trope for western attitudes toward death, so that Stoker's text represents not only an ambivalent desire for/fear of sexuality but also the same ambivalence toward mortality with the theme of sexuality put forward to veil that of death. His narrative presents the mourning for a woman, whose death poses as an enigma – what took out the blood of four strong men put into her veins? (p. 151) – equivalent to detecting and obliterating the source of death. Decathexis is here completed once a preserved corpse has been transformed into a decomposing one, replaced with a secondary double, a funeral symbol.

Stoker illustrates that after death the body can return in a fascinatingly dangerous or a soothingly safe form: the former a material somatic return, the vampire as body double, the latter an immaterial semiotic return, with documents, headstone inscriptions and memory images standing in for the absent body, doubling it not in an iconic/indexic but rather a symbolic mode. While the vampire penetrates the body, sucks blood to preserve itself as a death-bringer, the vampire-hunters also incite the body with their staking and decapitation, yet this act of penetration preserves the social body against death. As an undead body, disseminating an uncanny state of living-death with each body he bites, Dracula embodies a form of death which threatens two aspects of the paternal symbolic order. In a cultural sense the vampire's false death is a serious. falsification of Christian notions of death as the sleep before Judgement Day. The empty grave of the vampire, with its permeable plate, suggests that these bodies are not waiting for any teleologically oriented resurrection but, based on a cyclic notion of return, reappear prematurely in the world of the living, with their bodies preserved whole. In a semiotic sense the vampire traces the return to inscriptions on the body and counteracts the process of culturation, where language, as the cornerstone of paternal law, is a 'murder of the soma', where the body's contingent form of signification is replaced by arbitrary symbolisation. The language of the vampire keeps the originary exchange between life and death open to undermine the hegemony of secondary symbolic exchanges.

Vampire plots serve as narratives about the trauma that death poses once it is returned to the living, inscribed within the community, on the bodies of its members, and that the response that death – traced by Count Dracula's presence – elicits can be divided into a hysteric and an obsessional discourse.[2]

The hysteric recognises a lack or void in the symbolic order of laws and knows her non-existence. She exists within her cultural system by evoking the presence of a double; a rhetorical articulation of death. In this relation the hysteric is protean, able to appear in more than one guise, hiding the knowledge of her non-existence even as the fluidity of her position, because of which she is not fixed by any one cultural master signifier, is such that one of her relations is to radical Otherness outside the symbolic, as the site of her truth. Responding to the vampire can be read as the trope for the hysteric's relation to that radical Otherness beyond the social, the acknowledgement of the real void of death as one of her points of reference.[3]

While the hysteric accepts her division, feeds off her lack of a fixed identity, and preserves a fluid boundary to the unconscious, the obsessional tries to repress the real void of death by erecting clear divisions. He uses language and knowledge in an effort to exclude radical Otherness, lest it allow the lacks and gaps, which make him anxious, to appear. Against the hysteric's celebration of duplicity and her fluid relation to the unconscious, he fears duplicity, seeks to control the indeterminate and identifies with dead objects to close out death as the truth in his unconscious. The aim is to keep the ego impenetrable, the fantasies intact, even if this means killing off all living desire and difference within oneself, for any fixity is preferable to acknowledging death's presence in life. To block out fluidity, multiplicity and instability as remnants of the impossible burden emanating from Otherness as real death, the obsessional clings to the death-like fixity of mastery and certain knowledge. Desire, in being illicit, bringing surprises and subverting control is his enemy, and Woman as the instigator and object of desire, especially the hysteric's fluidity of appearances, must be petrified and purified of any taints. She can be a safe object for identification when she is no longer an uncanny figure representing death but rather cannily dead. The obsessional masters death as an uncanny difference within by fixing an ambivalent, fluid, oscillating body to a stable signifier, and precisely for this process, the vampire hunt with its staking is a trope.

In Stoker's text the hysterical discourse is embodied by the two brides, Lucy Westenra and Mina Murray, who respond to the trace of death the vampire evokes and, once bitten, hover uncannily between wakeful conscious and death-like unconscious states. Their psychosomatic symptoms signify that death's Otherness speaks through the medium of their bodies. Apart from histrionics, emotional lability and simulation, early psychoanalysis also saw as descriptive traits of the hysteric character 'demanding dependency', 'excessive excitability', and a proclivity toward semi-conscious states, towards 'suggestibility' as an acceptance and acting out of the desires others have induced in hypnosis.[4] Freud and Breuer's discussion of the hysteric's double conscience as a split in consciousness (between a daytime lucidity, favouring a cure and a nocturnal irrationality, resisting the analyst's efforts at healing), as well as hypnoid conditions, somnambulism, hallucinations and amnesia, evoke both Lucy's and Mina's behaviour as they oscillate between responding to Dracula's call and to that of their men.[5] The position of the obsessional is in turn assumed by the suitors and doctors, who hunt and destroy vampires to redraw the separation between bodies beneath the graveplate and funerary signs, between unconscious desires and conscious deeds. They precisely do not respond to death's call except to expel its living presence and identify instead with dead objects – mutilated corpses, memory images, the documents reduplicating their investigation.

These two responses to death are debated over the bodies of the two brides. Lucy and Mina respond hysterically in the form of a double conscience to death's incision (Dracula's bite) even as their bodies are the sites at which the men attempt symbolic restitution in the form of blood transfusions and second burials. Detecting Dracula is coterminous with obliterating the difference death traces in the community, even as his destruction along with that of the vampire Lucy serves to fix the disruption of the symbolic by the semiotic chora that the dying and dead feminine body enacts. The two brides are positioned between the paternal law and radical Otherness as their two points of reference, with the death of Dracula putting closure on this oscillation by placing Mina securely in relation to the phallus (as wife and mother) and Lucy in relation to canny death (as decomposing corpse). What returns with the vampire's bite are the two repressed enigmas – femininity and death – while a solution of the uncanniness of both is here, too, coterminous.

At the outset of Stoker's novel, both Mina and Lucy are in the premarital state, waiting for their future husbands. Mina remains rationally controlled in the absence of Jonathan Harker, in fact writes in her diary to exercise her conscious memory, practises stenography and typewriting. Lucy is psychosomatically disturbed by this 'waiting' (p. 72) and gives her liminality as bride the figure of the somnambulist. Even before Dracula has appeared she walks in her sleep, has an 'anaemic look', is 'excitable', 'supersensitive' to influences, and has chosen as her favourite seat, which she 'cannot leave', the grave of a boy suicide (p. 67). To a degree this restlessness can be seen as the banal symptomatisation of her uncertainty about her upcoming marriage to Arthur Holmwood. The fact that her symptoms – heavy, lethargic sleep, frightening dreams which she forgets – do not correspond to any bodily illness lets Dr Seward conclude 'it must be something mental' (p. 111). Though Mina started the habit of visiting the churchyard, she initially resists the call of death. Sleepwalking Lucy, in turn, immediately responds to the desire or call of the Other, like the sexton Swales, who says 'if (Death) should come this very night I'd not refuse to answer his call' (p. 74) and who is Dracula's first victim. She enacts that a desire for death is located in her unconscious, even if her conscious self cheerfully anticipates the return of her future husband. This conjunction is made explicit by the fact that Lucy is waiting for Arthur to take him to her seat on the churchyard cliff, while it is at precisely this 'favourite seat' that she is bitten by her other suitor, Dracula. The duplicity Lucy's self-division initially entails is that though her rest-lessness and her nocturnal yielding to an unconscious desire suggest a fluidity between various states of the self, this knowledge is fore-closed or rejected by her conscious self. She does not, in Mina's words, understand her restlessness nor will she admit to any cause. Once bitten she implores Mina 'not to say a word to any one ... about her sleep-walking adventure' (p. 92), and as her friend notes, exposure could cause not only her health but also her reputation to suffer.

The text gives Lucy two doubles: her own split-self which will eventually return as a vampire, and her friend Mina. The latter shares her oscillation between semi-conscious states that articulate a desire for death and a conscious desire for marriage, yet unlike Lucy, who withholds her secret from the vampire-hunters, Mina is more clearly an accomplice of the paternal law. She writes down her unconscious dreams, transcribes the other documents. As secretary she helps undo Lucy's somatic resurrection as revenant and is instrumental in replacing it with a textual resurrection. This semiotic restitution helps Mina redraw a boundary between herself and her dead friend as well as between her actions and her own unconscious response to death.

Throughout her illness, as she grows more languid and weak, as she fades away, the enigma Lucy poses is located in this enactment of a split self; on the one hand her unconscious attempts to get out of her room to the spot in the graveyard, her 'half-dreamy state', her hallucinations, and on the other her suddenly becoming 'her old self again', in 'gay spirits' and 'full of life and cheerfulness' (p. 97). Her own description of her illness repeatedly invokes images of Otherness that contradict her conscious sense of self – 'a great press of water', noises, distant voices, coming from 'I know not where and commanding me to do I know not what' (p. 135). Her description of her first encounter with Dracula emphasises that a near-death experience is one of division. While she is drawn inexplicably to the churchyard, she seems to be asleep though the experience seems to be real. The bite of the vampire is 'very sweet and very bitter', accompanied by a sense of sinking and of singing in her ears, her soul leaving her body and floating in the air, only to return finally to her body (p. 98).

The four blood transfusions meant to undo the vampire's death work, as it manifests itself in her corpse-like, ghastly waxen pallor, in her wan-like motionless body, do not only raise the issue of an implicit sexual exchange. Arthur feels that giving his blood to Lucy is a form of marriage, 'she was his wife in the sight of God' (p. 174), just as the other donors never speak of their gift, afraid to 'enjealous' him (p. 128). The operation also reveals that Lucy's body serves as a medium between the men and death, Dracula sucking their blood by virtue of this detour, as he will later speak to them through Mina's hypnotised body. This substitution allows for the displaced articulation of a repressed desire for death. Lucy's body is uncanny not only as the site of a dual exchange – she feeds Dracula even as she receives the gift of vampirism – but also as that of a double signature, his red marks on her neck countersigned by the men's mark on her arms. At stake in the repeated depletion and rejuvenation of her dying body, and later the mutilation of her corpse, is the question of which signature – Dracula's somatic or the men's symbolic form of signification – will be privileged. This artificial reanimation is also a representation of paternal birthgiving ('a feeling of personal pride' [p. 128]), pitched against natural decay, and implicitly against the maternal function. Lucy's mother unwittingly counteracts their intentions by removing the garlic and she dies in Lucy's bed having torn the protective wreath from her daughter's neck, exposing her once more to the vampire's bite.

Once vampirism sets in, the duplicity of Lucy's split self becomes bodily more manifest – sleeping she looks stronger, though more haggard, her breathing stertorous, her teeth longer and sharper; awakening, the softness of her eyes changes her expression back into the earlier Lucy, 'her own self'. In the end, because death gives her 'back part of her beauty' Lucy makes a 'very beautiful corpse' (p. 162). Once death has set in, the earliest self-division now articulates itself in an uncanny restoration of her previous beauty against the natural process of 'decay's effacing fingers' (p. 164). Every hour in fact 'seemed to be enhancing her loveliness' (p. 168). Seward's duplicitous response to this sight – 'It frightened and amazed me' – voices the survivors' ambivalence of feeling. Even as her lovers want to preserve her in life they also need her decomposition to complete their mourning.

Though in one sense she is a figure for sexualised death – Arthur repeatedly kisses the corpse – the trajectory of Van Helsing's detection is to put closure on any necrophilic desire. Unlike Heathcliff, who wished to open the coffin of his beloved so as to embrace both her and death, to preserve her death in life, Van Helsing opens her coffin to mutilate her body – to stake her heart and decapitate her – so as to begin the process of decomposition. He wishes to arrest the uncanniness which began with her oscillation between conscious and unconscious self, to resolve the duplicity of a body's beauty hiding that it is in fact decaying, to undo the split between angel and demon, to obliterate the perversion of the maternal that her biting of children entails. If the ill Lucy was safely pure during the day while dangerously semi-conscious at night, once undead her dual life is such that she is doubly threatening, 'more radiantly beautiful' while lying in her coffin and violently sexualised at night, her sweetness an 'adamantine heartless cruelty', her purity 'voluptuous wantonness' (p. 211).

The second killing or paternal resurrection Van Helsing instigates – Arthur staking the vampire Lucy in the presence of the other men – is a counterpart to the blood-transfusions and this operation again appears like a covert sexual act. As they confront the vampire, she is likened to Medusa, a figuration of death – 'If ever a face meant death – if looks could kill – we saw it at that moment' (p. 212). The effort of staking is meant to separate into two canny opposites what is so threateningly intertwined – death's and a beautiful woman's face – and this operation will work if the death-beauty can be proved to be false rather than inextricably intertwined with femininity. The vampire is designated as a 'nightmare of Lucy ... the whole carnal and unspiritual appearance, seeming like a devilish mockery of Lucy's sweet purity' (p. 214). At stake in the mutilation of this mock Lucy is the effort to counteract the false death of the undead ('working wickedness by night', 'growing more debased by day') and to arrest any further dissemination of death by her bite. By restituting the 'true Lucy', with her soul released, her dead body doubled as an angel in heaven because her earthly double, her corpse is safely decomposed, they have material proof for their Christian notion of true death. Here, too, the turn to the sheer materiality of the body serves to antidote a crisis in belief.

The staking will also restore that image of Lucy which they require as a safeguard of their own sense of stability. They aim 'to restore Lucy ... as a holy, and not an unholy, memory' (p. 215). This operation expels the image of the 'foul Thing' and leaves a Lucy, 'as we had seen her in her life, with her face of unequalled sweetness and purity'. The traces of death her face now draws, 'pain and waste', are no longer a mockery of death. Her long phase of oscillation is fixed in the aspect of the 'holy calm' that lies over what is now no longer a grinning devil but 'God's true dead' (p. 308).[6] This staking fixes semantic instability which the vampire Lucy enacted in two ways – as a dead body mocking a living woman, and as a woman who is superlatively beautiful while sleeping yet who mocks this beauty by exhibiting violent feminine wantonness while awake. Her semantic duplicity is arrested as she is resurrected as an angel and a holy image. The secondary form of representational double, used to obliterate the primary body-double, however, affords a second form of arrestation in that it covers up the traces of death's material work with inanimate signs. If Lucy, lying so radiantly beautiful in her coffin, resonates with the image of Snow White, her body may not awaken to become once again the bride. Rather it is replaced with a safe, purified memory image, over which a separation of the living and the dead, the exchange of the difference of death and femininity within, for a canny image of difference located outside can be fulfilled.

The last part of the narrative seeks to conclude what this second burial begins. The detection plot, the tracing and destruction of the vampire, completes the mourning plot. Having solved the duplicity and oscillation of the feminine body, the hunters must now solve death. Repeatedly they justify their mission by claiming to undertake it 'For dear Lucy's sake'. Implicitly she continues to haunt their imagination and will be completely decathected only when the agent of death is also seemingly destroyed. Lucy's other double, Mina, undergoes the same near-death experiences as her deceased friend before the two can be fully separated. She too is bitten in her sleep, polluted with his blood; she has the same visions as Lucy, the same symptoms of fatigue, pallor and disquietude. Yet unlike Lucy, who withheld her knowledge, 'who did not speak, even when she wrote that which she wished to be known later' (p. 323), Mina is more clearly on the side of the paternal law. She relates her near-death experiences to the vampire hunters and is a seminal accomplice in their search. Unlike Lucy, whose desire for death is coterminous with an insecurity about her status as bride, she accepts her fixture within the symbolic order and resists the call of death, despite her initial response to it.

The transparency and purity of women's bodies serves in both cases as the proof that the abject, toward which they are shown to incline more than men, has been expelled. The touch of the paternal sign – the holy wafer – leaves a 'red scar' on Mina's forehead to indicate that her body is tainted though her soul is pure. Killing the vampire will be coterminous with purifying her forehead, 'all white as ivory and with no stain'. Before this restitution, however, Mina doubles Lucy's somnambulism in her hypnotic trances during which Dracula, as death, speaks through the medium of her body. While initially she transcribed events in shorthand and typed them in order to help the men in their documentation, she later also translates that Otherness to which they have no access, because her hysteric proclivity toward semi-conscious states endows her with the 'power of reading the Count's sensations'. In her trances, Van Helsing notes, she is 'as though she were interpreting something. I have heard her use the same tone when reading her notes' (p. 312). Under hypnosis Otherness speaks through her and this Other is death's trace. Identifying with Dracula's sleep, she speaks the state of death – 'I am still – oh, so still. It is like death' (p. 313). She is, however, also the muse who leads the men to the vampire, as 'scribe ... writing him all down', so that they 'shall know' that which they bar from their conscious (p. 343). Though in the course of the journey she becomes ever more like Lucy, split between being the familiar 'old self', 'alert and wakeful' and falling silent, enveloped in lethargy and pallor, she nevertheless remains in complicity with the symbolic order of the living. In a 'strange scene', impressive for 'its solemnity, its gloom, its sadness, its horror and withal its sweetness', she has them read the Burial Service for her to assure the purity of her soul.

The moment of solution, the final staking of Count Dracula, is quite literally a moment of final dissolution as his 'whole body crumbled into dust and passed from our sight' (p. 377) and Mina's forehead is once again 'stainless', the 'curse ... passed away'. With the source of death that provoked uncanny duplicity and oscillation in the women gone, their memory of the dead Lucy becomes perfectly purified. She is completely severed from Mina, who can now give birth to a boy on this day's anniversary. Stoker presents three positions in relation to the figure of death Dracula traces. Firstly, Lucy's hysteria, her silence and her inability to resist death embodies a completely fluid boundary between the conscious sense of self-preservation and an unconscious desire for death. Secondly, Mina and Jonathan's responses to the call of death which, over the second killing of Lucy and Dracula, can be repressed. While Mina cedes to the vampire's call, the three women vampires at Castle Dracula excite Jonathan's imagination, evoke a 'burning desire that they would kiss me' (p. 37). The thought of being kissed by an undead feminine body which is 'both thrilling and repulsive' evokes an anticipation of 'languorous ecstasy'. To obliterate the source of death's call in life serves as a trope for the successful repression of that part of the self that responds, the unconscious, the imagination, for the foreclosure of the split in/of oneself, for an obsessive shutting out of death as one's truth. Finally, Van Helsing's unambiguous, obsessional identification with death is signified in his belief that he has a mastery over death. With the assistance of his instruments – his needles, his stakes, his wafers – he can revive dying brides and destroy the undead. This drawing of separations expels uncanny body doubles and uncanny semantic duplicity, as two signs of the difference death traces within and marks a complete lack of response to death's call.

Yet, even as, in Van Helsing's words 'the stake we play for is life and death' (p. 365), their detection was also meant to assure the supersession of documentation, of secondary transcriptions believed to be semantically stable over primary sensations, over unconscious desires and dreams. For the 'horrible imaginings', as Jonathan notes at Castle Dracula, will be his destruction unless he can shield himself by taking down 'prosaic notes' (p. 25). Throughout the novel, the danger of an unhinged mind, of the unconscious desires triumphing is apotropaically soothed by accurate documentation. Mina significantly starts typing Jonathan's journal once she realises Dracula is in England so as to set this typescript against the figure of death that takes hold of the imagination and 'tinges everything with something of its own colour' (p. 180). Stoker's text ends on an image of fathers, a son Quincy and a text, the papers documenting their detection. The intention behind this collection is that by translating a primary exchange with death into a secondary one, the resulting interpretation lets death cease to have a grip on the body; transforms conscious death anxiety into repressed unconscious desire even as the violence used to bring about this transformation is also repressed.

Stoker, however, brilliantly undermines the obsessional discourse of his protagonists not only in the banal sense that his entire text works by exciting the reader's imagination, drawing her or him into the dangerous realm of uncanniness, duplicity and longing for Otherness. He also explicitly states that the semiotic double replacing the somatic double is not stable, that the truth the men seek can not be fixed. While the true dead are such only when buried beneath a graveplate, turned to dust and irrevocably eliding the grip of the survivors, the documents representing them are equally elusive. As Jonathan notes, 'in all the mass of material of which the record is composed, there is hardly one authentic document! nothing but a mass of type-writing ... We could hardly ask anyone ... to accept these as proofs of so wild a story' (p. 378). Though these documents are meant to afford stability, the sema can not transparently reproduce the soma, making the papers a secondary form of signification, with difference and distance inscribed between the sign and the real events, while the real, the authentic eludes this signification. These papers ironically enact precisely the duplicity and impurity between signifier (appearance) and signified (truth), for whose effacement the men resorted to the process of documentation in the first place.

Though their aim is to close the crack on the gravestone, to obliterate all doubling and all uncanny otherness by killing the agent of difference, they end up with fragments of transcripts and ruins – decaying bodies, ashes, gravestones. In that there is nothing to assure their desire for purity and wholeness except Mina's cleared forehead and her boy, Stoker's text ends on the note of disjunction which I have argued is figured by allegory. Indeed, Swales's earlier discussion of the duplicity of gravestones suggests how the replacement of the bad double, the dead soma returned as vampire, with the good double, its semiotic representation, is in fact equally a mockery. He describes the tombstones as 'steans "simply tumblin" down with the weight o' the lies wrote on them, "Here lies the body" or "Sacred to the memory" wrote on all of them, an' yet in nigh half of them there bean't no bodies at all; an the memories of them bean't cared a pinch of snuff about, much less sacred. Lies all of them, nothin' but lies of one kind or another' (p. 65). He evokes an image of the Day of Judgement not as a moment of clarity but as a 'quare scowderment' with the dead dragging their tombstones to prove 'how good they was'. His disclosure focuses on two aspects of duplicity and deception. In those instances where no body has been placed beneath the ground so that the headstone marks an empty grave, its inscription 'here lies' indeed lies about the question of the dead body's place, conceivably to ward off the fear of wandering ghosts. For another, because the signifier 'in the memory of' may falsify the actual relation between deceased and mourner, it uses the site of death to produce a fictional version of the deceased. As Swales relates about Lucy's favourite grave, its headstone asserts that a sorrowing mother commemorates a beloved son to hide the fact that a man committed suicide to anger a mother who hated him. By implication the textual representation duplicitously reveals what Lucy's headstone hides – that her sacred memory could emerge only from a violent mutilation of her corpse and the desecration of her grave.

The feminine bodies in liminality – premarital brides, somnambulists, vampires and hypnotised mediums – are the very image of death's work in life, driving men to distance themselves obsessively from any erotically encoded experience of disintegration even as these images drive the text, the compilation of their papers tracing and reduplicating their obsessional discourse, toward a self-reflexivity by revealing its figurative hysteria.[7] Given that textual self-reflexivity is also achieved because the text serves as a trope for the allegorical process, this figurative hysteria resides in the fact that the text duplicitously enacts a real void which it cannot consciously acknowledge. The allegorical disjunction produced by the textuality of the compiled papers, analogous with the headstone inscriptions, traces Otherness so that paradoxically the real, which on the thematic level returns with the vampires and is effaced in the course of the second killings, remains rhetorically. That documentation and transcription occurs while the vampirised women and the detecting men are in a position of liminality, of near death or in mourning, articulates the possibility that writing, meant to assure a division of death from life, originates in precisely the marginal realm in between.

From Elisabeth Bronfen, *Over Her Dead Body: Death, Femininity and the Aesthetic* (Manchester, 1992), pp. 313–22.

NOTES

[In *Over Her Dead Body: Death, Femininity and the Aesthetic*, Elisabeth Bronfen draws upon Lacanian psychoanalysis, semiotics, and deconstruction to consider western representations of the dead feminine body from the mid-eighteenth century onwards. According to Lacan, we only define our sense of self by leaving behind the 'Imaginary' stage (or what Kristeva calls the 'semiotic') and entering the symbolic, by moving into language, into the law of the father. As 'undead', Dracula threatens this paternal order, eluding signification, and so do the women he infects, who lack fixed identity, whose position becomes more clearly fluid, related not just to the symbolic but to the radical Otherness outside the symbolic. They are associated with what Lacan called 'hysteric' discourse. The 'obsessional', usually encoded masculine, and here associated with the vampire hunters, uses language in an attempt to control, define, fix, and ultimately exclude this otherness. For Bronfen, the staking of the vampire becomes a trope for this fixing of an ambivalent fluid body to a stable signifier. As for poststructuralist critics there is always instability between signifier and signified, Bronfen finds the apparent success of the obsessional ultimately undermined: the documents meant to fix the truth are elusive, the papers with which they are left enact precisely the instability and impurity that they sought to efface. All quotations from Stoker's *Dracula* in this essay are taken from the Oxford World's Classics 1983 edition. Ed.]

1. See Margaret Carter's excellent collection of recent criticism, *Dracula: The Vampire and the Critics* (Ann Arbor, MI, 1988). For an overview of vampires in literature, see James Twitchell, *The Living Dead: A Study of the Vampire in Romantic Literature* (Durham, NC, 1981).

2. Explicating Lacan, Ellie Ragland-Sullivan argues that the hysteric's discourse is usually encoded as a feminine, the obsessional's as a masculine one. Where the hysteric's desire is related to the Otherness, and she accepts death's presence in life, the obsessional uses language and knowledge in an effort to avoid desire, a rejection coterminous with excluding Otherness as this also signifies death. *Jacques Lacan and the Philosophy of Psychoanalysis* (Urbana, IL, 1987).

3. As an aside it is interesting to note that physicians in the nineteenth century themselves used the analogy between hysteria and vampirism, though in a different sense. Oliver Wendell Holmes, for example, judged that 'a hysterical girl is a vampire who sucks the blood of the healthy people about her'. Quoted in Caroll Smith-Rosenberg, *Disorderly Conduct: Visions of Gender in Victorian America* (New York, 1986), p. 207.

4. See Stavros Mentzos, *Hysterie: Zur Psychodynamik unbewusymbol Inszenierungen* (Munich, 1980). I use this term not as a description of illness but rather to discuss discursive positions in Lacan's sense, as well as to point out correspondences between aesthetic and psychoanalytic imagery.

5. In *Woman and the Demon: The Life of a Victorian Myth* (Cambridge, MA, 1982), Nina Auerbach explicitly draws an analogy between Lucy mesmerised by Dracula and the hysteric women hypnotised by Freud, suggesting that Stoker could conceivably have known the work of the Viennese doctor through reports at the Society for Psychical Research in London in 1893.

6. Christopher Craft, discussing the connection between sexuality and textuality, calls this a post-penetrative peace meant to stabilise both woman's body and her semantic fluidity. See '"Kiss Me with Those Red Lips": Gender and Inversion in Bram Stoker's *Dracula*' [reprinted in this volume – Ed.].

7. Charles Bernheimer makes a similar point for the death of Zola's prostitute Nana. See *Figures of Ill Repute: Representing Prostitution in Nineteenth-Century France* (Cambridge, 1989).

5

Writing and Biting in *Dracula*

REBECCA A. POPE

We routinely read Bram Stoker's *Dracula* (1897) as a study of erotic desire. Recent work on the novel, quite correctly, has begun to put the strange and conflicted workings of eros there into its *fin de siècle* historical context, an age, Elaine Showalter notes, which saw the erosion of imperialism and patriarchy and thus a time of 'crisis in masculinity and ... sexual anarchy' (p. 9).[1] One glance at the novel's extravagant narrative structure, however, suggests that it is as concerned with textuality as with sexuality.[2] *Dracula* presents itself as a compilation of a vast array of assorted genres – letter, journal, medical case history, to name but a few – by a number of different writers, both men and women. This variegated structure, this flaunted textuality, invites an examination of how *Dracula* represents and critiques the conditions, processes, and motivations upon which the production, circulation, and exchange of its discourses depend. Because the texts which make up the novel vary in genre and their writers differ in gender, part of this project must attend to *Dracula*'s preoccupation with the framing – structuring and delimiting – work of both gender and genre. In short, I am interested here in the novel's preoccupation with textuality, and especially in the ways it brings together sex and text, discourse and desire.

As a discourse that lives off other discourses, *Dracula* represents the novel as a parasitic and appropriating genre and offers vampirism as a model. The resonance extends further: the novel consists of a series of texts which are, to use the characters' own term, 'knitted' together, and to piece together, as in patchwork, is to 'vamp'. This modelling of the genre as a vamping together of different discourses attributed to different voices neatly anticipates and illustrates Bakhtin's sense of the novel as a composite of different discourses and 'languages' – ideological languages, for example – in dialogical rather than hierarchical relations to each other.[3]

Harker provides a paradigm in his polyglot dictionary, a text which, like Stoker's novel in its stress on the writing and reading of texts as a way of producing knowledge, locates meaning in the relations between one sign, or group of signs, and another. For Bakhtin, the many voices of the dialogic novel make language and, when they are inserted into the novel, genres into objects of representation.[4] Similarly, the polyphony of languages and voices in the polyglot dictionary highlights language and discourse as such, apart from their mimetic function. The spectacular array of speakers and genres in the novel achieves the same effect: we can argue that if *Dracula* 'represents' anything at all, it represents language and textuality. In the way that it brings together so many languages, literal and metaphorical – 'languages' of gender, class, and ethnicity, for example – and so many varieties of discourse (each with its own framework of conventions, values, and assumptions), *Dracula* is one of the best examples of Bakhtin's dialogism in the tradition of the British novel.

According to Bakhtin, the dialogic novel does not bring together discordant voices in order to achieve concord or to subsume the many into a greater, transcendent and authoritative one. The characteristic energies of both the gothic and the dialogic subvert unities and hierarchies, and we find these energies operating in Stoker's novel from its start. *Dracula*'s inclusion of so many voices and discursive genres tends to relativise them and their world views: there is neither a supreme voice nor a master discourse in *Dracula*. The narrative structure and the dialogism it implies can thus be read as challenges to traditional structures of authority and thought founded on the single, the logocentric, the teleological: the theological, the patriarchal, the hierarchical, and the law and ideologies based upon them.

Thus Bakhtin's dialogism implies not just a dialogue among voices, but also a conflict between 'logics',[5] and in this tendency to challenge traditional orders (the established frameworks of thought, logic, and social organisation, for example) the dialogic and the

gothic converge. I want to devote the remaining pages of this essay
to tracing out, in the context of the novel's preoccupation with
textuality, the threads of one of the conflicts of logics/ideologies we
find in *Dracula* by turning to the relations between gender and
textuality in the novel.[6]

First, however, given the long debate over whether *Dracula* is,
finally, a feminist or misogynist text, it seems necessary to do some
preliminary framing of my own discussion. That years of debate
have not satisfactorily resolved this issue is symptomatic of the
extent to which Stoker's novel is deeply conflicted in matters of
gender. Further, this is not the only of Stoker's texts in which what
we would now term as a feminist recognition of women's social disabilities seems in conflict with attitudes and rhetoric associated with
the traditional gender code which promotes these disabilities. In a
late and little-known non-fiction work, *Famous Impostors* (1910),
many of the themes and preoccupations we find in *Dracula* reappear
– doubling, usurpation, appropriation, for example – but what is
most striking for our purposes is the way Stoker writes about
women and gender there. Throughout the book he is interested in
'gender impostors' and in issues of gender reversal and slippage
called up by transvestism. He even devotes an entire section to
'Women as Men'.

We might expect the writer of such a sensationalist novel as
Dracula to treat the topic in a sensationalist manner or perhaps,
suitably for the creator of Harker and Van Helsing, in a manner pa-
tronising and sentimental. What is thus surprising (and perhaps a
warning to us not to collapse automatically Stoker's attitudes into
those of his male characters) is the extent to which he openly
admires such (traditionally masculine) traits in women as intelligence, resourcefulness, and a taste for adventure, and recognises and
deplores the limitations an oppressive gender code has placed on
their lives. What is so odd, and so reminiscent of *Dracula*, is the
way he limits his own insights and reinscribes the terms and attitudes which contribute to the very disabilities he sincerely laments:

> One of the commonest forms of imposture – so common that it
> seems rooted in a phase of human nature – is that of women who
> disguise themselves as men. It is not to be wondered that such at-
> tempts are made; or that they were made more formerly when
> social advancement had not enlarged the scope of work available
> for women. The legal and economic disabilities of the gentler sex
> stood then so fixedly in the way of working opportunity that

women desirous of making an honest livelihood took desperate
chances to achieve their object.[7]

The key phrase is 'legal and economic disabilities of the gentler sex'.
It recognises the inequalities, and yet the use, without irony, of a
rhetoric of sentimental chivalry reinscribes one of the representations of women used to justify the very inequities Stoker deplores.
The pattern repeats itself throughout, as when he admires these
women's resourcefulness and ambition in the face of oppressive
gender roles and then proceeds to claim that the brave and clever
expedient of dressing like a man was often motivated by desires
traditionally 'feminine': 'In many of these cases are underlying romances, as of women making search for lost or absconding husbands, or of lovers making endeavours to regain the lost paradise of
life together'.[8]

Of course we see similar incongruities in *Dracula*. For example,
the novel consistently sympathises with and admires Mina, even
when her behaviour is untraditional or she is frustrated with the
conventional 'woman's role', yet there is also a sympathy for the
men's oppressive protectiveness, and a violence and attention to
detail in the staking scene which exceeds what would be necessary if
the scene were there solely to display male violence and female
victims. It is as if both texts were playing out the tensions of their
historical moment – an age when, as the Showalter quotation with
which I began suggests, certainties of all kinds, including those of
the traditional gender ideology, were breaking down.

Significantly, the two texts show a Stoker very aware of historical
moment, process, and change. In *Famous Impostors* he claims,
perhaps overconfidently, that the ages-old legal and economic op-
pression of women has come to an end, and in *Dracula* gender relations are placed in a historical context of changing roles and the
weakening of patriarchy; Mina, for example, writes about that late
Victorian challenge to the traditional gender code, the New
Woman. For Bakhtin, the novel thrives during such periods when
certainties are eroding, when the reigning powers and ideologies are
weakening and being called into question.[9] Thus the novel's sensitiv-
ity to its historical moment, as well as its narrative structure's highlighting of a polyphony of voices and its interest in representing
language and discourse, invites a Bakhtinian critical orientation
toward the novel. This critical framework allows us to explore the
gender issues and the relations between gender and textuality in the

novel without feeling obliged, as many earlier critics have felt, to smooth over conflicts in order to claim that the novel is ultimately feminist or misogynist. Further, by refocusing our efforts away from such goals as a closing critical mastery, a Bakhtinian 'framing' allows us to remain faithful to the gothic tradition's deep suspicion of the monologism and strong closure to which realism aspires.

What follows, then, is a look at the relations between gender and textuality in *Dracula* which is oriented less toward making final pronouncements that cover over conflicting voices and logics than toward uncovering these conflicting ideological voices and gender 'logics' as they play themselves out in the context of the novel's interest in textuality. This is not to say, however, that I have not made some choices in emphasis. I am especially interested in following Peter Schwenger's counsel that 'with writers of both sexes, we should take into account their tendencies to work against the sexual grain'.[10] In other words, I am interested in those intersections of gender and textuality which seem to openly dramatise, and thus hold up for critique, the strategies and representations that patriarchy uses to sustain itself, and in those moments which explore the relations between women and textuality under patriarchy.

Dracula stresses the process of textual production as much as it does textual product, highlighting the vast number of discursive modes, as well as the varied modes of making a text. For example, it repeatedly presents writing as a process in which a man or woman marks or inscribes various media: letters are chiselled into stone; script, typewriting, or shorthand symbols mark paper; wax cylinders receive voice impressions. So many ways of marking on so many different surfaces, including marking on human flesh.[11] In *Dracula* it is primarily women who are marked, who receive the impressions of another, usually male, which function as symbols to be read. Significantly, not only are none of the male protagonists bitten, but the only one who is ever in danger of being bitten, Jonathan Harker, is saved by Dracula himself. The major male figures in the novel, both human and vampire, do at times band together.[12]

Both Dracula and the human males in league against him textualise women, and it is important to see that their literal marking of women's physical bodies is only part of a wider enterprise in which men make women repositories for their own projected, interested, representations. For example, Van Helsing, who serves as a father-figure for the humans, tends to see women as symbolic objects, as signifiers in a masculine gender code. After reading Mina's writings, he exclaims.

> Oh, Madame Mina, good women tell all their lives, and by day and by hour and by minute, such things that angels can read; and we men who wish to know have in us something of angel's eyes.
>
> (p. 184)

In context, Van Helsing is praising both Mina's writings and the womanly woman he 'reads' there in her account of her concern for Lucy and Jonathan. By the end of this conversation, however, we see that reading Mina's writing has become a 'writing' of her: he makes her into signifier. Revealing both the deep investment these men have in maintaining patriarchy and their sense that passionate women like Lucy threaten it, he says to Mina.

> I come here full of respect for you, and you have given me hope – hope, not in what I am seeking of, but that there are good women still left to make life happy – good women, whose lives and whose truths may make good lesson for the children that are to be.
>
> (p. 185)

Requiring reassurance that the traditional gender ideology is not breaking down, he projects his hope onto Mina, transforming her into a sign in a patriarchal gender code, the 'good lesson', to be passed (and read) from generation to generation.

Van Helsing completes his transformation of woman into signifier when he makes Mina into a sign of ideal womanhood for all the human males. 'You must be our star and our hope', he tells her as he excludes, as it were erases, her from active participation in the hunt for the vampire (p. 242). In so doing, he sentences her to the female passivity and safekeeping that the traditional gender code prescribes, a prescription which, because such confinement makes Mina and Lucy vulnerable to Dracula, the novel represents as ultimately destructive to women. The framing work of gender ideology, this novel shows, is, at least for women, a frame-up as well. Women tell and men read, runs Van Helsing's version of the traditional gender code, but men usually read on women what men project.

One of the dangers of being marked out as a sign in someone else's discourse is the possibility of being silenced oneself. Mina recognises that this idealisation by which she is 'simultaneously apotheosized and nullified' is also a silencing,[13] and she locates such silencing in a long line of masculine representations of women: 'I could say nothing, save accept their chivalrous care of me' (p. 242). Stoker's novel quite wonderfully literalises all this. After she has been sentenced to inactivity and confined to 'safety', Mina is marked out by the vampire and assaulted by him. The response of the human males is reminiscent of their earlier staking of Lucy, a marking of the female body that simultaneously punishes and reclaims the woman who transgresses the traditional code of feminine behaviour. Van Helsing touches a host to Mina's forehead, burning her and leaving her marked like Cain. Males battle to mark and claim her, and consequently Mina becomes less and less able to speak for herself and more and more able to serve as a medium through which the vampire patriarch reads the minds of the male vampire hunters and vice versa. Like a letter, Mina carries information between sets of male minds. Indeed, when, like a playback of Seward's phonograph recorder, she relays this information during one of her hypnotic trances, she even sounds as if she is reading back from a text. 'I have heard her use the same tone when reading her notes', Harker observes, failing to notice, however, that a male's text had displaced a female's (p. 312).

The predominantly metaphorical marking and marking out of women by men that we see in Mina's case is more consistently literal in Lucy's. It is upon Lucy's body that the males most obviously and violently make their marks and send messages to each other, grim and literal reminders that, as Dale Spender and others have observed, under patriarchy masculinity is always the unmarked form and femininity the marked.[14] As a number of critics have observed, Lucy rebels against the plot line, sacred to patriarchy, that society has marked out and scripted for her. 'Why can't they let a girl marry three men, or as many as want her, and save all the trouble? But this is heresy and I must not say it', she writes in a letter to Mina (p. 59). Reading and writing in *Dracula* are ways of asserting and maintaining community, and thus the vampire's mark on Lucy's neck can be read as his sign that he has read in her their commonality as desiring creatures reluctant or unable to channel their desires toward a single object. The nightstalker sees himself in the nightwalker and by biting her claims her as his own. The mode of marking here, the puncture wound, is significant as well. Like an hysterical symptom, Dracula's bite is the sign that desire – vampire's and victim's – writes on the body. Moreover, a vampire bite on a female body is for all practical purposes a mimetic representation of what the novel, or at least the male characters in it, defines as female sexuality: a hole to be filled and/or made by men. The bite stands for what is usually framed out of the 'representable' in this culture and, at times, in this text. Mina's post-wedding sexual initiation, for example, is never mentioned; it is represented only by its absence, by a gap or hole in her journal and the compilation. Thus Dracula writes out the sign of gender and desire on Lucy's body; he makes darkness visible.

In a text filled with issues simultaneously sexual and generational that features women in trance-like states, the novel's many references to *Hamlet* are not surprising. Significantly, Lucy identifies not only with Ophelia, but with Desdemona as well. 'I sympathise with poor Desdemona when she had such a dangerous stream poured into her ear', writes Lucy of the proposal from Quincey Morris, in the same letter in which she takes such unconventional unrepressed pleasure in receiving three offers of marriage and expresses such unconventional and unrepentant regret that she cannot have all three men (p. 57). For Lucy, the points of similarity between herself and Desdemona are desire and temptation inspired by a foreign male, but the parallels do not end here. Like the final act of *Othello*, Stoker's novel repeatedly raises issues of killing out of love and male murder of females as a sacrifice to a patriarchal gender ideology. Moreover, both the sacrificed women are fatally textualised by men. 'Was this fair paper, this most goodly book / Made to write "whore" on?' demands Othello, articulating the male anxiety over female sexuality that underlies the human males' textualising of women in *Dracula* as well (IV.ii. 70–1). Othello's murder of Desdemona, a consequence of misreading his wife, can be seen as an attempt to erase or destroy the text of sexual transgression that another male has, as a frame-up, projected there for Othello to read. Similarly, the staking of Lucy is another attempt by a group of males to edit and rewrite another male's writing across a female body that the first claims as its own.

In a significant contrast to the care that the characters take to preserve even the most insignificant written papers, the scene of revisionary writing that is the staking scene shows none of this respectful attitude toward textuality. The human males edit and supplement Dracula's text by making their own marks on Lucy, by inscribing their own will on her in an attempt to erase the effects of the vampire's mark and to keep her from, as Van Helsing puts it, 'age after age adding new victims and multiplying the evils of the world' (p. 214). Similarly, Othello feels himself called to protect the world from a passionate woman who makes others – especially men – her victims. He is convinced that his wife 'must die, else she'll betray more men' (V.ii. 6.), and he rejects her protestations of innocence as attempts to make him 'call what [he] intend[s] to do / A murder which [he] thought a sacrifice' (V.ii. 64–5).

One might argue that the parallels I have been drawing here are limited because Desdemona is quite willing to direct her desire to a single object, Othello, whereas Lucy, as her letter to Mina shows, has three objects in mind. Lucy may thus be a transgressor against the gender code in a way that Desdemona is not, but there are limits: Lucy may complain about the constraints the gender code places on her desire and actions, but in her letter she submits to them nonetheless. The novel's references to *Othello* should be read in conjunction with those it makes to the *Arabian Nights*, another text in which an enraged patriarchal power sentences a woman to death for a perceived sexual transgression. We read those works as tales of excessive and oppressive abuse of male power as it enforces a patriarchal gender code. By calling them up, *Dracula* invites us to read the attitudes and actions of the human males as a representation of the workings of patriarchy – its logics and investments, its strategies for maintaining itself – that is also, because placed in a literary context of male excess, a critique.

Lucy's medical treatment and staking are striking examples of how the marking or 'textualising' of women is used to maintain patriarchy. As the sexualisation of her medical treatment implies, the underlying issue in Lucy's case, as it is in Desdemona and Scheherazade's, is erotic transgression. Her treatment, blood transfusions from the men, requires puncturing her with needles, a marking by the human males in response to the vampire's bite-marks. The men view the transfusions as metaphors for intercourse, and Van Helsing proclaims that they have made her a polyandrist. The married Van Helsing admits that he has, as well, become a bigamist, but because his mad wife is, he claims, 'dead' to him and thus 'now-no-wife', the overall effect of the passage is to cast, to frame, the unconscious Lucy, not the men, as the sole sexual transgressor (p. 176). The staking of Lucy in her crypt is the final male marking of her, an inscription that kills as it appropriates and signifies possession. Arthur is chosen to do the deed; Lucy's fiancé is thus cast as Othello: a man who perceives himself wronged by a passionate woman and consequently uses violence to reassert the patriarchal gender code.

Like Othello, the men represent the staking as an act of love not destruction, a liberation of her innocent spirit by a sacrifice of her corrupt body. Significantly, Arthur drives the stake into Lucy's breast, the same place where Lucy had earlier hidden the memorandum of her illness – her attack of 'vampiric' desire – and thus a place on her body already associated with both sex and text. That the staking occurs in Lucy's burial crypt further allies, in good gothic fashion, writing, the (subversively) desiring (female) body, and death.

Seward's account of the staking and its aftermath provides a sense of what the men believe is at stake in Dracula's attempt to appropriate Lucy for himself and in Lucy's reluctance, both before and after the vampire bites her, to channel her desire toward a single object:

> There in the coffin lay no longer the foul Thing that we had so dreaded and grown to hate that the work of her destruction was yielded as a privilege to the one best entitled to it, but Lucy as we had seen her in life, with her face of unequalled sweetness and purity. True that there was there, as we had seen them in life, traces of care and pain and waste; but these were all dear to us, for they marked her truth to what we knew. One and all we felt the holy calm that lay like sunshine over the wasted face and form and was only an earthly token and symbol of the calm that was to reign for ever.
>
> (pp. 216–17)

In the case of both Mina and Lucy, the female body in *Dracula* is the site of a battle between opposing males who seek to stake their claims for her and, by marking her body, on her. In her study of body issues in Victorian culture, Helena Michie has shown how the female body was often the focal point for the construction of women's roles, and we can see here that the battle is a matter of gender ideology. As a desiring creature, Lucy is not 'Lucy' or a 'woman', but a 'foul Thing'. For these men, as Seward's narrative makes clear, the point of the staking is to turn Lucy into the pure and angelic being their gender code requires her to be – only then can she be 'Lucy'.

A rhetoric of writing – traces, marks, tokens, symbols – pervades Seward's description. In presenting the female body as the place where social and gender meanings are written – projected, inscribed, disfigured, erased and reinscribed – the staking scene is as much about text as about sex. According to *Dracula*, the tale patriarchy tells is this: whatever women can tell (and the marks on Lucy's neck suggest that they can tell a number of different stories), good women tell the traditional gender ideology that men project there. Thus Seward can claim that Lucy's changed appearance 'marked her truth to what we knew'. As the final picture of Lucy as silent, passive, beautiful but violently marked corpse framed within a coffin makes clear, the framing work of gender ideology sets the female body off, like any framed space, as a field for representations. The cryptal setting, moreover, further implies how much artifice and patriarchy as *Dracula* presents it have in common – they both kill for the sake of their own existence.

As the experience of both Lucy and Mina suggests, under patriarchy women are to be marked and read, and if the text of the traditional gender ideology becomes defaced there, they are to be quickly and aggressively re-marked because the marked, like the vampire and the sign, always threatens infinite repetition. The framing work of gender frames in the womanly woman and frames out the passionate, sexual, independent and rebellious ones. But, as Lucy's letter suggests and as Mina's speculation that 'some of the taste of the original apple ... remains still in our mouths', makes clear, such boundaries – interested, constructed fictions – are difficult, if not impossible, to maintain (p. 183). Thus the enormous time and energy the men devote to reading Mina and Lucy's bodies; they study their wounds, teeth, complexions and behaviour. These men as – lawyer, scientist and physician, aristocrat, and scholar with special ties to the Church – are apt representatives of patriarchal power who monitor women for deviance to be erased and serve as guardians of the traditional gender code. The men who can read women, Van Helsing claims, are those who have 'angel's eyes'. Calling on a higher authority, they assert theirs as border police who patrol and guard the framework of traditional gender roles and relations.

The staking is, then, a staking of claim, and as such calls up a thematics of property exchange and circulation. These are, of course, the themes which open the novel: both the narrating and the action start with Harker's Transylvanian journey to complete the paperwork necessary for the transfer to Dracula of an estate in England. The act of transferring reminds us that the logic of the novel depends on movements of displacement – the metonymic movement of desire to text, for example, and the chain of displacements from Lucy's breast to her memorandum to the marks from the stake. And thus it is fitting that the text sets up another chain of displacements

– property, texts (textualised) women – within an economy of circulation and exchange among, for the most part, men. For example, during a visit to Seward's asylum, Dracula attacks both Mina and the narratives she has typed and complied as equal threats to him. The point of this interchangeability is not simply that Mina, by having the most intimate knowledge of the narratives has the most knowledge that can be used against him, but that women and texts are both elements in a male economy of exchange which mediates power relations, perhaps even erotic ones, among them.

To best see how women are not only textualised here, but have as well much the same status and function as texts, we must first look at the way actual texts, both written and oral, create communities among men and mediate relations between them. At first glance, the exchange and circulation of texts does not seem to be a gendered activity. A woman is, after all, among the group of humans who exchange texts as a way of banding together and fighting the vampire. However, Harker's stage-setting opening narrative – which seems to present his writing as a link between himself and Mina but quickly makes narrating reflexive, a therapy to keep his sanity – gives way to an early model of the circulation of texts as a way of sustaining community that is highly gendered. After Harker's journal breaks off, we find a letter from Quincey Morris to Arthur Holmwood which begins,

> We've told yarns by the camp-fire in the prairies; and dressed one another's wounds after trying a landing at the Marquesas; and drunk healths on the shore of the Titicaca. There are more yarns to be told, and other wounds to be healed, and another health to be drunk. Won't you let this be at my campfire to-morrow night? I have no hesitation in asking you, as I know a certain lady is engaged to a certain dinner party, and that you are free. There will only be one other, our old pal at the Korea, Jack Seward. He's coming, too, and we both want to mingle our weeps over the wine-cup, and to drink a health with all our hearts to the happiest man in all the wide world ...
>
> (p. 61)

The most striking feature of the novel's first model of communal bonding through the exchange of narratives – trading yarns around the campfire – is its maleness. The making and exchanging of narratives takes its place as one male activity among others, hunting, adventuring, and exploring, for example. Indeed, the hunting of the vampire who has preyed upon Mina and Lucy can be seen as just the latest example of the adventures which have bound these men together long before they meet Mina and Lucy.

Significantly, the occasion for this 'men only' gathering is a woman. Morris plans the party to celebrate Arthur's engagement to Lucy and to console himself and Seward on the loss of her. As they share stories, they share Lucy and come together through her; all three will toast her, and two will 'mingle [their] weeps' over her. The moment looks forward to the time when Lucy is ill after Dracula's assault: then again she will serve as the pretext for further communal action and bonding among these men as they mingle their bloods in and through her by giving her transfusions. The men look at these transfusions as separate and individual instances of metaphorical intercourse with Lucy, but the multiple transfusions can also be seen as an instance of males bonding with each other in and through a woman.[15] As *Dracula* presents the structures and strategies of patriarchy, women, like texts, make and mediate relations – comradely and hostile, homosocial and homoerotic – among men. Women are marked like texts because they serve to mark relations – especially those of power and property – between men.

The vampire patriarch also sees women primarily as vehicles for mediating male relations. From the early scene in which he forbids the vampire women any contact with Harker – 'How dare you touch him', he exclaims, 'This man belongs to me' (p. 39) – a moment of male solidarity that looks forward to the human male's exclusion of Mina from the hunt, to the close of the novel, Dracula seems, despite his preying upon women, more invested in men and more interested in maintaining power over them. For example, when he assaults Mina, he seems most preoccupied with hurting the male hunters:

> You would help these men to hunt me and frustrate my designs! You know now, and they know in part already, and will know in full before long, what it is to cross my path. They should have kept their energies for use closer to home. Whilst they played their wits against me – against me who commanded nations and who intrigued for them and fought for them, hundreds of years before they were born – I was countermining them. And you, their best beloved one, are now flesh of my flesh; blood of my blood; kin of my kin ...
>
> (pp. 287–8)

The parody of the wedding service – a communal text used to mark the 'giving' of a woman by one man (father) to another (husband) –

calls up the institution charged with maintaining traditional gender roles and casts it into a context which suggests the extent to which marriage is an institution designed to maintain regulated bonds between men. Dracula is most preoccupied with the male vampire hunters, and he views himself not, as we might expect here, as an amorous and conquering lover, but as a commander of armies and nations. The emphasis is on male relations and male activities. This 'marriage' is less a romantic or erotic one than a political alliance in which a woman is forcibly circulated among men to define, mediate, and regulate their relations. Thus Dracula can taunt them, 'Your girls that you all love are mine already; and through them you and others shall yet be mine. ...' (p. 306).

Under patriarchy, Stoker's novel suggests, women and texts have a similar function and status: their sharing, circulation and/or exchange serve to constitute and maintain bonds, especially male bonds and relations. Moreover, as the relations between Dracula and his human hunters isolated above imply, these activities also regulate power between one person or group and another. The novel consistently inscribes language and writing as ways of gaining and keeping power: Dracula believes that his plans to master the human race depend on his ability to master English, and his hunters trust that the writing and circulating of texts will produce knowledge that will help them defeat the vampire. The relations between textuality and power extend to gender issues as well, of course: men mark women to stake a claim, to assert, the opening thematics of property ownership and exchange suggests, 'property rights'; and, as Mina's sense that the men's chivalry silences her implies, the traditional gender code which idealises women and makes them dependent on male power simultaneously silences them.

But this is only part of the story. What then of the relations between women themselves and language and writing in *Dracula*? The first important mention of women writing occurs surprisingly early, before Lucy and Mina's letters, in Harker's Transylvanian journal. Throughout this narrative Harker is almost as preoccupied with his writing as with his host; he even speculates about how and where his own writing figures in the discursive tradition:

> Here I am, sitting at a little oak table where in old times possibly some fair lady sat to pen, with much thought and many blushes, her ill-spelt love-letter, and writing in my diary in shorthand all that has happened since I closed it last. It is the nineteenth century up-to-date

with a vengeance. And yet, unless my sense deceive me, the old centuries had, and have powers of their own which mere 'modernity'
cannot kill.

(p. 36)

Harker's imagining of a woman writing a love letter yields two levels
of resonance. On a more general level, the image reminds us of
Dracula's debt to the epistolary novel, fictions which also present
themselves as collections of texts by diverse hands. Stoker's novel especially recalls Richardson's fiction, not just in its stress on reading
and writing as part of the action, but in its highlighting of reading
and writing 'to the moment' and under threat. In Stoker's tale of
female virtue and desire in the face of male predatory passion the
Richardsonian resonances are thematic as well, and from this vantage
point we can begin to glimpse the discursive tradition that Jonathan
calls up only to displace by his own narrative reportage: amorous
epistolary discourse. In *Discourses of Desire* Linda Kauffman traces
the history of the genre from Ovid on, showing how it is assimilated
into the novel, especially through Richardson, and how deeply the
gothic is indebted to it, even for features we have thought of as
defining characteristics of the gothic tradition.[16] Moreover, the parallels extend further than shared character types and a common interest
in the workings of erotic desire. Like the gothic, amorous epistolary
discourse 'questions mimesis, draws attention to the ambiguous implications of the signature, and exposes the artifice involved in critical
perceptions of gender'.[17] Indeed, many of the motifs and preoccupations Kauffman finds in these discourses of desire – transgression,
contract, identity, authority and authorship, lineage and paternity –
pervade as well the gothic in general and *Dracula* in particular.[18]

What interests me here is Kauffman's reading of the women
writers and their letters, the figures and the texts Harker believes he
and his writing have displaced. The letters of these desiring women
are acts of 'rebellion against the tyranny of fathers and lovers', cen-
sures of 'their control of women and speech' and critiques of their
'distorted representations of women'.[19] They are texts of protest
and passion in which women speak and augment their desire and, in
the process, rebel against the terms of the patriarchal gender code.
The letters are, in other words, supplements to the texts which,
Dracula shows, men would write on women.

What Harker sees his writing displacing, then, is the discourse of
female passion. His ominous tone at the close – 'the old centuries

had, and have powers of their own which mere "modernity" cannot kill' – allies female passion with vampirism as transgressive; it is, after all, Dracula, the lord of the manor from an earlier age, who represents the 'old centuries' in battle against the modernity of the nineteenth-century bourgeoisie which Harker represents. Harker is, of course, correct to worry that suppressed female passion might return, as we see only a few pages later in Lucy's proposal letter.

Harker's calling up of the amorous epistolary tradition gives us a context and interpretive frame for reading Lucy's and Mina's texts. The letter in which Lucy lovingly details to Mina the multiple proposals of marriage can certainly be placed in the tradition Kauffman traces out. Lucy's lament, 'Why can't they let a girl marry three men, or as many as want her, and save all the trouble? But this is heresy and I must not say it' (p. 59), is a good example of how discourses of desire are less exercises in wish-fulfilment than wish-formation; the woman letter writer takes up her pen because her desires have been thwarted and reconstitutes them in narrative metonymies.[20] Lucy's letter, the novel's most striking text of female passion, functions much like the mouldering manuscripts of so many gothic novels in the way it brings to light what has been repressed, here, a female desire at odds with a masculinist gender code.

Significantly, the letter is addressed not to one of her suitors, but to Mina. As its contents show, Lucy takes full advantage of the familiar letter as a private, expressive, and confidential genre, and, by addressing it to another woman, she further removes it from what the novel presents as a male-dominated textual circuit and from the strictures of a masculinist gender ideology. Texts written by women and for women become places of freedom where the powers and desires framed out by culture find a place and a language. But, as Van Helsing's reading of Mina's letters to Lucy and his probable reading of Lucy's to Mina demonstrates, texts by women for women are not necessarily protected from men's ('Angel') eyes. From this perspective, the staking is not only the males' editing of the marks which Dracula inscribed on Lucy's body, but also and by extension, an erasing and repressive revision of the text of her desire as it appears in her letter.

Stoker's novel vividly displays the strategies patriarchy uses to sustain itself and, as we have seen, these strategies include the literal and metaphorical textualising of women and the scripting of their roles and lives. Although she resigns herself to the traditional gender code and never consciously sets out to have all three men, thanks to the tradition of amorous epistolary discourse which Harker calls up, we can still read Lucy's letter-writing as an act of protest and rebellion, an attempt to rewrite the terms of the traditional gender code to another logic, a logic which recognises and accommodates female desire. This reading gains force when we see that Lucy's letter is not the only instance in *Dracula* of female reappropriation of textuality as a mode of resistance and revision.

Lucy's text of protest and desire joins those of other women called up by the novel who are already rewriting the terms of the gender code. For example, Mina speculates,

> Some of the 'New Women' writers will some day start an idea that men and women should be allowed to see each other asleep before proposing or accepting. But I suppose the New Woman won't condescend in future to accept; she will do the proposing herself. And a nice job she will make of it, too! There's some consolation in that.
>
> (p. 89)

As a transgressive text, then, the letter that speaks Lucy's desire is allied with those of New Woman writers who, as Mina reads them, are already rewriting the terms of gender relations. Clearly the New Woman, that 'powerful evolutionary type, harbinger of new worlds, new futures', is not quite what Harker has in mind for his 'modernity', but we can see here that she is the daughter of the female letter-writer Harker believes he has displaced.[21]

Moreover, as Mina presents her, the New Woman writer offers a slightly different way of using textuality to resist the script patriarchy writes on and for women. Lucy writes an alternative text with different logic – 'Why can't they let a girl marry three men, or as many as want her' – while the New Woman writer appropriates a male text – 'will you marry me' – for herself. The novel's narrative structure – a series of texts taken from a number of different 'contexts' collected and reframed as *Dracula* – shows that discourses can always be detached from their original contexts/speakers and reframed to serve other purposes, and the New Woman writer takes advantage of this to reframe as an expression of female desire and self-determination a text central to the discourse of male supremacy in gender relations.

Mina's own reaction to the New Woman writer's appropriation of texts traditionally masculine is ambiguous, but given her generally conservative rhetoric on gender matters, we can read it as disapproving. We should, however, draw some distinctions between, on the one hand, the conventional idealising rhetoric the men use about her and her own vocabulary of domestic duty and marital devotion, and on the other hand her own activities as text-maker and text-manager.

As transcriber, typist, compiler, and writer in her own right, Mina is, of all the group fighting the vampire, the one who most consistently and devotedly facilitates the circulation of texts that produces the knowledge so helpful in fighting the vampire. From the beginning she frames her textual work as an act of feminine duty and devotion:

> I have been working very hard lately, because I want to keep up with Jonathan's studies, and I have been practising shorthand very assiduously. When we are married I shall be able to be useful to Jonathan, and if I can stenograph well enough I can take down what he wants to say in this way and write it out for him on the typewriter, at which I am also practising very hard.
>
> (p. 53)

The passage recalls Dorothea Brooke's strategy of expanding the terms of wifely duty in ways that serve aspirations greater than those traditionally allowed a woman. Mina describes her idea to begin typing Harker's diary, an enterprise which leads to the grander scheme of typing and compiling all the texts, in very similar terms: 'I shall get my typewriter this very hour and start transcribing ... then, perhaps if I am ready, poor Jonathan may not be upset, for *I can speak for him* and never let him be worried or troubled at all' (p. 179, my italics). In both instances traditionally male interests and prerogatives are taken up by a woman in the name of traditionally female duties and interests. What Mina supposes the New Woman writer will do with texts traditionally male, she herself seems to be doing with actions.

Later, on her own initiative, Mina begins the typing and arranging of texts which eventually produces the compilation that we read. Harker, who as a solicitor is a professional manager of documents, helps her with this work, but the idea is Mina's and she is given full credit for the work and its success. Significantly, Harker praises her work not in terms associated with the feminine and domestic, but in terms of the intellectual and traditionally masculine – the production of knowledge through textual work is, after all, a traditionally masculine province. 'It is due to her energy and brains and foresight that the whole story is put together in such a way that every point tells', praises Harker (pp. 247–8). Van Helsing echoes the sentiment, and suggests what is at stake for the traditional gender code:

> Ah! that wonderful Madame Mina! She has man's brain – a brain that a man should have were he much gifted – and woman's heart. The good God fashioned her for a purpose, believe me when He made that so good combination.
>
> (pp. 234–5)

Just as striking as Van Helsing's praise of what he sees as Mina's 'masculine' intellectual gifts is his investment in maintaining the traditional gender ideology that Mina, as she and her textual work are described here, calls into question. This earthly patriarch represents Mina as an exception to womankind especially fashioned by the divine patriarch, and in so doing reinscribes the binary framework of traditional gender roles. Whether by violence, as in Lucy's case, or by the sort of idealising we see here, she who transgresses the boundaries is ultimately reappropriated to re-mark and reassert the very boundaries upon which patriarchy depends.[22]

The males recognise Mina's intelligence, and she herself enjoys exercising it, as her making of the compilation shows and her disappointment and depression over the men's excluding her from active participation in the hunt for Dracula suggests (a job too dangerous for a woman, they maintain) (p. 257). But Mina is not only smart – before she married she was a teacher – she is also canny. Sensing that their traditional gender roles are too narrow to encompass her, the men maintain them by making Mina a divine exception; but Mina, as we have seen, takes another tack, revising the terms of feminine activity and wifely duty to accommodate her wider aspirations. The best example of this strategy is Mina's casting of her textual work as textile work.

In his diary Seward notes, 'Mrs Harker says that they are knitting together in chronological order every scrap of evidence that they have' (p. 225). Although Seward may be the one characterising the writing and compiling as 'knitting' – his comments on the staking of Lucy suggest that he is deeply invested in maintaining traditional gender roles for women – the narrators' devotion to recording everything as accurately as possible suggests that the term was originally Mina's. Indeed, even if the term is Seward's, Mina's own actions have invited him to see her activity in such terms because Mina stores her typewriting in her workbasket (p. 183). If the novel had not already called up a tradition of women writers and narrators –

from Scheherazade to Harker's writer of love-letters to Mina's New Woman writers – we might see this likening of textual work to needlework solely as a reduction and trivialising of Mina. But given these allusions, to do so is critically reductive.

The analogy between the text and the textile which we see in such earlier gothic texts as Hogg's *Private Memoirs and Confessions* and Maturin's *Melmoth the Wanderer* has a long literary history and is now a critical commonplace. The knitting and weaving of Arachne, Penelope, Philomela, and the Lady of Shalott, for example, can all be read as *mise-en-abymes* of the texts in which they appear. Expanding on this phenomenon, deconstructive critics hold up the threadwork of Ariadne and Arachne as models of textuality, and in response feminist critics reinscribe the forgotten gender issues which the model calls up.[23]

Because the men decide – wrongly and to their detriment, it turns out – to keep Mina from active participation in the vampire hunt, we may be tempted to see her textual knitting as akin to the weaving of the Lady of Shalott, who weaves because a mysterious curse forbids her from taking part in the teeming life beyond her imprisoning island. Or we might see Mina as a latter-day Erinna, 'spin[ning] the byssus drearily / In insect-labour, while the throng / Of gods and men wrought deeds that poets wrought in song'. Such parallels have the appeal of being faithful to our final glimpse of Mina, in Harker's epilogue, where she is consigned to silence and traditional domesticity, but this end is itself problematic, and such a collapsing of textual work and women's work neglects the tradition of women writers/narrators the novel has already called up, women who use textuality to protest and even rewrite the traditional gender code which would silence them.

These lines describing Erinna's weaving are part of the epigraph of chapter 51 of *Daniel Deronda*, in which the Princess Halm-Eberstein defends herself for putting herself before the dictates of the gender code. What interests me here is Eliot's linking of weaving with female resistance to patriarchy, a link also implicit in 'insect-labour', an allusion to Arachne. Arachne wove a tapestry depicting human women (Europe and Leda, for example) who had been appropriated, at times violently, by male gods, and was consequently punished for representing the workings of divine (male) power. Her strategy is similar to that of the silenced Philomela, who, after she was raped by King Tereus and after he had cut out her tongue so she could not tell of the deed, cannily wove her story into a tapestry and in this way made it known.

As 'narrative' weavers, Arachne and Philomela have the most in common with Mina. Moreover, when we read Mina's textual work in the representational tradition called up when her work is characterised as 'knitting', we see that all three women produce works which tell tales of the abuse of patriarchal power, gendered narratives of the appropriation and suppression of women. The theme is woven throughout *Dracula*, from the treatment of Lucy and Mina by males human and vampiric, to the allusions to Othello and the Sultan of the *Arabian Nights*, and thus the irony of Harker's comment that it is thanks to Mina that every point in what comes to be the novel 'tells'. Like the women of the amorous epistolary tradition, Lucy plainly writes out both her passion and her frustration with the gender code, and her punishment for this act of resistance is to be made a place where men violently write their own texts. Mina uses a more subtle and covert strategy which is in keeping with both her cautious temperament and the novel's interest in coding and encryption (Jonathan writes in shorthand so that Dracula will not be able to read his journal; the staking of Lucy takes place in her crypt, and the marks on her body are thus a 'cryptic' sort of writing). Like Arachne and Philomela, Mina sets out for all to see the strategies and logics patriarchy uses to sustain itself – for example, the textualising of women on the one hand and the silencing of them on the other – and in this way representation becomes critique, a mode of silent resistance.

Indeed, from one vantage point this textual knitting even serves as a mode of subtle redress and revision. For example, the story Mina's textual work ultimately tells casts her and her work as not merely helpful but indispensable. Only after the men invite Mina back into active participation in the hunt do they succeed; her ability to read Dracula's mind when under hypnosis gives the humans the winning advantage. Even the form and structure of her compilation is subtly anti-patriarchal because it is not hierarchical. The structure does not privilege a single, unitary, voice or one voice above a rank of others, but refuses to subordinate either discourses, or writers, one to another. Mina's text has no master discourse.

Of all the women weavers and knitters, Mina may finally have the most in common with Philomela who, her tongue forever silenced by the king, was finally transformed into a nightingale, the idealised bird which male writers have for centuries celebrated as a figure for their poetic inspiration. As the nightingale sings but the male poets have the last word, so Harker has the last word in *Dracula*. As framing discourses, epilogues are often places of maximum repression, and

Harker's close both describes and enacts the reinscription of Mina into the terms of the traditional gender code. As Lucy was ultimately consigned to the silence and celibacy of the grave, so Mina is consigned to the silence and monogamy of traditional marriage and motherhood. Once again the men make her the object of their chivalrous care and rhetoric, the same idealising care which she earlier claimed rendered her without a voice. Our last glimpse of her is as homemaker, not text-maker, her energy, brains, and foresight no longer devoted to producing texts, but to producing and nurturing a son whose 'bundle of names', Harker notes with paternal pride, 'links all our little band of men together' (p. 378). Even here, in the son's name, we find a final reassertion of the primacy of men and male bonds under patriarchy, and consequently of the function of women and (the products of) their bodies as mediating relations among men.[24] No longer a means by which narrative is produced and transmitted, Mina becomes the means by which male power is transmitted from fathers to sons.

The novel's multiple-voice narrative strategy, I have argued, invites us to read it through a Bakhtinian framework which is suspicious of master discourses and 'final words'. Moreover, no matter how strong the appearance of closure, endings in gothic fiction rarely provide resolution; they are merely places where we begin to re-enter the text. The text's consistent weaving of two (opposing) logics – represented by the patriarchal textualising of women on the one hand and, on the other, a female appropriation of textuality as a means of resisting patriarchy and its strategies – into a single work should warn us not to read it as merely making a final choice here, as endorsing once and for all the traditional gender code and celebrating the bourgeois family that code fosters. Harker frames off the novel with a picture of happy domesticity, but the text which Mina has vamped together and helped to write tells clearly what price women, and perhaps even men, pay for the sake of this picture.

From *LIT*, 1 (1990), 199–216.

NOTES

[In this essay, Rebecca Pope traces the conflict of ideologies in *Dracula* through a Bakhtinian analysis of the relations between gender and textuality. Bakhtin, a Marxist, recognised that words were carriers of values, sites of class struggles; literary texts, he demonstrated, were constructed from different discourses in dialogue. Meaning was dependent on context since language is 'dialogic' or 'polyphonic': there is a multiplicity of voices. In *Dracula*, Pope demonstrates, the patriarchal textualising of women, seen most strikingly in the way the men inscribe, mark, the body of Lucy, is set against the women's appropriation of textuality as a means of resisting such patriarchal strategies. In spite of the restoration of patriarchal values in the final scene of happy domesticity, the polyphonic nature of the text remains resistant to any such closure. All quotations from Stoker's *Dracula* in this essay are taken from the Oxford World's Classics 1983 edition. Ed.]

1. Elaine Showalter, 'Introduction: The Rise of Gender', in *Speaking of Gender*, ed. Elaine Showalter (New York, 1989), p. 9.

2. Most critics mention the novel's striking narrative structure, but few of the many critics who have written on the novel offer a detailed and sustained analysis of it. Exceptions, in varying degrees, are Carol Senf's 'Dracula: The Unseen Face in the Mirror', *Journal of Narrative Technique*, 19 (1979), 160–70; David Seed's 'The Narrative Method of *Dracula*', *Nineteenth-Century Fiction*, 40 (1985), 61–75; and Geoffrey Wall's 'Different from Writing: *Dracula* in 1897', *Literature and History*, 10 (1984), 15–23. Their emphases differ from mine.

3. The most helpful of Bakhtin's texts here is *The Dialogic Imagination: Four Essays*, ed. Michael Holquist, trans. Michael Holquist and Caryl Emerson (Austin, TX, 1981). Tzvetan Todorov's *Bakhtin: The Dialogical Principle*, trans. Wlad Godzich (Minneapolis, 1984) and Julia Kristeva's *Desire in Language*, ed. Leon S. Roudiez, trans. Thomas Gora, Alice Jardine, and Leon S. Roudiez (New York, 1980) provide helpful readings of Bakhtin.

4. Bakhtin, *The Dialogic Imagination*, p. 49.

5. Kristeva, *Desire in Language*, p. 71.

6. Linda Kauffman's *Discourses of Desire* (Ithaca, NY, 1986) employs Bakhtin's notion of an alternative logic that challenges official (patriarchal) thought and ideology in its study of gender issues and the genre of amorous epistolary discourse. While she does not discuss *Dracula*, some of her insights have aided my own work here.

7. Bram Stoker, *Famous Imposters* (New York, 1910), p. 227.

8. Ibid., p. 230.

9. Todorov, *Bakhtin: The Dialogical Principle*, p. 58.

10. Peter Schwenger, 'The Masculine Mode', in *Speaking of Gender*, ed. Elaine Showalter, p. 102.

11. In the course of his examination of the text's anxieties over eroticism between men and the way the novel uses monstrous heterosexual bonds to talk covertly about homoerotic ones, Christopher Craft, in '"Kiss Me

with Those Red Lips": Gender and Inversion in Bram Stoker's *Dracula*'
[reprinted in this volume – Ed.], makes some of the same observations
upon which my own differently framed and motivated argument
depends: that women mediate bonds between men; that, for men,
women are passive signs in a masculine gender code; that, as Lucy's fate
shows, men inscribe and reinscribe the female body in order to assert
the distinctions of gender that Victorian culture fears might dissolve.
The classic essay on the textualisation of the female body is Susan
Gubar's '"The Blank Page" and the Issues of Female Creativity', *Critical
Inquiry*, 8 (1981), 243–63. In *The Flesh Made Word: Female Figures
and Women's Bodies* (Oxford, 1987), Helena Michie discusses the
'reading' of women's bodies in Victorian texts, including *Dracula*.

12. Some readers may argue that Renfield, whose behaviour bears the mark
of his having been impressed by Dracula and pressed into his service,
upsets the gendered pattern I establish here. But Renfield's status and
much of his behaviour are, from the first time we meet him, markedly
'feminine' and thus rather off the scale to begin with. For example, as a
mad person locked away, he takes a place in Victorian fiction usually
occupied by women – Bertha in *Jane Eyre* and Laura in *The Woman in
White* for example.

13. Alan P. Johnson, '"Dual Life": The Status of Women in Stoker's
Dracula', in *Sexuality and Victorian Literature*, ed. Don Richard Cox
(Knoxville, TN, 1984), p. 21.

14. Dale Spender, *Man Made Language*, 2nd edn (London, 1985), p. 20.

15. René Girard's *Deceit, Desire, and the Novel*, trans. Yvonne Freccero
(Baltimore, MD, 1965), sets out the notion of a triangular structure of
mimetic desire which informs my reading of *Dracula*. Eve Sedgwick's
Between Men: English Literature and Male Homosocial Desire (New
York, 1985) builds upon this triangular structure to analyse the range
of male bonds from the homosocial to the homoerotic. Only recently
have critical readings of *Dracula* begun to note the homoeroticism that
subtends the relentlessly heterosexual surface of the novel. See especially the readings by Christopher Craft and Robin Wood, 'Burying the
Undead: The Use and Obsolescence of Count Dracula', *Mosaic*, 16
(1983), 175–87.

16. Kauffman, *Discourses of Desire*, pp. 120, 176.

17. Ibid., p. 21.

18. Ibid., pp. 229, 262.

19. Ibid., p. 122.

20. Ibid., pp. 214–15.

21. Nina Auerbach, *Woman and the Demon: The Life of a Victorian
Myth* (Cambridge, MA, 1982), p. 43. A number of critics look at the

appearance of the New Woman in the novel; see David Punter's *The Literature of Terror: A History of Gothic Fiction from 1765 to the Present Day* (London, 1980) [excerpt reprinted in this volume – Ed.] and Carol Senf's '*Dracula*: Stoker's Response to the New Woman', *Victorian Studies*, 26 (1982), 33–49.

22. For a reading of the mixing of gender traits in the novel as a distortion of an ideal androgyny, see William Patrick Day, *In the Circles of Fear and Desire: A Study of Gothic Fantasy* (Chicago, 1985).

23. J. Hillis Miller, in both 'Ariachne's Broken Woof', *Georgia Review*, 31 (1977), 44–60, and 'Ariadne's Thread: Repetition and the Narrative Line', in *Interpretation of Narrative*, ed. Mario J. Valdes and Owen J. Miller (Toronto, 1978), pp. 148–66, illustrates well deconstruction's use of thread and knitting imagery. In her 'Arachnologies: The Woman, The Critic, and the Text', in *Speaking of Gender*, ed. Elaine Showalter, pp. 270–85, Nancy K. Miller sums up and furthers feminist criticism's corrective.

24. 'Mina' is short for 'Wilhelmina' – a feminisation of 'Wilhelm' and thus the child could have been given a form of his mother's name but was not.

6

'Kiss Me with Those Red Lips': Gender and Inversion in Bram Stoker's *Dracula*

CHRISTOPHER CRAFT

When Joseph Sheridan Le Fanu observed in *Carmilla* (1872) that 'the vampire is prone to be fascinated with an engrossing vehemence resembling the passion of love' and that vampiric pleasure is heightened 'by the gradual approaches of an artful courtship', he identified clearly the analogy between monstrosity and sexual desire that would prove, under a subsequent Freudian stimulus, paradigmatic for future readings of vampirism.[1] Modern critical accounts of *Dracula*, for instance, almost universally agree that vampirism both expresses and distorts an originally sexual energy. That distortion, the representation of desire under the defensive mask of monstrosity, betrays the fundamental psychological ambivalence identified by Franco Moretti when he writes that 'vampirism is an excellent example of the identity of desire and fear'.[2] This interfusion of sexual desire and the fear that the moment of erotic fulfilment may occasion the erasure of the conventional and integral self informs both the central action in *Dracula* and the surcharged emotion of the characters about to be kissed by 'those red lips'.[3] So powerful an ambivalence, generating both errant erotic impulses and compensatory anxieties, demands a strict, indeed an almost schematic formal management of narrative material. In *Dracula* Stoker borrows from Mary Shelley's *Frankenstein* and Robert Louis Stevenson's *Dr Jekyll and Mr Hyde* a narrative strategy characterised by a predictable, if variable, triple rhythm. Each of these texts first invites or admits a monster, then entertains and is entertained by monstrosity for some extended duration, until in its closing pages it expels or repudiates the monster and all the disruption that he/she/it brings.

Obviously enough, the first element in this triple rhythm corresponds formally to the text's beginning or generative moment, to its need to produce the monster, while the third element corresponds to the text's terminal moment, to its need both to destroy the monster it has previously admitted and to end the narrative that houses the monster. Interposed between these antithetical gestures of admission and expulsion is the gothic novel's prolonged middle,[4] during which the text affords its ambivalence a degree of play intended to produce a pleasurable, indeed a thrilling anxiety. Within its extended middle, the gothic novel entertains its resident demon – is, indeed, entertained by it – and the monster, now ascendent in its strength, seems for a time potent enough to invert the 'natural' order and overwhelm the comforting closure of the text. That threat, of course, is contained and finally nullified by the narrative requirement that the monster be repudiated and the world of normal relations restored; thus, the gesture of expulsion, compensating for the original irruption of the monstrous, brings the play of monstrosity to its predictable close. This narrative rhythm, whose tripartite cycle of admission-entertainment-expulsion enacts sequentially an essentially simultaneous psychological equivocation, provides aesthetic management of the fundamental ambivalence that motivates these texts and our reading of them.

While such isomorphism of narrative method obviously implies affinities and similarities among these different texts, it does not argue identity of meaning. However similar *Frankenstein*, *Dr Jekyll and Mr Hyde*, and *Dracula* may be, differences nevertheless obtain, and these differences bear the impress of authorial, historical, and institutional pressures. This essay therefore offers not a reading of monstrosity in general, but rather an account of Bram Stoker's particular articulation of the vampire metaphor in *Dracula*, a book whose fundamental anxiety, an equivocation about the relationship between desire and gender, repeats, with a monstrous difference, a pivotal anxiety of late Victorian culture. Jonathan Harker, whose diary opens the novel, provides *Dracula*'s most precise articulation of this anxiety. About to be kissed by the 'weird sisters' (p. 64), the incestuous vampiric daughters who share Castle Dracula with the Count, a supine Harker thrills to a double passion:

All three had brilliant white teeth, that shone like pearls against the ruby of their voluptuous lips. There was something about them that made me uneasy, *some longing and at the same time some deadly fear*. I felt in my heart a wicked, burning desire that they would kiss me with those red lips.

(p. 51; emphasis added)

Immobilised by the competing imperatives of 'wicked desire' and 'deadly fear', Harker awaits an erotic fulfilment that entails both the dissolution of the boundaries of the self and the thorough subversion of conventional Victorian gender codes, which constrained the mobility of sexual desire and varieties of genital behaviour by according to the more active male the right and responsibility of vigorous appetite, while requiring the more passive female to 'suffer and be still'. John Ruskin, concisely formulating Victorian conventions of sexual difference, provides us with a useful synopsis: 'The man's power is active, progressive, defensive. He is eminently the doer, the creator, the discoverer, the defender. His intellect is for speculation and invention; his energy for adventure, for war, and for conquest. ...' Woman, predictably enough, bears a different burden: 'She must be enduringly, incorruptibly, good; instinctively, infallibly wise – wise, not for self-development, but for self-renunciation ... wise, not with the narrowness of insolent and loveless pride, but with the passionate gentleness of an infinitely variable, because infinitely applicable, modesty of service – the true changefulness of woman.'[5] Stoker, whose vampiric women exercise a far more dangerous 'changefulness' than Ruskin imagines, anxiously inverts this conventional pattern, as virile Jonathan Harker enjoys a 'feminine' passivity and awaits a delicious penetration from a woman whose demonism is figured as the power to penetrate. A swooning desire for an overwhelming penetration and an intense aversion to the demonic potency empowered to gratify that desire compose the fundamental motivating action and emotion in *Dracula*.

This ambivalence, always excited by the imminence of the vampiric kiss, finds its most sensational representation in the image of the Vampire Mouth, the central and recurring image of the novel: 'There was a deliberate voluptuousness which was both thrilling and repulsive ... I could see in the moonlight the moisture shining on the red tongue as it lapped the white sharp teeth' (p. 52). That is Harker describing one of the three vampire women at Castle

Dracula. Here is Dr Seward's description of the Count: 'His eyes flamed red with devilish passion; the great nostrils of the white aquiline nose opened wide and quivered at the edges; and the white sharp teeth, behind the full lips of the blood-dripping mouth, champed together like those of a wild beast' (p. 336). As the primary site of erotic experience in *Dracula*, this mouth equivocates, giving the lie to the easy separation of the masculine and the feminine. Luring at first with an inviting orifice, a promise of red softness, but delivering instead a piercing bone, the vampire mouth fuses and confuses what Dracula's civilised nemesis, Van Helsing and his Crew of Light,[6] works so hard to separate – the gender-based categories of the penetrating and the receptive, or, to use Van Helsing's language, the complementary categories of 'brave men' and 'good women'. With its soft flesh barred by hard bone, its red crossed by white, this mouth compels opposites and contrasts into a frightening unity, and it asks some disturbing questions. Are we male or are we female? Do we have penetrators or orifices? And if both, what does that mean? And what about our bodily fluids, the red and the white? What are the relations between blood and semen, milk and blood? Furthermore, this mouth, bespeaking the subversion of the stable and lucid distinctions of gender, is the mouth of all vampires, male and female.

Yet we must remember that the vampire mouth is first of all Dracula's mouth, and that all subsequent versions of it (in *Dracula* all vampires other than the Count are female)[7] merely repeat as diminished simulacra the desire of the Great Original, that 'father or furtherer of a new order of beings' (p. 360). Dracula himself, calling his children 'my jackals to do my bidding when I want to feed', identifies the systematic creation of female surrogates who enact his will and desire (p. 365). This should remind us that the novel's opening anxiety, its first articulation of the vampiric threat, derives from Dracula's hovering interest in Jonathan Harker; the sexual threat that this novel first evokes, manipulates, sustains, but never finally represents is that Dracula will seduce, penetrate, drain another male. The suspense and power of *Dracula's* opening section, of that phase of the narrative which we have called the invitation to monstrosity, proceeds precisely from this unfulfilled sexual ambition. Dracula's desire to fuse with a male, most explicitly evoked when Harker cuts himself shaving, subtly and dangerously suffuses this text. Always postponed and never directly enacted, this desire finds evasive fulfilment in an important series of heterosexual displacements.

Dracula's ungratified desire to vamp Harker is fulfilled instead by his three vampiric daughters, whose anatomical femininity permits, because it masks, the silently interdicted homoerotic embrace between Harker and the Count. Here, in a displacement typical both of this text and the gender-anxious culture from which it arose, an implicitly homoerotic desire achieves representation as a monstrous heterosexuality, as a demonic inversion of normal gender relations. Dracula's daughters offer Harker a feminine form but a masculine penetration:

> Lower and lower went her head as the lips went below the range of my mouth and chin and seemed to fasten on my throat. ... I could feel the soft, shivering touch of the lips on the supersensitive skin of my throat, and the hard dents of the two sharp teeth, just touching and pausing there. I closed my eyes in a langorous ecstasy and waited – waited with a beating heart.
>
> (p. 52)

This moment, constituting the text's most direct and explicit representation of a male's desire to be penetrated, is governed by a double deflection: first, the agent of penetration is nominally and anatomically (from the mouth down, anyway) female; and second, this dangerous moment, fusing the maximum of desire and the maximum of anxiety, is poised precisely at the brink of penetration. Here the 'two sharp teeth', just 'touching' and 'pausing' there, stop short of the transgression which would unsex Harker and toward which this text constantly aspires and then retreats: the actual penetration of the male.

This moment is interrupted, this penetration denied. Harker's pause at the end of the paragraph ('waited – waited with a beating heart'), which seems to anticipate an imminent piercing, in fact anticipates not the completion but the interruption of the scene of penetration. Dracula himself breaks into the room, drives the women away from Harker, and admonishes them: 'How dare you touch him, any of you? How dare you cast eyes on him when I had forbidden it? Back, I tell you all! This man belongs to me' (p. 53). Dracula's intercession here has two obvious effects: by interrupting the scene of penetration, it suspends and disperses throughout the text the desire maximised at the brink of penetration, and it repeats the threat of a more direct libidinous embrace between Dracula and Harker. Dracula's taunt, 'This man belongs to me', is suggestive enough, but at no point subsequent to this moment does Dracula kiss Harker, preferring instead to pump him for his knowledge of English law, custom, and language. Dracula, soon departing for England, leaves Harker to the weird sisters, whose final penetration of him, implied but never represented, occurs in the dark interspace to which Harker's journal gives no access.

Hereafter *Dracula* will never represent so directly a male's desire to be penetrated; once in England Dracula, observing a decorous heterosexuality, vamps only women, in particular Lucy Westenra and Mina Harker. The novel, nonetheless, does not dismiss homoerotic desire and threat; rather it simply continues to diffuse and displace it. Late in the text, the Count himself announces a deflected homoeroticism when he admonishes the Crew of Light thus: 'My revenge is just begun! I spread it over the centuries, and time is on my side. Your girls that you all love are mine already; and *through them you and others shall yet be mine ...*' (p. 365; italics added). Here Dracula specifies the process of substitution by which 'the girls that you all love' mediate and displace a more direct communion among males. Van Helsing, who provides for Lucy transfusions designed to counteract the dangerous influence of the Count, confirms Dracula's declaration of surrogation; he knows that once the transfusions begin, Dracula drains from Lucy's veins not her blood, but rather blood transferred from the veins of the Crew of Light: 'even we four who gave our strength to Lucy it also is all to him [*sic*]' (p. 244). Here, emphatically, is another instance of the heterosexual displacement of a desire mobile enough to elude the boundaries of gender. Everywhere in this text such desire seeks a strangely deflected heterosexual distribution; only through women may men touch.

The representation of sexuality in *Dracula*, then, registers a powerful ambivalence in its identification of desire and fear. The text releases a sexuality so mobile and polymorphic that Dracula may be best represented as bat or wolf or floating dust; yet this effort to elude the restrictions upon desire encoded in traditional conceptions of gender then constrains that desire through a series of heterosexual displacements. Desire's excursive mobility is always filtered in *Dracula* through the mask of a monstrous or demonic heterosexuality. Indeed, Dracula's mission in England is the creation of a race of monstrous women, feminine demons equipped with masculine devices. This monstrous heterosexuality is apotropaic for two reasons: first, because it masks and deflects the anxiety consequent to a more direct representation of same sex eroticism; and second, because in imagining a sexually aggressive woman as a demonic penetrator, as a usurper of a prerogative belonging 'naturally' to the other gender, it justifies, as we shall see later, a violent expulsion of this deformed femininity.

In its particular formulation of erotic ambivalence, in its contrary need both to liberate and constrain a desire indifferent to the prescriptions of gender by figuring such desire as monstrous heterosexuality, *Dracula* may seem at first idiosyncratic, anomalous, merely neurotic. This is not the case. *Dracula* presents a characteristic, if hyperbolic, instance of Victorian anxiety over the potential fluidity of gender roles, and this text's defensiveness toward the mobile sexuality it nonetheless wants to evoke parallels remarkably other late Victorian accounts of same sex eroticism, of desire in which the 'sexual instincts' were said to be, in the words of John Addington Symonds, 'improperly correlated to [the] sexual organs'.[8] During the last decades of the nineteenth century and the first of the twentieth, English writers produced their first sustained discourse about the variability of sexual desire, with a special emphasis upon male homoerotic love, which had already received indirect and evasive endorsement from Tennyson in 'In Memoriam' and from Whitman in the 'Calamus' poems. The preferred taxonomic label under which these writers categorised and examined such sexual desire was not, as we might anticipate, 'homosexuality' but rather 'sexual inversion', a classificatory term involving a complex negotiation between socially encoded gender norms and a sexual mobility that would seem at first unconstrained by those norms. [...]

ENGENDERING GENDER

Our strong game will be to play our masculine against her feminine.
(Stoker, *The Lair of the White Worm*)

The portion of the gothic novel that I have called the prolonged middle, during which the text allows the monster a certain dangerous play, corresponds in *Dracula* to the duration beginning with the Count's arrival in England and ending with his flight back home; this extended middle constitutes the novel's prolonged moment of equivocation, as it entertains, elaborates, and explores the very anxieties it must later expel in the formulaic resolution of the plot. The action within this section of *Dracula* consists, simply enough, in an extended battle between two evidently masculine forces, one identifiably good and the other identifiably evil, for the allegiance of a woman (two women actually – Lucy Westenra and Mina Harker nee Murray).[9] This competition between alternative potencies has the apparent simplicity of a black and white opposition. Dracula ravages and impoverishes these women, Van Helsing's Crew of Light restores and 'saves' them. As Dracula conducts his serial assaults upon Lucy, Van Helsing, in a pretty counterpoint of penetration, responds with a series of defensive transfusions; the blood that Dracula takes out Van Helsing then puts back. Dracula, isolated and disdainful of community, works alone; Van Helsing enters this little English community, immediately assumes authority, and then works through surrogates to cement communal bonds. As critics have noted, this pattern of opposition distils readily into a competition between antithetical fathers. 'The vampire Count, centuries old', Maurice Richardson wrote twenty-five years ago, 'is a father figure of huge potency' who competes with Van Helsing, 'the good father figure'.[10] The theme of alternate paternities is, in short, simple, evident, unavoidable.

This oscillation between vampiric transgression and medical correction exercises the text's ambivalence toward those fundamental dualisms – life and death, spirit and flesh, male and female – which have served traditionally to constrain and delimit the excursions of desire. As doctor, lawyer, and sometimes priest ('The Host. I brought it from Amsterdam. I have an indulgence.'), Van Helsing stands as the protector of the patriarchal institutions he so emphatically represents and as the guarantor of the traditional dualisms his religion and profession promote and authorise.[11] His largest purpose is to reinscribe the dualities that Dracula would muddle and confuse. Dualities require demarcations, inexorable and ineradicable lines of separation, but Dracula, as a border being who abrogates demarcations, makes such distinctions impossible. He is *nosferatu*, neither dead nor alive but somehow both, mobile frequenter of the grave and boudoir, easeful communicant of exclusive realms, and as such as he toys with the separation of the living and the dead, a distinction critical to physician, lawyer, and priest alike. His mobility and metaphoric power deride the distinction between spirit and flesh, another of Van Helsing's sanctified dualisms. Potent enough to ignore death's terminus, Dracula has a spirit's freedom and mobility, but that mobility is chained to the most mechanical of appetites: he and his children rise and fall for a drink and for nothing else, for nothing else matters. This con- or inter-fusion of spirit and appetite, of eternity and sequence, produces a madness of activity and a mania of unceasing desire. Dracula lives an eternity of sexual repetition, a lurid wedding of desire and satisfaction that parodies both.

But the traditional dualism most vigorously defended by Van Helsing and most subtly subverted by Dracula is, of course, sexual: the division of being into gender, either male or female. Indeed, as we have seen, the vampiric kiss excites a sexuality so mobile, so insistent, that it threatens to overwhelm the distinctions of gender, and the exuberant energy with which Van Helsing and the Crew of Light counter Dracula's influence represents the text's anxious defence against the very desire it also seeks to liberate. In counterposing Dracula and Van Helsing, Stoker's text simultaneously threatens and protects the line of demarcation that ensures the intelligible division of being into gender. This ambivalent need to invite the vampiric kiss and then to repudiate it defines exactly the dynamic of the battle that constitutes the prolonged middle of this text. The field of this battle, of this equivocal competition for the right to define the possible relations between desire and gender, is the infinitely penetrable body of a somnolent woman. This interposition of a woman between Dracula and Van Helsing should not surprise us; in England, as in Castle Dracula, a violent wrestle between males is mediated through a feminine form.

The Crew of Light's conscious conception of women is, predictably enough, idealised – the stuff of dreams. Van Helsing's concise description of Mina may serve as a representative example: 'She is one of God's women fashioned by His own hand to show us men and other women that there is a heaven we can enter, and that its light can be here on earth' (p. 226). The impossible idealism of this conception of women deflects attention from the complex and complicitous interaction within this sentence of gender, authority, and representation. Here Van Helsing's exegesis of God's natural text reifies Mina into a stable sign or symbol ('one of God's women') performing a fixed and comfortable function within a masculine sign system. Having received from Van Helsing's exegesis her divine impress, Mina signifies both a masculine artistic intention ('fashioned by His own hand') and a definite didactic purpose ('to show us men and other women' how to enter heaven), each of which constitutes an enormous constraint upon the significative possibilities of the sign or symbol that Mina here becomes. Van Helsing's reading of Mina, like a dozen other instances in which his interpretation of the sacred determines and delimits the range of activity permitted to women, encodes woman with a 'natural' meaning composed according to the textual imperatives of anxious males. Precisely this complicity between masculine anxiety, divine textual authority, and a fixed conception of femininity – which may seem benign enough in the passage above – will soon be used to justify the destruction of Lucy Westenra, who, having been successfully vamped by Dracula, requires a corrective penetration. To Arthur's anxious importunity 'Tell me what I am to do', Van Helsing answers: 'Take this stake in your left hand, ready to place the point over the heart, and the hammer in your right. Then when we begin our prayer for the dead – I shall read him; I have here the book, and the others shall follow – strike in God's name ...' (p. 259). Here four males (Van Helsing, Seward, Holmwood, and Quincey Morris) communally read a masculine text (Van Helsing's mangled English even permits Stoker the unidiomatic pronominalisation of the genderless text: 'I shall read him')[12] in order to justify the fatal correction of Lucy's dangerous wandering, her insolent disregard for the sexual and semiotic constraint encoded in Van Helsing's exegesis of 'God's women'.

The process by which women are construed as signs determined by the interpretive imperatives of authorising males had been brilliantly identified some fifty years before the publication of *Dracula* by John Stuart Mill in *The Subjection of Women*. 'What is now called the nature of women', Mill writes, 'is an extremely artificial thing – the result of forced repression in some directions, unnatural stimulation in others.'[13] Mill's sentence, deftly identifying 'the nature of women' as an 'artificial' construct formed (and deformed) by 'repression' and 'unnatural stimulation', quietly unties the lacings that bind something called 'woman' to something else called 'nature'. Mill further suggests that a correct reading of gender becomes almost impossible, since the natural difference between male and female is subject to cultural interpretation: '... I deny that anyone knows, or can know, the nature of the two sexes, as long as they have only been seen in their present relation to one another.' Mill's agnosticism regarding 'the nature of the sexes' suggests the societal and institutional quality of all definitions of the natural, definitions which ultimately conspire to produce 'the imaginary and conventional character of women'.[14] This last phrase, like the whole of Mill's essay, understands and criticises the authoritarian nexus that arises when a deflected or transformed desire ('imaginary'), empowered by a gender-biased societal agreement ('conventional'), imposes itself upon a person in order to create a 'character'. 'Character' of course functions in at least three senses: who and what one 'is', the role one plays in society's supervening script, and the sign or letter that is intelligible only within the constraints of a larger sign system. Van Helsing's exegesis of 'God's women' creates just such an imaginary and conventional character. Mina's body/character may indeed be feminine, but the signification it bears is written and interpreted solely by males. As Susan Hardy Aiken has written, such a symbolic system takes 'for granted the role of women as passive objects or signs to be manipulated in the grammar of privileged male interchanges'.[15]

Yet exactly the passivity of this object and the ease of this manipulation are at question in *Dracula*. Dracula, after all, kisses these women out of their passivity and so endangers the stability of Van Helsing's symbolic system. Both the prescriptive intention of Van Helsing's exegesis and the emphatic methodology (hypodermic needle, stake, surgeon's blade) he employs to ensure the durability of his interpretation of gender suggest the potential unreliability of Mina as sign, an instability that provokes an anxiety we may call fear of the mediatrix. If, as Van Helsing admits, God's women provide the essential mediation ('the light can be here on earth') between the divine but distant patriarch and his earthly sons, then God's intention may be distorted by its potentially changeable vehicle. If woman-as-signifier wanders, then Van Helsing's whole cosmology, with its founding dualisms and supporting texts, collapses. In short, Van Helsing's interpretation of Mina, because endangered by the proleptic fear that his mediatrix might destabilise and wander, necessarily imposes an *a priori* constraint upon the significative possibilities of the sign 'Mina'. Such an authorial gesture, intended to forestall the semiotic wandering that Dracula inspires, indirectly acknowledges woman's dangerous potential. Late in the text, while Dracula is vamping Mina, Van Helsing will admit, very uneasily, that 'Madam Mina, our poor, dear Madam Mina is changing' (p. 384). The potential for such a change demonstrates what Nina Auerbach has called this woman's 'mysterious amalgam of imprisonment and power'.[16]

Dracula's authorising kiss, like that of a demonic Prince Charming, triggers the release of this latent power and excites in these women a sexuality so mobile, so aggressive, that it thoroughly disrupts Van

Helsing's compartmental conception of gender. Kissed into a sudden sexuality,[17] Lucy grows 'voluptuous' (a word used to describe her only during the vampiric process), her lips redden, and she kisses with a new interest. This sexualisation of Lucy, metamorphosing woman's 'sweetness' to 'adamantine, heartless cruelty, and [her] purity to voluptuous wantonness' (p. 252), terrifies her suitors because it entails a reversal or inversion of sexual identity; Lucy, now toothed like the Count, usurps the function of penetration that Van Helsing's moralised taxonomy of gender reserves for males. *Dracula*, in thus figuring the sexualisation of woman as deformation, parallels exactly some of the more extreme medical uses of the idea of inversion. Late Victorian accounts of lesbianism, for instance, superscribed conventional gender norms upon sexual relationships to which those norms were anatomically irrelevant. Again the heterosexual norm proved paradigmatic. The female 'husband' in such a relationship was understood to be dominant, appetitive, masculine, and 'congenitally inverted'; the female 'wife' was understood to be quiescent, passive, only 'latently' homosexual, and, as Havelock Ellis argued, unmotivated by genital desire. Extreme deployment of the heterosexual paradigm approached the ridiculous, as George Chauncey explains:

> The early medical case histories of lesbians thus predictably paid enormous attention to their menstrual flow and the size of their sexual organs. Several doctors emphasised that their lesbian patients stopped menstruating at an early age, if they began at all, or had unusually difficult and irregular periods. They also inspected the women's sexual organs, often claiming that inverts had unusually large clitorises, which they said the inverts used in sexual intercourse as a man would his penis.[18]

This rather pathetic hunt for the penis-in-absentia denotes a double anxiety: first, that the penis shall not be erased, and if it is erased, that it shall be reinscribed in a perverse simulacrum; and second, that all desire repeat, even under the duress of deformity, the heterosexual norm that the metaphor of inversion always assumes. Medical professionals had in fact no need to pursue this fantasised amazon of the clitoris, this 'unnatural' penetrator, so vigorously, since Stoker, whose imagination was at least deft enough to displace that dangerous simulacrum to an isomorphic orifice, had by the 1890s already invented her. His sexualised women are men too.

Stoker emphasises the monstrosity implicit in such abrogation of gender codes by inverting a favourite Victorian maternal function.

His new Lady Vampires feed at first only on small children, working their way up, one assumes, a demonic pleasure thermometer until they may feed at last on full-blooded males. Lucy's dietary indiscretions evoke the deepest disgust from the Crew of Light:

> With a careless motion, she flung to the ground, callous as a devil, the child that up to now she had clutched strenuously to her breast, growling over it as a dog growls over a bone. The child gave a sharp cry, and lay there moaning. There was a cold-bloodedness in the act which wrung a groan from Arthur; when she advanced to him with outstretched arms and a wanton smile, he fell back and hid his face in his hands.
>
> She still advanced, however, and with a langorous, voluptuous grace, said:
>
> 'Come to me Arthur. Leave those others and come to me. My arms are hungry for you. Come, and we can rest together. Come, my husband, come!'
>
> (pp. 253–4)

Stoker here gives us a *tableau mordant* of gender inversion: the child Lucy clutches 'strenuously to her breast' is not being fed, but is being fed upon. Furthermore, by requiring that the child be discarded that the husband may be embraced, Stoker provides a little emblem of this novel's anxious protestation that appetite in a woman ('My arms are hungry for you') is a diabolic ('callous as a devil') inversion of natural order, and of the novel's fantastic but futile hope that maternity and sexuality be divorced.

The aggressive mobility with which Lucy flaunts the encasements of gender norms generates in the Crew of Light a terrific defensive activity, as these men race to reinscribe, with a series of pointed instruments, the line of demarcation which enables the definition of gender. To save Lucy from the mobilisation of desire, Van Helsing and the Crew of Light counteract Dracula's subversive series of penetrations with a more conventional series of their own, that sequence of transfusions intended to provide Lucy with the 'brave man's blood' which 'is the best thing on earth when a woman is in trouble' (p. 180). There are in fact four transfusions, which begin with Arthur, who as Lucy's accepted suitor has the right of first infusion, and include Lucy's other two suitors (Dr Seward, Quincey Morris) and Van Helsing himself. One of the established observations of *Dracula* criticism is that these therapeutic penetrations represent displaced marital (and martial) penetrations; indeed, the text is emphatic about this substitution of medical for sexual penetration. After the first transfusion, Arthur feels as if he and Lucy 'had been really married and that she was his wife in the sight of God' (p. 209); and Van Helsing, after his donation, calls himself a 'bigamist' and Lucy 'this so sweet maid ... a polyandrist' (pp. 211–12). These transfusions, in short, are sexual (blood substitutes for semen here)[19] and constitute, in Nina Auerbach's superb phrase, 'the most convincing epithalamiums in the novel'.[20]

These transfusions represent the text's first anxious reassertion of the conventionally masculine prerogative of penetration; as Van Helsing tells Arthur before the first transfusion, 'You are a man and it is a man we want' (p. 148). Countering the dangerous mobility excited by Dracula's kiss, Van Helsing's penetrations restore to Lucy both the stillness appropriate to his sense of her gender and 'the regular breathing of healthy sleep', a necessary correction of the loud 'stertorous' breathing, the animal snorting, that the Count inspires. This repetitive contest (penetration, withdrawal; penetration, infusion), itself an image of *Dracula*'s ambivalent need to evoke and then to repudiate the fluid pleasures of vampiric appetite, continues to be waged upon Lucy's infinitely penetrable body until Van Helsing exhausts his store of 'brave men', whose generous gifts of blood, however efficacious, fail finally to save Lucy from the mobilisation of desire.

But even the loss of this much blood does not finally enervate a masculine energy as indefatigable as the Crew of Light's, especially when it stands in the service of a tradition of 'good women whose lives and whose truths may make good lesson [*sic*] for the children that are to be' (p. 222). In the name of those good women and future children (very much the same children whose throats Lucy is now penetrating), Van Helsing will repeat, with an added emphasis, his assertion that penetration is a masculine prerogative. His logic of corrective penetration demands an escalation, as the failure of the hypodermic needle necessitates the stake. A woman is better still than mobile, better dead than sexual:

> Arthur took the stake and the hammer, and when once his mind was set on action his hands never trembled nor even quivered. Van Helsing opened his missal and began to read, and Quincey and I followed as well as we could. Arthur placed the point over the heart, and as I looked I could see its dint in the white flesh. Then he struck with all his might.
> The Thing in the coffin writhed; and a hideous, blood-curdling screech came from the opened red lips. The body shook and quivered

and twisted in wild contortions; the sharp white teeth champed together till the lips were cut and the mouth was smeared with a
crimson foam. But Arthur never faltered. He looked like the figure of
Thor as his untrembling arm rose and fell, driving deeper and deeper
the mercy-bearing stake, whilst the blood from the pierced heart
welled and spurted up around it. His face was set, and high duty
seemed to shine through it; the sight of it gave us courage, so that our
voices seemed to ring through the little vault.

And then the writhing and quivering of the body became less, and
the teeth ceased to champ, and the face to quiver. Finally it lay still.
The terrible task was over.

(pp. 258–9)

Here is the novel's real – and the woman's only – climax, its most
violent and misogynistic moment, displaced roughly to the middle
of the book, so that the sexual threat may be repeated but its ultimate success denied: Dracula will not win Mina, second in his series
of English seductions. The murderous phallicism of this passage
clearly punishes Lucy for her transgression of Van Helsing's gender
code, as she finally receives a penetration adequate to ensure her
future quiescence. Violence against the sexual woman here is intense,
sensually imagined, ferocious in its detail. Note, for instance, the terrible dimple, the 'dint in the white flesh', that recalls Jonathan
Harker's swoon at Castle Dracula ('I could feel ... the hard dents of
the two sharp teeth, just touching and pausing there') and anticipates
the technicolour consummation of the next paragraph. That paragraph, masking murder as 'high duty', completes Van Helsing's penetrative therapy by 'driving deeper and deeper the mercy-bearing
stake'. One might question a mercy this destructive, this fatal, but
Van Helsing's actions, always sanctified by the patriarchal textual tradition signified by 'his missal', manage to 'restore Lucy to us as a
holy and not an unholy memory' (p. 258). This enthusiastic correction of Lucy's monstrosity provides the Crew of Light with a double
reassurance: it effectively exorcises the threat of a mobile and hungering feminine sexuality, and it counters the homoeroticism latent
in the vampiric threat by reinscribing (upon Lucy's chest) the line
dividing the male who penetrates and the woman who receives. By
disciplining Lucy and restoring each gender to its 'proper' function,
Van Helsing's pacification programme compensates for the threat of
gender indefinition implicit in the vampiric kiss.

The vigour and enormity of this penetration (Arthur driving the
'round wooden stake', which is 'some two and a half or three inches

thick and about three feet long', resembles 'the figure of Thor') do not bespeak merely Stoker's personal or idiosyncratic anxiety but suggest as well a whole culture's uncertainty about the fluidity of gender roles. Consider, for instance, the following passage from Ellis's contemporaneous *Studies in the Psychology of Sex*. Ellis, writing on 'The Mechanism of Detumescence' (i.e., ejaculation), employs a figure that Stoker would have recognised as his own:

> Detumescence is normally linked to tumescence. Tumescence is the piling on of the fuel; detumescence is the leaping out of the devouring flame whence is lighted the torch of life to be handed on from generation to generation. The whole process is double yet single; it is exactly analogous to that by which a pile is driven into the earth by the raising and the letting go of a heavy weight which falls on the head of the pile. In tumescence the organism is slowly wound up and force accumulated; in the act of detumescence the accumulated force is let go and by its liberation the sperm-bearing instrument is driven home.[21]

Both Stoker and Ellis need to imagine so homely an occurrence as penile penetration as an event of mythic, or at least seismographic, proportions. Ellis's pile driver, representing the powerful 'sperm-bearing instrument', may dwarf even Stoker's already outsized member, but both serve a similar function: they channel and finally 'liberate' a tremendous 'accumulated force' that itself represents a trans- or supra-natural intention. Ellis, employing a Darwinian principle of interpretation to explain that intention, reads woman's body (much as we have seen Van Helsing do) as a natural sign – or, perhaps better, as a sign of nature's overriding reproductive intention:

> There can be little doubt that, as one or two writers have already suggested, the hymen owes its development to the fact that its influence is on the side of effective fertilisation. It is an obstacle to the impregnation of the young female by immature, aged, or feeble males. *The hymen is thus an anatomical expression of that admiration of force which marks the female in her choice of a mate.* So regarded, it is an interesting example of the intimate matter in which sexual selection is really based on natural selection.[22] (italics added)

Here, as evolutionary teleology supplants divine aetiology and as Darwin's texts assume the primacy Van Helsing would reserve for God's, natural selection, not God's original intention, becomes the interpretive principle governing nature's text. As a sign or 'anatomical expression' within that text, the hymen signifies a woman's presumably natural 'admiration of force' and her invitation to 'the sperm-bearing instrument'. Woman's body, structurally hostile to 'immature, aged, or feeble males', simply begs for 'effective fertilisation'. Lucy's body, too, reassures the Crew of Light with an anatomical expression of her admiration of force. Once fatally staked, Lucy is restored to 'the so sweet that was'. Dr Seward describes the change:

> There in the coffin lay no longer the foul Thing that we had so dreaded and grown to hate that the work of her destruction was yielded to the one best entitled to it, but Lucy as we had seen her in her life, with her face of unequalled sweetness and purity. ... One and all we felt that the holy calm that lay like sunshine over the wasted face and form was only an earthly token and symbol of the calm that was to reign for ever.
>
> (p. 259)

This post-penetrative peace[23] denotes not merely the final immobilisation of Lucy's body, but also the corresponding stabilisation of the dangerous signifier whose wandering had so threatened Van Helsing's gender code. Here a masculine interpretive community ('One and all we felt') reasserts the semiotic fixity that allows Lucy to function as the 'earthly token and symbol' of eternal beatitude, of the heaven we can enter. We may say that this last penetration is doubly efficacious: in a single stroke both the sexual and the textual needs of the Crew of Light find a sufficient satisfaction.

Despite its placement in the middle of the text, this scene, which successfully pacifies Lucy and demonstrates so emphatically the efficacy of the technology Van Helsing employs to correct vampirism, corresponds formally to the scene of expulsion, which usually signals the end of the gothic narrative. Here, of course, this scene signals not the end of the story but the continuation of it, since Dracula will now repeat his assault on another woman. Such displacement of the scene of expulsion requires explanation. Obviously this displacement subserves the text's anxiety about the direct representation of eroticism between males: Stoker simply could not represent so explicitly a violent phallic interchange between the Crew of Light and Dracula. In a by now familiar heterosexual mediation, Lucy receives the phallic correction that Dracula deserves. Indeed, the actual expulsion of the Count at novel's end is a disappointing anticlimax. Two rather perfunctory knife strokes suffice to dispatch him, as *Dracula* simply forgets the elaborate ritual of correction that vampirism previously required. And the displacement of this scene performs at least two other functions: first, by establishing early the ultimate efficacy of Van Helsing's corrective technology, it reassures everyone – Stoker, his characters, the reader – that vampirism may indeed be vanquished, that its sexual threat, however powerful and intriguing, may be expelled; and second, in doing so, in establishing this reassurance, it permits the text to prolong and repeat its flirtation with vampirism, its ambivalent petition of that sexual threat. In short, the displacement of the scene of expulsion provides a heterosexual locale for Van Helsing's demonstration of compensatory phallicism, while it also extends the duration of the text's ambivalent play.

This extension of the text's flirtation with monstrosity, during which Mina is threatened by but not finally seduced into vampirism, includes the novel's only explicit scene of vampiric seduction. Important enough to be twice presented, first by Seward as spectator and then by Mina as participant, the scene occurs in the Harker bedroom, where Dracula seduces Mina while 'on the bed lay Jonathan Harker, his face flushed and breathing heavily as if in a stupor'. The Crew of Light bursts into the room; the voice is Dr Seward's:

> With his left hand he held both Mrs Harker's hands, keeping them away with her arms at full tension; his right hand gripped her by the back of the neck, forcing her face down on his bosom. Her white nightdress was smeared with blood, and a thin stream trickled down the man's bare breast, which was shown by his torn-open dress. The attitude of the two had a terrible resemblance to a child forcing a kitten's nose into a saucer of milk to compel it to drink.
>
> (p. 336)

In this initiation scene Dracula compels Mina into the pleasure of vampiric appetite and introduces her to a world where gender distinctions collapse, where male and female bodily fluids intermingle terribly. For Mina's drinking is double here, both a 'symbolic act of enforced fellation'[24] and a lurid nursing. That this is a scene of enforced fellation is made even clearer by Mina's own description of the scene a few pages later; she adds the graphic detail of the 'spurt':

> With that he pulled open his shirt, and with his long sharp nails opened a vein in his breast. When the blood began to spurt out, he took my hands in one of his, holding them tight, and with the other seized my neck and pressed my mouth to the wound, so that I must

either suffocate or swallow some of the – Oh, my God, my God!
What have I done?

(p. 343)

That 'Oh, my God, my God!' is deftly placed: Mina's verbal ejaculation supplants the Count's liquid one, leaving the fluid unnamed
and encouraging us to voice the substitution that the text implies –
this blood is semen too. But this scene of fellation is thoroughly displaced. We are at the Count's breast, encouraged once again to substitute white for red, as blood becomes milk: 'the attitude of the two
had a terrible resemblance to a child forcing a kitten's nose into a
saucer of milk.' Such fluidity of substitution and displacement
entails a confusion of Dracula's sexual identity, or an interfusion of
masculine and feminine functions, as Dracula here becomes a lurid
mother offering not a breast but an open and bleeding wound. But if
the Count's sexuality is double, then the open wound may be yet
another displacement (the reader of *Dracula* must be as mobile as
the Count himself). We are back in the genital region, this time a
woman's, and we have the suggestion of a bleeding vagina. The
image of red and voluptuous lips, with their slow trickle of blood,
has, of course, always harboured this potential.

We may read this scene, in which anatomical displacements and
the confluence of blood, milk, and semen forcefully erase the demarcation separating the masculine and the feminine, as *Dracula*'s
most explicit representation of the anxieties excited by the vampiric
kiss. Here *Dracula* defines most clearly vampirism's threat of gender
indefinition. Significantly, this scene is postponed until late in the
text. Indeed, this is Dracula's last great moment, his final demonstration of dangerous potency; after this, he will vamp no one. The
novel, having presented most explicitly its deepest anxiety, its fear
of gender dissolution, now moves mechanically to repudiate that
fear. After a hundred rather tedious pages of pursuit and flight,
Dracula perfunctorily expels the Count. The world of 'natural'
gender relations is happily restored, or at least seems to be.

A FINAL DISSOLUTION

If my last sentence ends with an equivocation, it is because *Dracula*
does so as well; the reader should leave this novel with a troubled
sense of the difference between the forces of darkness and the forces
of light. Of course the plot of *Dracula*, by granting ultimate victory

to Van Helsing and a dusty death to the Count, emphatically ratifies the simplistic opposition of competing conceptions of force and desire, but even a brief reflection upon the details of the war of penetrations complicates this comforting schema. A perverse mirroring occurs, as puncture for puncture the Doctor equals the Count. Van Helsing's doubled penetrations, first the morphine injection that immobilises the woman and then the infusion of masculine fluid, repeat Dracula's spatially doubled penetrations of Lucy's neck. And that morphine injection, which subdues the woman and improves her receptivity, curiously imitates the Count's strange hypnotic power; both men prefer to immobilise a woman before risking a penetration. Moreover, each penetration announces through its displacement this same sense of danger. Dracula enters at the neck, Van Helsing at the limb; each evades available orifices and refuses to submit to the dangers of vaginal contact. The shared displacement is telling: to make your own holes is an ultimate arrogance, an assertion of penetrative prowess that nonetheless acknowledges, in the flight of its evasion, the threatening power imagined to inhabit woman's available openings. Woman's body readily accommodates masculine fear and desire, whether directly libidinal or culturally refined. We may say that Van Helsing and his tradition have polished teeth into hypodermic needles, a cultural refinement that masks violation as healing. Van Helsing himself, calling his medical instruments 'the ghastly paraphernalia of our beneficial trade', employs an adjectival oxymoron (ghastly/beneficial) that itself glosses the troubled relationship between paternalism and violence (p. 146). The medical profession licenses the power to penetrate, devises a delicate instrumentation, and defines canons of procedure, while the religious tradition, with its insistent idealisation of women, encodes a restriction on the mobility of desire (who penetrates whom) and then licenses a tremendous punishment for the violation of the code.

But it is all penetrative energy, whether re-fanged or refined, and it is all libidinal; the two strategies of penetration are but different articulations of the same primitive force. *Dracula* certainly problematises, if it does not quite erase, the line of separation signifying a meaningful difference between Van Helsing and the Count. In other words, the text itself, in its imagistic identification of Dracula and the Crew of Light, in its ambivalent propensity to subvert its own fundamental differences, sympathises with and finally domesticates vampiric desire; the uncanny, as Freud brilliantly observed, always comes home. Such textual irony, composed of simultaneous but contrary impulses to establish and subvert the fundamental differences between violence and culture, between desire and its sublimations, recalls Freud's late speculations on the troubled relationship between the id and the superego (or ego ideal). In the two brief passages below, taken from his late work *The Ego and the Id*, Freud complicates the differentiation between the id and its unexpected effluent, the superego:

> There are two paths by which the contents of the id can penetrate into the ego. The one is direct, the other leads by way of the ego ideal.

And:

> From the point of view of instinctual control, of morality, it may be said of the id that it is totally non-moral, of the ego that it strives to be moral, and of the super-ego that it can be supermoral and then become as cruel as only the id can be.[25]

It is so easy to remember the id as a rising energy and the superego as a suppressive one, that we forget Freud's subtler argument. These passages, eschewing as too facile the simple opposition of the id and superego, suggest instead that the id and the superego are variant articulations of the same primitive energy. We are already familiar with the 'two paths by which the contents of the id penetrate the ego'. 'The one is direct', as Dracula's penetrations are direct and unembarrassed, and the other, leading 'by way of the ego ideal', recalls Van Helsing's way of repression and sublimation. In providing an indirect path for the 'contents of the id' and in being 'as cruel as only the id can be', the superego may be said to be, in the words of Leo Bersani, 'the id which has become its own mirror'.[26] This mutual reflectivity of the id and superego, of course, constitutes one of vampirism's most disturbing features, as Jonathan Harker, standing before his shaving glass, learns early in the novel: 'This time there could be no error, for the man was close to me, and I could see him over my shoulder. But there was no reflection of him in the mirror! The whole room behind me was displayed; but there was no sign of a man in it, except myself' (p. 37). The meaning of this little visual allegory should be clear enough: Dracula need cast no reflection because his presence, already established in Harker's image, would be simply redundant; the monster, indeed, is no one 'except myself'.

A dangerous sameness waits behind difference: tooth, stake, and hypodermic needle, it would seem, all share a point.

This blending or interfusion of fundamental differences would seem, in one respect at least, to contradict the progress of my argument. We have, after all, established that the Crew of Light's penetrative strategy, subserving Van Helsing's ideology of gender and his heterosexual account of desire, counters just such interfusions with emphatic inscriptions of sexual difference. Nonetheless, this penetrative strategy, despite its purposive heterosexuality, quietly erases its own fundamental differences, its own explicit assumptions of gender and desire. It would seem at first that desire for connection among males is both expressed in and constrained by a traditional articulation of such fraternal affection, as represented in this text's blaring theme of heroic or chivalric male bonding. The obvious male bonding in *Dracula* is precipitated by action – a good fight, a proud ethic, a great victory. Dedicated to a falsely exalted conception of woman, men combine fraternally to fulfil the collective 'high duty' that motivates their 'great quest' (p. 261). Van Helsing, always the ungrammatical exegete, provides the apt analogy: 'Thus we are ministers of God's own wish. ... He have allowed us to redeem one soul already, and we go out as the old knights of the Cross to redeem more' (p. 381). Van Helsing's chivalric analogy establishes this fraternity within an impeccable lineage signifying both moral rectitude and adherence to the limitation upon desire that this tradition encodes and enforces.

Yet beneath this screen or mask of authorised fraternity a more libidinal bonding occurs as male fluids find a protected pooling place in the body of a woman. We return, for a last time, to those serial transfusions, which, while they pretend to serve and protect 'good women', actually enable the otherwise inconceivable interfusion of the blood that is semen too. Here displacement (a woman's body) and sublimation (these are medical penetrations) permit the unpermitted, just as in gang rape men share their semen in a location displaced sufficiently to divert the anxiety excited by a more direct union. Repeating its subversive suggestion that the refined moral conceptions of Van Helsing's Crew of Light express obliquely an excursive libidinal energy, an energy much like the Count's, *Dracula* again employs an apparently rigorous heterosexuality to represent anxious desire for a less conventional communion. The parallel here to Dracula's taunt ('Your girls that you all love are mine already; and through them you ... shall be mine') is inescapable; in each case

Lucy, the woman in the middle, connects libidinous males. Here, as in the Victorian metaphor of sexual inversion, an interposed difference – an image of manipulable femininity – mediates and deflects an otherwise unacceptable appetite for sameness. Men touching women touch each other, and desire discovers itself to be more fluid than the Crew of Light would consciously allow.

Indeed, so insistent is this text to establish this pattern of heterosexual mediation that it repeats the pattern on its final page. Jonathan Harker, writing in a postscript that compensates clearly for his assumption at Castle Dracula of a 'feminine' passivity, announces the text's last efficacious penetration:

> Seven years ago we all went through the flames; and the happiness of some of us since then is, we think, well worth the pain we endured. It is an added joy to Mina and to me that our boy's birthday is the same day as that on which Quincey Morris died. His mother holds, I know, the secret belief that some of our brave friend's spirit has passed into him. His bundle of names links all our little band of men together; but we call him Quincey.
>
> (p. 449)

As offspring of Jonathan and Mina Harker, Little Quincey, whose introduction so late in the narrative ensures his emblematic function, seemingly represents the restoration of 'natural' order and especially the rectification of conventional gender roles. His official genesis is, obviously enough, heterosexual, but Stoker's prose quietly suggests an alternative paternity: 'His bundle of names links all our little band of men together.' This is the fantasy child of those sexualised transfusions, son of an illicit and nearly invisible homosexual union. This suggestion, reinforced by the preceding pun of 'spirit', constitutes this text's last and subtlest articulation of its 'secret belief' that 'a brave man's blood' may metamorphose into 'our brave friend's spirit'. But the real curiosity here is the novel's last-minute displacement, its substitution of Mina, who ultimately refused sexualisation by Dracula, for Lucy, who was sexualised, vigorously penetrated, and consequently destroyed. We may say that Little Quincey was luridly conceived in the veins of Lucy Westenra and then deftly relocated to the purer body of Mina Harker. Here, in the last of its many displacements, *Dracula* insists, first, that successful filiation implies the expulsion of all 'monstrous' desire in women and, second, that all desire, however mobile and omnivorous it may secretly be, must subject itself to the heterosexual configuration that alone defined the Victorian sense of the normal. In this regard, Stoker's fable, however hyperbolic its anxieties, represents his age. As we have seen, even polemicists of same sex eroticism like Symonds and Ellis could not imagine such desire without repeating within their metaphor of sexual inversion the basic structure of the heterosexual paradigm. Victorian culture's anxiety about desire's potential indifference to the prescriptions of gender produces everywhere a predictable repetition and a predictable displacement: the heterosexual norm repeats itself in a mediating image of femininity – the Count's vampiric daughters. Ulrichs's and Symonds's *anima muliebris*, Lucy Westenra's penetrable body – that displaces a more direct communion among males. Desire, despite its propensity to wander, stays home and retains an essentially heterosexual and familial definition. The result in *Dracula* is a child whose conception is curiously immaculate, yet disturbingly lurid: child of his fathers' violations. Little Quincey, fulfilling Van Helsing's prophecy of 'the children that are to be', may be the text's emblem of a restored natural order, but his paternity has its unofficial aspect too. He is the unacknowledged son of the Crew of Light's displaced homoerotic union, and his name, linking the 'little band of men together', quietly remembers that secret genesis.

From *Representations*, 8 (1984), 107–30.

NOTES

[The influence of Christopher Craft's seminal essay on *Dracula* criticism cannot be underestimated; he has influenced not only our interpretations of the text, by disturbing previously accepted gendered readings, but even the language we use to discuss the text; for all post-Craftian *Dracula* critics, the band of vampire hunters has simply become, in Craft's term, the 'Crew of Light'. Placing *Dracula* in the context of the Victorian fin de siècle, his historicist reading draws on late-nineteenth-century constructions of homoeroticism to demonstrate the way in which the text uses monstrous heterosexual relationships to talk covertly about homoerotic ones, and reveals the anxiety of an age over the fluidity of gender roles. A section of this essay has been edited for reasons of space. Ed.]

1. Joseph Sheridan Le Fanu, *Carmilla*, in *The Best Ghost Stories of J. S. Le Fanu* (New York, 1964), p. 337. This novella of lesbian vampirism, which appeared first in Le Fanu's *In a Glass Darkly* (1872), predates *Dracula* by 25 years.

2. Franco Moretti, *Signs Taken For Wonders* (London, 1983), p. 100 [excerpted in this volume – Ed.].

3. Bram Stoker, *Dracula* (New York, 1979), p. 51. All further references to *Dracula* appear within the essay in parentheses.

4. Readers of Tzvetan Todorov's *The Fantastic* (Ithaca, NY, 1975) will recognise that my argument about the Gothic text's extended middle derives in part from his idea that the essential condition of fantastic fiction is a duration characterised by readerly suspension of uncertainty.

5. John Ruskin, *Sesame and Lilies* (New York, 1974), pp. 59–60.

6. This group of crusaders includes Van Helsing himself, Dr John Seward, Arthur Holmwood, Quincey Morris, and later Jonathan Harker; the title Crew of Light is mine, but I have taken my cue from Stoker: Lucy, *lux*, light.

7. Renfield, whose 'zoophagy' precedes Dracula's arrival in England and who is never vamped by Dracula, is no exception to this rule.

8. John Addington Symonds, *A Problem in Modern Ethics* (London, 1906), p. 74.

9. This bifurcation of woman is one of the text's most evident features, as critics of *Dracula* have been quick to notice. See Phyllis Roth, 'Suddenly Sexual Women in Bram Stoker's *Dracula*', *Literature and Psychology*, 27 (1977), 117 [reprinted in this volume – Ed.], and her full-length study *Bram Stoker* (Boston, 1982). Roth, in an argument that emphasises the pre-Oedipal element in *Dracula*, makes a similar point: '... one recognises that Lucy and Mina are essentially the same figure: the Mother. Dracula is, in fact, the same story told twice with different outcomes'. Perhaps the most extensive thematic analysis of this split in Stoker's representation of women is Carol A. Senf's '*Dracula*: Stoker's Response to the New Woman', *Victorian Studies*, 26 (1982), 33–9, which sees this split as Stoker's 'ambivalent reaction to a topical phenomenon – the New Woman'.

10. Maurice Richardson, 'The Psychoanalysis of Ghost Stories', *The Twentieth Century*, 166 (1959), 427–8.

11. On this point see Stephanie Demetrakopoulos, 'Feminism, Sex Role Exchanges, and Other Subliminal Fantasies in Bram Stoker's *Dracula*', *Frontiers*, 2:3 (1977), 104.

12. In this instance at least Van Helsing has an excuse for his ungrammatical usage; in Dutch, Van Helsing's native tongue, the noun *bijbel* (Bible) is masculine.

13. John Stuart Mill, *The Subjection of Women*, in *Essays on Sex Equality*, ed. Alice Rossi (Chicago, 1970), p. 148.

14. Ibid., p. 187.

15. Susan Hardy Aiken, 'Scripture and Poetic Discourse in *The Subjection of Women*', *PMLA*, 98 (1983), 354.

16. Nina Auerbach, *Woman and the Demon: The Life of a Victorian Myth* (Cambridge, MA, 1982), p.11.

17. Roth, 'Suddenly Sexual Women', 116.

18. George Chauncey, Jr, 'From Sexual Inversion to Homosexuality: Medicine and the Changing Conceptualization of Female Deviance', *Salmagundi*, 58–9 (1982), 132.

19. The symbolic interchangeability of blood and semen in vampirism was identified as early as 1931 by Ernest Jones in *On the Nightmare* (London, 1931), p. 119: 'in the unconscious mind blood is commonly an equivalent for semen ...'.

20. Auerbach, *Woman and the Demon*, p. 22.

21. Havelock Ellis, *Erotic Symbolism*, Vol. 5 of *Studies in the Psychology of Sex* (Philadelphia, 1906), p. 142.

22. Ibid., p. 140.

23. Roth correctly reads Lucy's countenance at this moment as 'a thank you note' for the corrective penetration; 'Suddenly Sexual Women', 116.

24. C. F. Bentley, 'The Monster in the Bedroom: Sexual Symbolism in Bram Stoker's *Dracula*', *Literature and Psychology*, 22 (1972), 30.

25. Sigmund Freud, *The Ego and the Id* (New York, 1960), pp. 44–5.

26. Leo Bersani, *Baudelaire and Freud* (Berkeley, CA, 1977), p. 92.

7

The Occidental Tourist: *Dracula* and the Anxiety of Reverse Colonisation

STEPHEN D. ARATA

> Fashions in monsters do change.
> (Joseph Conrad)

Bram Stoker's *Dracula* (1897) participates in that 'modernising' of Gothic which occurs at the close of the nineteenth century. Like Stevenson's *Dr Jekyll and Mr Hyde* (1886) and Wilde's *Picture of Dorian Gray* (1891), Stoker's novel achieves its effects by bringing the terror of the Gothic home. While Gothic novelists had traditionally displaced their stories in time or locale, these later writers root their action firmly in the modern world. Yet critics have until recently ignored the historical context in which these works were written and originally read. Most notably, criticism has persistently undervalued *Dracula*'s extensive and highly visible contacts with a series of cultural issues, particularly those involving race, specific to the 1890s.[1] This neglect has in part resulted from the various psychoanalytic approaches taken by most critics of Gothic. While such approaches have greatly enriched our understanding of *Dracula*, and while nothing in psychoanalytic critical theory precludes a 'historicist' reading of literary texts, that theory has in practice been used almost exclusively to demonstrate, as Stoker's most recent critic puts it, that *Dracula* is a 'representation of fears that are more universal than a specific focus on the Victorian background would allow'.[2]

Yet the novel's very attachment to the 'Victorian background' – what *The Spectator* in 1897 called its 'up-to-dateness' – is a primary source of Stoker's continuing power.[3] Late-Victorian Gothic in general, and *Dracula* in particular, continually calls our attention to the cultural context surrounding and informing the text, and insists that we take that context into account.

In the case of *Dracula*, the context includes the decline of Britain as a world power at the close of the nineteenth century; or rather, the way the perception of that decline was articulated by contemporary writers. *Dracula* appeared in a Jubilee year, but one marked by considerably more introspection and less self-congratulation than the celebration of a decade earlier. The decay of British global influence, the loss of overseas markets for British goods, the economic and political rise of Germany and the United States, the increasing unrest in British colonies and possessions, the growing domestic uneasiness over the morality of imperialism – all combined to erode Victorian confidence in the inevitability of British progress and hegemony. Late-Victorian fiction in particular is saturated with the sense that the entire nation – as a race of people, as a political and imperial force, as a social and cultural power – was in irretrievable decline. What I will be examining is how that perception is transformed into narrative, into stories which the culture tells itself not only to articulate and account for its troubles, but also to defend against and even to assuage the anxiety attendant upon cultural decay.

I

Dracula enacts the period's most important and pervasive narrative of decline, a narrative of reverse colonisation. Versions of this story recur with remarkable frequency in both fiction and nonfiction texts throughout the last decades of the century. In whatever guise, this narrative expresses both fear and guilt. The fear is that what has been represented as the 'civilised' world is on the point of being colonised by 'primitive' forces. These forces can originate outside the civilised world (in Rider Haggard's *She*, Queen Ayesha plans to sack London and depose Queen Victoria) or they can inhere in the civilised itself (as in Kurtz's emblematic heart of darkness). Fantasies of reverse colonisation are particularly prevalent in late-Victorian popular fiction. [...] In each case, a terrifying reversal has occurred:

the coloniser finds himself in the position of the colonised, the exploiter becomes exploited, the victimiser victimised. Such fears are linked to a perceived decline – racial, moral, spiritual – which makes the nation vulnerable to attack from more vigorous, 'primitive' peoples.

But fantasies of reverse colonisation are more than products of geopolitical fears. They are also responses to cultural guilt. In the marauding, invasive Other, British culture sees its own imperial practices mirrored back in monstrous forms. H. G. Wells located the germ of his *War of the Worlds* in a discussion with his brother Frank over the extermination of the indigenous Tasmanian population under British rule.[4] Reverse colonisation narratives thus contain the potential for powerful critiques of imperialist ideologies, even if that potential usually remains unrealised. As fantasies, these narratives provide an opportunity to atone for imperial sins, since reverse colonisation is often represented as deserved punishment. [...]

Reverse colonisation narratives are obsessed with the spectacle of the primitive and the atavistic. The 'savagery' of Haggard's Amahaggers and Wells's Morlocks both repels and captivates; their proximity to elemental instincts and energies, energies seen as dissipated by modern life, makes them dangerous but also deeply attractive. Patrick Brantlinger has linked this interest in the primitive to the late-Victorian fascination with the occult and the paranormal, and by extension to the Gothic. The primitive and the occultist alike operated beyond or beneath the threshold of the 'civilised' rational mind, tapping into primal energies and unconscious resources as well as into deep-rooted anxieties and fears. Brantlinger identifies a body of fiction he terms 'imperial Gothic' in which the conjunction of imperialist ideology, primitivism, and occultism produces narratives that are at once self-divided and deeply 'symptomatic of the anxieties that attended the climax of the British Empire'. The 'atavistic descents into the primitive' characteristic of imperial Gothic 'seem often to be allegories of the larger regressive movement of civilisation' and of the ease with which it could be overcome by the forces of barbarism.[5] What Brantlinger finally shows is how, in late-Victorian Britain, political and cultural concerns about empire become gothicised. The novel of empire and the adventure story especially become saturated with Gothic motifs: Kipling's 'The Phantom Rickshaw' and 'At the End of the Passage', Conan Doyle's 'The Brown Hand', Edgar Wallace's *Sanders of the River*, and Haggard's *She* are representative in this respect. Unlike dynamite or invasion-scare narratives, which generally aim at a documentary-like realism, turn-of-the-century fictions involving the empire often inhabit the regions of romance and the supernatural. [...]

Stoker maps his story not simply onto the Gothic but also onto a second, equally popular late-Victorian genre, the travel narrative. By examining how and to what extent *Dracula* participates in these two genres, we can illuminate the underlying fear and guilt characteristic of reverse colonisation narratives. Like late-century Gothic, the travel narrative clearly displays aspects of imperial ideology. Like Gothic, too, the travel narrative concerns itself with boundaries – both with maintaining and with transgressing them. The blurring of psychic and sexual boundaries that occurs in Gothic is certainly evident in Dracula (and is one reason the novel is so accessible to psychoanalytic interpretation), but for Stoker the collapse of boundaries resonates culturally and politically as well. The Count's transgressions and aggressions are placed in the context, provided by innumerable travel narratives, of late-Victorian forays into the 'East'. For Stoker, the Gothic and the travel narrative problematise, separately and together, the very boundaries on which British imperial hegemony depended: between civilised and primitive, coloniser and colonised, victimiser (either imperialist or vampire) and victim. By problematising those boundaries, Stoker probes the heart of the culture's sense of itself, its ways of defining and distinguishing itself from other peoples, other cultures, in its hour of perceived decline.

II

In many respects, *Dracula* represents a break from the Gothic tradition of vampires. It is easy, for instance, to forget that the 'natural' association of vampires with Transylvania begins with, rather than predates, *Dracula*. The site of Castle Dracula was in fact not determined until well after Stoker had begun to write. As Joseph Bierman points out, Stoker originally signalled his debt to his countryman Le Fanu's *Carmilla* (1872) by locating the castle in 'Styria', the scene of the earlier Gothic novella.[6] In rewriting the novel's opening chapters, however, Stoker moved *his* Gothic story to a place that, for readers in 1897, resonated in ways Styria did not. Transylvania was known primarily as part of the vexed 'Eastern Question' that so obsessed British foreign policy in the 1880s and '90s. The region was first and foremost the site, not of superstition and Gothic romance, but of political turbulence and racial strife. Victorian readers knew the Carpathians largely for its endemic cultural upheaval and its fostering of a dizzying succession of empires. By moving Castle Dracula there, Stoker gives distinctly political overtones to his Gothic narrative. In Stoker's version of the myth, vampires are intimately linked to military conquest and to the rise and fall of empires. According to Dr Van Helsing, the vampire is the unavoidable consequence of any invasion: 'He have follow the wake of the berserker Icelander, the devil-begotten Hun, the Slav, the Saxon, the Magyar.'[7]

Nowhere else in the Europe of 1897 could provide a more fertile breeding ground for the undead than the Count's homeland. The Western accounts of the region that Stoker consulted invariably stress the ceaseless clash of antagonistic cultures in the Carpathians.[8] The cycle of empire – rise, decay, collapse, displacement – was there displayed in a particularly compressed and vivid manner. 'Greeks, Romans, Huns, Avars, Magyars, Turks, Slavs, French and Germans, all have come and seen and gone, seeking conquest one over the other', opens one late-century account.[9] The Count himself confirms that his homeland has been the scene of perpetual invasion: 'there is hardly a foot of soil in all this region that has not been enriched by the blood of men, patriots or invaders', he tells Harker (p. 33). His subsequent question is thus largely rhetorical: 'Is it a wonder that we were a conquering race?' (p. 41).

The 'race' in which Dracula claims membership is left ambiguous here. He refers at once to his Szekely warrior past and to his vampiric present. The ambiguity underscores the impossibility of untangling the two aspects of Dracula's essential nature, since his vampirism is interwoven with his status as a conqueror and invader. Here Stoker departs significantly from his literary predecessors. Unlike Polidori and Le Fanu, for instance, who depict their vampires as wan and enervated, Stoker makes Dracula vigorous and energetic. Polidori's Count Ruthven and Le Fanu's Carmilla represent the aristocrat as decadent aesthete; their vampirism is an extension of the traditional aristocratic vices of sensualism and conspicuous consumption. Dracula represents the nobleman as warrior. His activities after death carry on his activities in life; in both cases he has successfully engaged in forms of conquest and domination.

Racial conquest and domination, we should immediately add. Stoker continues a Western tradition of seeing unrest in Eastern Europe primarily in terms of racial strife. For Stoker, the vampire 'race' is simply the most virulent and threatening of the numerous warrior races – Berserker, Hun, Turk, Saxon, Slovak, Magyar, Szekely – inhabiting the area. Nineteenth-century accounts of the Carpathians repeatedly stress its polyracial character. The standard Victorian work on the region, Charles Boner's *Transylvania* (1865), begins by marvelling at this spectacle of variety:

> The diversity of character which the various physiognomies present that meet you at every step, also tell of the many nations which are here brought together. ... The slim, lithe Hungarian ... the more oriental Wallachian, with softer, sensuous air, – in her style of dress and even in her carriage unlike a dweller in the West; a Moldavian princess, wrapped in a Turkish shawl. ... And now a Serb marches proudly past, his countenance calm as a Turk's; or a Constantinople merchant sweeps along in his loose robes and snowy turban. There are, too, Greeks, Dalmatians, and Croats, all different in feature: there is no end to the variety.[10]

Transylvania is what Dracula calls the 'whirlpool of European races' (p. 41), but within that whirlpool racial interaction usually involved conflict, not accommodation. Racial violence could in fact reach appalling proportions, as in the wholesale massacres, widely reported by the British press, of Armenians by Turks in 1894 and 1896, the years in which *Dracula* was being written. For Western writers and readers, these characteristics – racial heterogeneity combined with racial intolerance considered barbaric in its intensity – defined the area east and south of the Danube, with the Carpathians at the imaginative centre of the turmoil.

By situating Dracula in the Carpathians, and by continually blurring the lines between the Count's vampiric and warrior activities, Stoker forges seemingly 'natural' links among three of his principal concerns: racial strife, the collapse of empire, and vampirism. It is important too to note the sequence of events. As Van Helsing says, vampires follow 'in [the] wake of' imperial decay (p. 286). Vampires are generated by racial enervation and the decline of empire, not vice versa. They are produced, in other words, by the very conditions characterising late-Victorian Britain.

Stoker thus transforms the materials of the vampire myth, making them bear the weight of the culture's fears over its declining status. The appearance of vampires becomes the sign of profound trouble. With vampirism marking the intersection of racial strife, political upheaval, and the fall of empire, Dracula's move to London indicates that Great Britain, rather than the Carpathians, is now the scene of these connected struggles. The Count has penetrated to the heart of modern Europe's largest empire, and his very presence seems to presage its doom:

> This was the being I was helping to transfer to London [Harker writes in anguish] where, perhaps for centuries to come, he might, amongst its teeming millions, satiate his lust for blood, and create a new and ever widening circle of semi-demons to batten on the helpless.
>
> (p. 67)

The late-Victorian nightmare of reverse colonisation is expressed succinctly here: Harker envisions semi-demons spreading through the realm, colonising bodies and land indiscriminately. The Count's 'lust for blood' points in both directions: to the vampire's need for its special food, and also to the warrior's desire for conquest. The Count endangers Britain's integrity as a nation at the same time that he imperils the personal integrity of individual citizens.

Harker's lament highlights the double thrust – political and biological – of Dracula's invasion, while at the same time conflating the two into a single threat. Dracula's twin status as vampire and Szekely warrior suggests that for Stoker the Count's aggressions against the body are also aggressions against the body politic. Indeed, the Count can threaten the integrity of the nation precisely because of the nature of his threat to personal integrity. His attacks involve more than an assault on the isolated self, the subversion and loss of one's individual identity. Again unlike Polidori's Count Ruthven or Le Fanu's Carmilla (or even Thomas Prest's Sir Francis Varney), Dracula imperils not simply his victims' personal identities, but also their cultural, political, and racial selves. In *Dracula* vampirism designates a kind of colonisation of the body. Horror arises not because Dracula destroys bodies, but because he appropriates and transforms them. Having yielded to his assault, one literally 'goes native' by becoming a vampire oneself. As John Allen Stevenson argues, if 'blood' is a sign of racial identity, then Dracula effectively deracinates his victims.[11] In turn, they receive a new racial identity, one that marks them as literally 'Other'. Miscegenation leads, not to the mixing of races, but to the biological and political annihilation of the weaker race by the stronger.

Through the vampire myth, Stoker gothicises the political threats to Britain caused by the enervation of the Anglo-Saxon 'race'. These threats also operate independently of the Count's vampirism, however, for the vampire was not considered alone in its ability to deracinate. Stoker learned from Emily Gerard that the Roumanians were themselves notable for the way they could 'dissolve' the identities of those they came in contact with:

> The Hungarian woman who weds a Roumanian husband will necessarily adopt the dress and manners of his people, and her children will be as good Roumanians as though they had no drop of Magyar blood in their veins; while the Magyar who takes a Roumanian girl for his wife will not only fail to convert her to his ideas, but himself, subdued by her influence, will imperceptibly begin to lose his nationality. This is a fact well known and much lamented by the Hungarians themselves, who live in anticipated apprehension of seeing their people ultimately dissolving into Roumanians.[12]

Gerard's account of the 'imperceptible' but inevitable loss of identity – national, cultural, racial – sounds remarkably like the transformations that Lucy and Mina suffer under Dracula's 'influence'. In life Dracula was a Roumanian (Gerard designates the Szekelys as a branch of the Roumanian race); his ability to deracinate could thus derive as easily from his Roumanian as from his vampire nature.

The 'anticipated apprehension' of deracination – of seeing Britons 'ultimately dissolving into Roumanians' or vampires or savages – is at the heart of the reverse colonisation narrative. For both Gerard and Stoker, the Roumanians' dominance can be traced to a kind of racial puissance that overwhelms its weaker victims. This racial context helps account for what critics routinely note about Dracula: that he is by his very nature vigorous, masterful, energetic, robust. Such attributes are conspicuously absent among the novel's British characters, particularly the men. All the novel's vampires are distinguished by their robust health and their equally robust fertility. The vampire serves, then, to highlight the alarming decline among the British, since the undead are, paradoxically, both 'healthier' and more 'fertile' than the living. Perversely, a vampiric attack can serve to invigorate its victim. 'The adventure of the night does not seem to have harmed her', Mina notes after Lucy's first encounter with Dracula; 'on the contrary, it has benefited her, for she looks better this morning than she has done in weeks' (p. 115). Indeed, after his attack, Lucy's body initially appears stronger, her eyes brighter, her cheeks rosier. The corresponding enervation that marks the British men is most clearly visible in Harker (he is 'pale', 'weak-looking', 'exhausted', 'nervous', 'a wreck'), but it can be seen in the other male British characters as well. Harker and Dracula in fact switch places during the novel; Harker becomes tired and white-haired as the action proceeds, while Dracula, whose white hair grows progressively darker, becomes more vigorous.

The vampire's vigour is in turn closely connected with its virility, its ability to produce literally endless numbers of offspring. Van Helsing's concern that the earth in Dracula's boxes be 'sterilised' (pp. 347, 355) underlines the connection between the Count's threat and his fecundity. In marked contrast, the nonvampires in the novel seem unable to reproduce themselves. Fathers in particular are in short supply: most are either dead (Mr Westenra, Mr Harker, Mr Murray, Mr Canon), dying (Mr Hawkins, Lord Godalming, Mr Swales), or missing (Mr Seward, Mr Morris), while the younger men, being unmarried, cannot father legitimately. Even Harker, the novel's only married man, is prohibited from touching Mina after she has been made 'unclean'. In *Dracula*'s lexicon, uncleanliness is closely related to fertility, but it is the wrong kind of fertility; Mina, the men fear, is perfectly capable of producing 'offspring', but not with Jonathan. The prohibition regarding Mina is linked to the fear of vampiric fecundity, a fecundity that threatens to overwhelm the far less prolific British men. Thus, as many critics have pointed out, the arrival of little Quincey Harker at the story's close signals the final triumph over Dracula, since the Harkers' ability to secure an heir – an heir whose racial credentials are seemingly impeccable – is the surest indication that the vampire's threat has been mastered. Even this triumph is precarious, however. Harker proudly notes that his son is named after each of the men in the novel, making them all figurative fathers (p. 449), yet Quincey's multiple parentage only underscores the original problem. How secure is any racial line when five fathers are needed to produce one son?

Such racial anxieties are clearest in the case of Lucy Westenra. If Dracula's kiss serves to deracinate Lucy, and by doing so to unleash what the male characters consider her incipiently monstrous sexual appetite, then the only way to counter this process is to 're-racinate' her by reinfusing her with the 'proper' blood. But Stoker is careful to establish a strict hierarchy among the potential donors. The men give blood in this order: Holmwood, Seward, Van Helsing, Morris. Arthur Holmwood is first choice ostensibly because he is engaged to Lucy, but also, and perhaps more importantly, because his blood is, in Van Helsing's words, 'more good than' Seward's (p. 149). As the only English aristocrat in the novel, Holmwood possesses a 'blood so pure' (p. 149) that it can restore Lucy's compromised racial identity. Dr Seward, whose blood though bourgeois is English nonetheless, comes next in line, followed by the two foreigners, Van Helsing and Morris. We should note that Van Helsing's old, Teutonic blood is still preferred over Morris's young, American blood, for reasons I will take up in a moment. Even foreign blood is better than lower-class blood, however. After Lucy suffers what proves to be the fatal attack by Dracula, Van Helsing, looking for blood donors, rejects the four apparently healthy female servants as unsafe: 'I fear to trust those women' (p. 180).

More precisely, Van Helsing's distrust of 'those women' marks a point of intersection between his usually covert class prejudices and his often overt misogyny. That Dracula propagates his race solely through the bodies of women suggests an affinity, or even an identity, between vampiric sexuality and female sexuality. Both are represented as primitive and voracious, and both threaten patriarchal hegemony. In the novel's (and Victorian Britain's) sexual economy, female sexuality has only one legitimate function, propagation within the bounds of marriage. Once separated from that function, as Lucy's desire is, female sexuality becomes monstrous. The violence of Lucy's demise is grisly enough, but we should not miss the fact that her subjection and Mina's final fate parallel one another. They differ in degree, not kind. By the novel's close, Mina's sexual energy has been harnessed for purely domestic use. In the end, women serve identical purposes for both Dracula and the Western characters. If in this novel blood stands for race, then women quite literally become the vehicles of racial propagation. The struggle between the two camps is thus on one level a struggle over access to women's bodies, and Dracula's biological colonisation of women becomes a horrific parody of the sanctioned exploitation practised by the Western male characters.

By considering the parallel fates of Lucy and Mina, moreover, we can see how the fear and guilt characteristic of reverse colonisation narratives begin to overlap. The fear generated by the Count's colonisation of his victims' bodies – a colonisation appropriately designated monstrous – modulates into guilt that his practices simply repeat those of the 'good' characters. Dracula's invasion and appropriation of female bodies does not distinguish him from his Western antagonists as much as at first appears. Instead of being uncannily Other, the vampire is here revealed as disquietingly familiar. And since the colonisations of bodies and territory are closely linked, the same blurring of distinctions occurs when we consider more closely the nature of the Count's invasion of Britain. Just as Dracula's vampirism mirrors the domestic practices of Victorian patriarchs, so his invasion of London in order to 'batten on the helpless' natives there mirrors British imperial activities abroad. [...]

In Count Dracula, Victorian readers could recognise their culture's imperial ideology mirrored back as a kind of monstrosity. Dracula's journey from Transylvania to England could be read as a reversal of Britain's imperial exploitations of 'weaker' races, including the Irish. This mirroring extends not just to the imperial practices themselves, but to their epistemological underpinnings. Before Dracula successfully invades the spaces of his victims' bodies or land, he first invades the spaces of their knowledge. The Count operates in several distinct registers in the novel. He is both the warrior nobleman, whose prowess dwarfs that of the novel's enfeebled English aristocrat, Lord Godalming, and the primitive savage, whose bestiality, fecundity, and vigour alternately repel and attract. But he is also what we might call an incipient 'Occidentalist' scholar. Dracula's physical mastery of his British victims begins with an intellectual appropriation of their culture, which allows him to delve the workings of the 'native mind'. As Harker discovers, the Count's expertise in 'English life and customs and manners' (p. 30) provides the groundwork for his exploitative invasion of Britain. Thus, in Dracula the British characters see their own ideology reflected back as a form of bad faith, since the Count's Occidentalism both mimics and reverses the more familiar Orientalism underwriting Western imperial practices.[13]

III

To understand fully how the Count's Occidentalism functions, however, we must relate it to the second literary genre visible in *Dracula*, the travel narrative. Jonathan Harker's initial journey to Castle Dracula constitutes a travel narrative in miniature, and the opening entries in his journal reproduce the conventions of this popular Victorian genre. Critics have occasionally noted the travel motifs in *Dracula*, but have not pursued the implications of Stoker's mixing of genres. To be sure, Gothic has always contained a strong travel component. The restless roaming found in many Gothic fictions – Victor Frankenstein's pursuit of his monster, Melmoth's wanderings, Mr Hyde's perambulations of London – suggests that an affinity between the two genres has always existed. Stoker's use of travel conventions is new, however. Earlier Gothic writers were interested primarily in the psychological dimensions of travel; the landscape traversed by the Gothic protagonist was chiefly psychological.[14] Stoker on the other hand is interested in the ideological dimensions of travel. Harker's early journal entries clearly reveal his Orientalist perspective, which structures what he sees and what he misses as he travels through the Carpathians. This perspective is embedded in the generic conventions that Harker deploys, conventions familiar to late-Victorian readers. Stoker's disruption of Harker's tourist perspective at Castle Dracula also calls into question the entire Orientalist outlook. Stoker thus expresses a telling critique of the Orientalist enterprise through the very structure of his novel.

Early in his stay at Castle Dracula, Harker to his great surprise finds his host stretched upon the library sofa reading, 'of all things in the world', an English *Bradshaw's Guide* (p. 34). We probably share Harker's puzzlement at the Count's choice of reading material, though like Harker we are apt to forget this brief interlude amid ensuing horrors. Why is Dracula interested in English train schedules? The Count's absorption in *Bradshaw's* echoes Harker's own obsessive interest in trains. (Later we discover that Mina, attempting to secure Harker's affections, has herself become a 'train fiend', memorising whole sections of *Bradshaw's* for his convenience.) Harker's journal opens with the terse note: 'should have arrived at 6.46, but train was an hour late' (p. 9). The next morning, more delays give him further cause to grumble: 'It seems to me that the further East you go the more unpunctual are the trains. What ought they to be in China?' (pp. 10–11).

An obsession with trains – or, as in Harker's case, an obsession with trains running on time – characterises Victorian narratives of travel in Eastern Europe. Even Emily Gerard, whose enthusiasm for all things Transylvanian seldom flagged, had little patience with its trains. 'The railway communications were very badly managed', she writes of one journey, 'so that it was only on the evening of the second day (fully forty-eight hours) that we arrived at Klausenberg. ... It would hardly have taken longer to go from Lemberg to London'.[15] Harker immediately invokes a second convention of the travel genre when, having crossed the Danube at Buda-Pesth, he invests the river with symbolic significance. 'The impression I had was that we were leaving the West and entering

the East; the most Western of splendid bridges over the Danube ...
took us among the traditions of Turkish rule' (p. 9). In crossing
the Danube, Harker maintains, he leaves 'Europe' behind, geo-
graphically and imaginatively, and approaches the first outpost of
the 'Orient'.[16]

Harker's first two acts – noting that his train is late, and then tra-
versing a boundary he considers symbolic – function as a kind of
shorthand, alerting readers that Harker's journal is to be set against
the background of late-Victorian travel narratives. Once the travel
genre is established, there is an inevitability about Harker's subsequent
gestures. Not only does he continue to gripe about the trains, he also
searches for quaint hotels (p. 12), samples the native cuisine (p. 10),
ogles the indigenous folk (p. 11), marvels at the breathtaking scenery
(p. 11), wonders at local customs (p. 15), and, interspersed throughout, provides pertinent facts about the region's geography, history,
and population. Harker's first three journal entries (ch. 1 of the novel)
are so thoroughly conventional as to parody the travel genre. Such
conventions constitute what Wolfgang Iser calls the 'repertoire of the
familiar' that readers can be expected to bring to texts.[17] Indeed,
Harker is so adept an imitator of travel narratives in part because he
has been such an assiduous reader of them. Like Stoker himself,
Harker 'had visited the British Museum, and made search among the
books and maps in the library regarding Transylvania' in order to gain
'some foreknowledge of the country' (p. 9).

This foreknowledge – the textual knowledge gathered before the
fact, the same knowledge that any casual reader of contemporary
travel narratives would also possess – structures Harker's subsequent
experiences. In assuming the role of the Victorian traveller in the
East, Harker also assumes the Orientalist perspective that allows
him to 'make sense' of his experiences there. For Harker, as for
most Victorian travel writers, that 'sense' begins with the assumption that an unbridgeable gap separates the Western traveller from
Eastern peoples. The contrast between British punctuality and
Transylvanian tardiness stands, in Harker's view, as a concrete instance of more fundamental and wide-ranging oppositions: between
Western progress and Eastern stasis, between Western science and
Eastern superstition, between Western reason and Eastern emotion,
between Western civilisation and Eastern barbarism. The 'backward-
ness' of the Carpathian races displayed itself most surely in what
one traveller called their inability to '[settle] themselves down to the
inexorable limits of timetables'.[18] As Harker moves further east

toward Castle Dracula, he leaves even the railroads behind and is forced to travel by stagecoach. Simultaneously, he leaves Western rationality behind: 'I read that every known superstition in the world is gathered into the horseshoe of the Carpathians' (p. 10).

Harker may marvel and wonder at this strange world he has entered, but he does not expect to be disconcerted. He trades extensively on his 'foreknowledge', which allows him to retain a comfortable distance from the scene. He views it simply as a diverting spectacle, imagining the 'barbarian' Slovaks he sees by the roadside as 'an Oriental band of brigands' performing 'on the stage' (p. 11). At first, Harker's descent into the dark heart of the Carpathians serves only to titillate, not to unsettle. His favourite word in this first section is 'picturesque', that stock term of the travel genre. Throughout his journey, he is able to reduce everything he encounters to an example of the picturesque or the poetic.

Until he reaches Castle Dracula, that is. There, everything is disrupted. Stoker undermines the conventions of the travel narrative, just as Dracula undermines all the stable oppositions structuring Harker's – and his readers' – foreknowledge of Eastern and Western races. For the fact is, by Harker's own criteria, Dracula is the most 'Western' character in the novel. No one is more rational, more intelligent, more organised, or even more punctual than the Count. No one plans more carefully or researches more thoroughly. No one is more learned within his own spheres of expertise or more receptive to new knowledge. A reading that emphasises only the archaic, anarchic, 'primitive' forces embodied by Dracula misses half the point. When Harker arrives at the end of his journey East, he finds, not some epitome of irrationality, but a most accomplished Occidentalist. If Harker has been diligently combing the library stacks, so too has the Count. Harker writes: 'In the library I found, to my great delight, a vast number of English books, whole shelves full of them, and bound volumes of magazines and newspapers. ... The books were of the most varied kind – history, geography, politics, political economy, botany, geology, law – all relating to England and English life and customs and manners' (p. 30). Displaying an epistemophilia to rival Harker's own, Dracula says: '"These friends" – and he laid his hand on some of the books – "have been good friends to me, and for some years past, ever since I had the idea of going to London, have given me many, many hours of pleasure. Through them I have come to know your great England"' (p. 31).

The novel thus sets up an equivalence between Harker and Dracula: one can be seen as an Orientalist travelling East, the other – unsettling thought for Stoker's Victorian readers – as an Occidentalist travelling West. Dracula's absorption in *Bradshaw*'s timetables echoes Harker's fetish for punctual trains, just as the Count's posture – reclining comfortably on a sofa – recalls the attitude of the casual Western reader absorbed in a late-Victorian account of the exotic.

But of course Dracula's preoccupation with English cultures is not motivated by a disinterested desire for knowledge; instead, his Occidentalism represents the essence of bad faith, since it both promotes and masks the Count's sinister plan to invade and exploit Britain and her people. By insisting on the connections between Dracula's growing knowledge and his power to exploit, Stoker also forces us to acknowledge how Western imperial practices are implicated in certain forms of knowledge. Stoker continually draws our attention to the affinities between Harker and Dracula, as in the oft-cited scene where Harker looks for Dracula's reflection in the mirror and sees only himself (p. 37). The text's insistence that these characters are capable of substituting for one another becomes most pressing when Dracula twice dons Harker's clothes to leave the Castle (pp. 59, 64). Since on both occasions the Count's mission is to plunder the town, we are encouraged to see a correspondence between the vampire's actions and those of the travelling Westerner. The equivalence between these two sets of actions is underlined by the reaction of the townspeople, who have no trouble believing that it really is Harker, the visiting Englishman, who is stealing their goods, their money, their children. The peasant woman's anguished cry – 'Monster, give me my child!' (p. 60) – is directed at him, not Dracula.

The shock of recognition that overtakes Harker, and presumably the British reader, when he sees Dracula comfortably decked out in Victorian garb is, however, only part of the terror of this scene. The truly disturbing notion is not that Dracula impersonates Harker, but that he does it so well. Here indeed is the nub: Dracula can 'pass'. To impersonate an Englishman, and do it convincingly, is the goal of Dracula's painstaking research into 'English life and customs and manners', a goal Dracula himself freely, if rather disingenuously, acknowledges. When Harker compliments him on his command of English, Dracula demurs:

> 'Well I know that, did I move and speak in your London, none there are who would not know me for a stranger. That is not enough for

> me. Here I am noble ... I am master. ... [In London] I am content if I am like the rest, so that no man stops if he sees me, or pause in his speaking if he hear my words, to say "Ha, ha! a stranger!" I have been so long master that I would be master still – or at least that none other should be master of me.'
>
> (p. 31)

To understand fully how disquieting Dracula's talents are, we have only to remember that in Victorian texts non-Western 'natives' are seldom – I am tempted to say never, since I have not come up with another example – permitted to 'pass' successfully. Those who try, as for instance some of Kipling's natives do, become the occasion for low comedy or ridicule, since Kipling never allows the possibility that their attempts could succeed to be seriously entertained. [...]

Dracula is different, however. A large part of the terror he inspires originates in his ability to stroll, unrecognised and unhindered, through the streets of London. As he tells Harker, his status as 'master' resides in this ability. So long as no one recognises him as a 'stranger', he is able to work his will unhampered. Like Richard Burton travelling disguised among the Arabs, or like Kipling's ubiquitous policeman Strickland passing himself off as a Hindu, Dracula gains power, becomes 'master', by striving 'to know as much about the natives as the natives themselves'.[19] The crucial difference is that in this case the natives are English.

Links between knowledge and power are evident enough in Kipling's work; his two great impersonators – Strickland and Kim – both work for the police, and each uses his talents in the service of colonial law and order. Dracula, too, understands how knowledge and power are linked. In this case, however, knowledge leads, not to the stability envisioned by Kipling's characters, but to anarchy: it undermines social structures, disrupts the order of nature, and ends alarmingly in the appropriation and exploitation of bodies. Stoker's text never explicitly acknowledges the continuity between Dracula's actions and British imperial practices, but it continually forces us to see the first as a terrifying parody of the second. In the Gothic mirror that Stoker holds up to late-Victorian culture, that culture, like Harker peering into the glass at Castle Dracula, cannot see, but is nevertheless intensely aware of, its monstrous double peering over its shoulder.

Dracula not only mimics the practices of British imperialists, he rapidly becomes superior to his teachers. The racial threat embodied by the Count is thus intensified: not only is he more vigorous, more fecund, more 'primitive' than his Western antagonists, he is also becoming more 'advanced'. As Van Helsing notes, Dracula's swift development will soon make him invincible:

> In some faculties of mind he has been, and is, only a child; but he is growing, and some things that were childish at the first are now of man's stature. ... That big child-brain of his is working. Well for us, it is, as yet, a child-brain; for had he dared, at the first, to attempt certain things he would long ago have been beyond our power.
>
> (p. 360)

Van Helsing's metaphor of the child growing into manhood is a familiar and homely way to explain Dracula's progress, but the image deflects attention from the notion of racial development that is the real source of the vampire's threat. Since Dracula's growth is not bound by a single lifetime, but instead covers potentially limitless generations, the proper analogy for his development is not that of an individual. He is in effect his own species, or his own race, displaying in his person the progress of ages. Dracula can himself stand in for entire races, and through him Stoker articulates fears about the development of those races in relation to the English.

A passage from Emily Gerard is relevant here, since Stoker seems to have had it in mind when he made his vampire a Roumanian. In discussing the various races in Transylvania, Gerard singles out the Roumanians as representing what she calls 'manhood in the future tense':

> It is scarcely hazardous to prophesy that this people have a great future before them, and that a day will come when, other nations having degenerated and spent their strength, these descendants of the ancient Romans, rising phoenix-like from their ashes, will step forward with a whole fund of latent power and virgin material, to rule as masters where formerly they have crouched as slaves.[20]

Gerard's 'prophesy' sounds much like Van Helsing's metaphor for Dracula's development. What Gerard again allows us to see is that the anxieties engendered by Count Dracula do not derive wholly from his vampirism. He is dangerous as the representative or embodiment of a race which, all evidence suggested, was poised to 'step forward' and become 'masters' of those who had already 'spent their strength'. Even Dracula's destruction (which, if he stands in for an entire race, becomes a fantasised genocide) cannot entirely erase the 'moral' endorsed by the rest of the story: that strong races inevitably weaken and fall, and are in turn displaced by stronger races. The novel provides an extraordinarily long list of once-proud people, now vanquished or vanished – not just the Huns, Berserkers, Magyars, and others who have passed through Carpathian history, but the Romans who gave their name, and perhaps their blood, to the modern Roumanians, as well as the Danes and Vikings who, Mina tells us, once occupied Whitby (pp. 80–1).

Do the British evade the fate of Huns, Danes, Vikings, and others, since Dracula is destroyed by novel's end? Critical consensus follows Christopher Craft when he suggests that *Dracula* embodies the 'predictable, if variable, triple rhythm' characteristic of Gothic novels: it 'first invites or admits a monster, then entertains or is entertained by monstrosity for some extended duration, until in its closing pages it expels or repudiates the monster and all the disruption that he/she/it brings'.[21] This triple rhythm also characterises many narratives of reverse colonisation. The mingled anxiety and desire evident in these texts is relieved when the primitive or exotic invader – Haggard's Ayesha, Wells's Martians, Kipling's Silver Man – is at last expelled and order is restored. *Dracula*, however, is finally divided against itself; it strives to contain the threat posed by the Count but cannot do so entirely. The novel in fact ends twice. The narrative proper closes with a fantasy of revitalised English supremacy: his invasion repulsed, the Count is driven back to Transylvania, and destroyed there. Along with this is what David Seed calls the 'diminishment in stature' suffered by Dracula over the final third of the novel, as he is transformed from the essence of evil to a 'disappointingly conventional embodiment of Nordau's and Lombroso's criminal type'.[22] But the satisfaction of closure brought about by Dracula's diminishment and death is immediately disrupted by Harker's 'Note', which constitutes *Dracula*'s second ending.

Dracula, appropriately, is subdued by the weapons of empire. Harker's 'great Kukri knife', symbol of British imperial power in India, and Morris's bowie knife, symbol of American westward expansion, simultaneously vanquish the Count (p. 447), apparently re-establishing the accustomed dominance of Western coloniser over Eastern colonised. The triumph extends even further for the British, since Dracula is not the book's only fatality. The American Quincey Morris dies too. His demise is not simply gratuitous, for the American represents, however obliquely, a second threat to British power hidden behind Dracula's more overt antagonism.[23] A shadowy figure throughout, Morris is linked with vampires and racial Others from his first appearance. When he courts Lucy, Morris reminds her of Othello; both aroused and frightened by his words, she compares herself to 'poor Desdemona when she had such a dangerous stream poured in her ear, even by a black man' (p. 74). Morris's dangerous hunting expeditions are a modern equivalent to the Count's warrior exploits, and Lucy's fascination with his stories of adventure repeats Harker's initial response to Dracula's tales. Later, it is left to Morris to pronounce the word 'vampire' for the first time in the novel, when he compares Lucy's condition to that of a mare on the Pampas 'after one of those big bats that they call vampires had got at her in the night' (p. 183). Morris's familiarity with vampirism apparently exceeds even Van Helsing's, since he correctly diagnoses the aetiology of Lucy's symptoms the first moment he sees her.[24]

There is even a suggestion that the American is at times leagued with Dracula against the others. Morris leaves, without explanation, the crucial meeting in which Van Helsing first names the Count as their enemy; a moment later he fires his pistol *into* the room where they are seated (pp. 288–9). He quickly explains that he was shooting at a 'big bat' sitting on the windowsill, but this very brief and easily missed tableau – Morris standing outside the window in the place vacated by Dracula, looking in on the assembled Westerners who have narrowly escaped his violence – suggests strongly that Stoker wants us to consider the American and the Roumanian together.

Morris thus leads a double life in *Dracula*. He stands with his allies in Anglo-Saxon brotherhood, but he also, as representative of an America about to emerge as the world's foremost imperial power, threatens British superiority as surely as Dracula does. 'If America can go on breeding men like that', Seward remarks, 'she will be a power in the world indeed' (p. 209).[25] If *Dracula* is about how vigorous races inevitably displace decaying races, then the real danger to Britain in 1897 comes not from the moribund Austro-Hungarian or Ottoman empires, but from the rising American empire. Without at all dismissing the powerful anxiety that the Count produces, we can say that Stoker's attention to Dracula screens his anxiety at the threat represented by Morris and America. Stoker insistently directs our gaze East, all the while looking back over his shoulder.[26] It is appropriate, then, that Morris's death, not Dracula's, closes the story proper; appropriate, too, that the confrontation between England and America is displaced to the

Balkans, traditionally the arena where Western powers conducted their struggles with one another indirectly, or by proxy.

England's triumph is immediately troubled and qualified, however, by Harker's appended 'Note', written seven years later. In announcing the birth of his son Quincey, Harker unwittingly calls attention to the fact that the positions of vampire and victim have been reversed. Now it is Dracula whose blood is appropriated and transformed to nourish a faltering race. As Mark Hennelly has noticed, in Quincey Harker flows the blood not only of Jonathan and Mina, but of Dracula as well (p. 23). Little Quincey, who is not conceived until after Mina drinks the Count's blood, is, moreover, born on the anniversary of Dracula's and Morris's demise. Through Roumania, the English race invigorates itself by incorporating those racial qualities needed to reverse its own decline. American energy is appropriated as well, since, as Jonathan tells us, Quincey Morris has also contributed to his namesake's racial makeup: 'His mother holds, I know, the secret belief that some of our brave friend's spirit has passed into' their son (p. 449). The 'little band of men' can thus rest assured that the threats to English power have been neutralised on both fronts, East and West, through the appropriation of Dracula's blood and Morris's spirit. The cost of such assurance is great, however. Quincey Harker stands as a mute reminder of the violence upon which the stability of the nation, as well as the family, rests.

The remainder of Harker's 'Note' is taken up with two related projects: his account of a return visit to Transylvania, and an apology for the 'inauthenticity' of the documents comprising the novel. These two projects point back, in different ways, to the two genres – travel and Gothic – in which *Dracula* participates. Harker first relates that he has recently revisited the Carpathians:

> In the summer of this year we made a journey to Transylvania, and went over the old ground which was, and is, to us so full of vivid and terrible memories. It was almost impossible to believe that the things we had seen with our own eyes and heard with our own ears were living truths. Every trace of all that had been was blotted out. The castle stood as before, reared high above a waste of desolation.
>
> (p. 449)

The text seems to have come full circle and returned securely to its starting point. The conventions of the travel genre are again invoked. Harker's return to Transylvania ostensibly re-enacts the trip that opened the novel; or rather, it attempts to reinstate the conditions and attitudes which preceded and, in a sense, enabled that trip. By returning simply as a tourist (this time he has not even the excuse of business to take him there), Harker implicitly asserts that nothing has intervened to make the tourist outlook problematic. The disruption caused by Dracula is entirely erased; the story ends where it began.

But Harker's words are strikingly tentative. In their general movement, his first two sentences assert that things have indeed returned to 'normal'. The old ground was (but is not now) full of vivid and terrible memories; we once believed (but do no longer) that what we experienced constituted a living truth. Yet each sentence is significantly qualified, and qualified in such a way as to reverse its effects. The ground not only was, but still is, full of terrible memories; the living truths are not impossible to believe, but almost impossible, which means that belief in them is, at bottom, almost inevitable. The overall effect of the sentences is to exacerbate the anxieties they are presumably intended to assuage. The unalloyed confidence and security of the novel's opening pages cannot be recaptured; any return to the beginning is barred.

The linchpin of the passage is Harker's overdetermined assertion, 'Every trace of all that had been was blotted out.' On the manifest level, Harker means simply that all evidence of the Count's horrific presence is gone from the land. His next comment contradicts this claim, however, since 'the castle stood as before'. We might see this 'blotting out', then, in psychological terms, as a repression of the insights, the 'living truths', revealed by the narrative as a whole. Alternately (or simply in addition), what has been 'blotted out' is precisely that vision of Transylvania – landscape, people, culture – which Harker, as a travelling Westerner secure in his 'foreknowledge' of the region, 'saw' on his initial visit. The ideological foundations of that vision having been disturbed, Harker can no longer perceive the land or its people in the same way. Significantly, he now sees nothing at all, only 'a waste of desolation'. The wasteland is the result, not of Dracula's activities – if that were the case, Harker would have noted such a wasteland on his earlier, not his later, visit – but of the desolation that has occurred to Harker's and the Victorian reader's accustomed modes of perception.

Finally, though, both these kinds of erasures, psychological and epistemological, lead to a different kind of obliteration. The 'blotting out' of 'traces' points to the cancellation of writing, to Harker's (though not necessarily Stoker's) attempt to disavow the Gothic narrative preceding the 'Note'. When he returns from Transylvania, Harker retrieves the mass of papers comprising the narrative – diaries, journals, letters, memoranda, and so on – which have remained buried and unread in a safe. 'We were struck by the fact', he writes in an oft-cited disclaimer, 'that, in all the mass of material of which the record is composed, there is hardly one authentic document!'

Such disclaimers are often found in Gothic fictions; in the same way, Harker's 'Note' invokes the narrative framing devices that are one of Gothic's distinctive features. But Harker uses this device to *repudiate* parts of his narrative, whereas in Gothic the function of the frame is precisely to *establish* the narrative's authenticity. Indeed, this is the function of the unsigned note that opens *Dracula*: to overcome readerly scepticism 'so that a history almost at variance with the possibilities of latter-day belief may stand forth as simple fact' (p. 8). For Harker, however, the inauthenticity of the documents (what would make for authenticity is unclear) casts further doubt on the veracity of portions of the narrative. 'We could hardly expect anyone, even did we wish to, to accept these [documents] as proofs of so wild a story' (p. 449). Not only does Harker not expect us to believe the collected accounts, he does not even 'wish [us] to'.

At the same time that he tries to recapture the comforting tourist outlook, Harker also tries to erase the 'wild' or Gothic parts of his 'story', to blot out all their traces. The two gestures are complementary. In effect, Harker asserts the story's 'truth' up until the moment he enters Castle Dracula; the moment, in other words, when his travel narrative, disrupted by the Count's Occidentalism, becomes a Gothic narrative. The trouble, in Harker's view, starts there. Once the dichotomies on which Harker's (and imperial Britain's) tourist perspective rest are exploded, anything is possible. The 'Note' tries to recontain the anxieties generated by that moment of rupture by invalidating what follows, by calling into question its 'authenticity' as narrative. The 'realism' of the travel narrative gives way to the fantasy constructions of the Gothic, which can be dismissed – as Harker urges us to do – as untrue. 'We want no proofs; we ask none to believe us', Van Helsing says in the novel's final moments, and his words sound remarkably like a plea.

From *Victorian Studies*, 33:4 (1990), 621–45.

NOTES

[Stephen Arata's historicist reading sees the specific anxieties articulated in *Dracula* as emanating from the decline of Britain as a world power and the accompanying concerns about cultural decay. The text, he argues, is permeated with anxiety about reverse colonisation, with the fear that the racial purity of England will be compromised by the invasion of the dark-skinned other. Drawing also on postcolonial theory, in particular on the long-standing European tradition of 'Orientalism', the term used by Edward Said to identify the way of fixing the East as Other and inferior, Arata demonstrates Stoker's critique of Orientalist ideology and British Imperial practices, suggesting that as Harker becomes an Orientalist travelling to the East, so the Count becomes an Occidentalist travelling West. This essay has been slightly edited for reasons of space. All quotations from Bram Stoker's *Dracula* are taken from the 1984 Penguin edition. Ed.]

For their advice and support, I would like to thank Andrea Atkin, Julie Early, Sheila Sullivan, and Orrin Wang. I owe a special debt to William Veeder for the time, patience, encouragement, insight, and general good sense he has provided in such generous quantitites.

1. The divorce of Gothic and 'history' goes back at least to Walter Scott's famous distinction between the two in the introduction to *Waverly* (1814). By contrast, I take as one of my starting points David Punter's sensible claim, in his *Literature of Terror: A History of Gothic Fictions from 1765 to the Present Day* (London, 1980) [exerpted in this volume – Ed.] that 'within the Gothic we can find a very intense, if displaced, engagement with political and social problems' (p. 62).

2. John Allen Stevenson, 'A Vampire in the Mirror: The Sexuality of *Dracula*', *PMLA*, 103 (1988), 139–49. Stevenson's remark is somewhat surprising, since his essay convincingly places *Dracula* in the context of late-century thought on marriage, race, and exogamy.

3. *The Spectator*, 79 (31 July 1897), 151.

4. Quoted in Bernard Bergonzi, *The Early H. G. Wells: A Study of the Scientific Romances* (Manchester, 1961), p. 124.

5. Patrick Brantlinger, *Rule of Darkness: British Literature and Imperialism, 1830–1914* (Ithaca, NY, 1988), pp. 228–9. For a somewhat different account of the conjunction of Gothic and imperialism, see Judith Wilt, 'The Imperial Mouth: Imperialism, the Gothic, and Science Fiction', *Journal of Popular Culture*, 14 (1981), 618–28. Wilt sees Britain's 'imperial anxieties' summoning up 'the great Gothic and science fiction tales of the 1880s and 1890s' (p. 620), which in turn do the cultural work of 'subverting' imperial ideology.

6. Joseph Bierman, 'The Genesis and Dating of *Dracula* from Bram
Stoker's Working Notes', *Notes and Queries*, 24 (1977), 39–41. For a
brief description of Stoker's manuscripts and notes for *Dracula*, including a 'List of Sources' that Stoker drew up, see Phyllis A.
Roth, *Bram Stoker* (Boston, 1982), pp. 145–6. Stoker gleaned his version of
Carpathian history and culture entirely from travel narratives, guide-
books, and various works on Eastern European superstitions, legends,
and folktales. Daniel Farson, one of Stoker's biographers, mentions his
'genius for research'. See *The Man Who Wrote Dracula: A Biography of
Bram Stoker* (London, 1975), p. 148. Stoker's debt to Le Fanu is most
immediately evident in a chapter deleted from *Dracula*, in which
Harker, travelling to Castle Dracula, discovers the mausoleum of a
'Countess Dolingen of Gratz in Styria'. The chapter was later reprinted
separately as 'Dracula's Guest'. See *The Bram Stoker Bedside Companion: Ten Stories by the Author of Dracula*, ed. Charles Osborne
(New York, 1973).

7. Bram Stoker, *Dracula* (Harmondsworth, 1984), p. 286. All further references given in the text.

8. I have based my observations on the standard Victorian and
Edwardian works in English on the region, which include John Paget,
Hungary and Transylvania (London, 1855); James O. Noyes,
Roumania (New York, 1857); Charles Boner, *Transylvania: Its
Products and Its People* (London, 1865); Andrew W. Crosse, *Round
About the Carpathians* (Edinburgh, 1878); C. Johnson, *On the Track
of the Crescent* (London, 1885); M. Edith Durham, *The Burden of
the Balkans* (London, 1905); Jean Victor Bates, *Our Allies and
Enemies in the Near East* (New York, n.d.); and especially Emily
Gerard, *The Land Beyond the Forest: Facts, Figures, and Fancies from
Transylvania*, 2 vols (Edinburgh, 1888).

9. Bates, *Allies and Enemies*, p. 3.

10. Boner, *Transylvania*, pp. 1–2.

11. Stevenson, 'Vampire in the Mirror', 144.

12. Gerard, *The Land Beyond the Forest*, Vol. 1, pp. 304–5. Scholars
have long recognised Stoker's reliance on Gerard. See Roth, *Bram
Stoker*, pp. 13–14, and Leonard Wolf, *The Annotated Dracula*
(New York, 1975), pp. xiii–xiv, and references in annotations
throughout.

13. See Edward Said, *Orientalism* (New York, 1979).

14. Critics who do address the travel motifs in *Dracula* generally emphasise
travel's connections to psychology rather than to politics. 'Transylvania
is Europe's unconscious', asserts Geoffrey Wall in '"Different from
Writing": *Dracula* in 1897', *Literature and History*, 10 (1984), 20.

Alan Johnson quotes Wall approvingly, and argues that Harker's journey to Transylvania is a 'symbolic journey into his own mind'. See 'Bent and Broken Necks: Signs of Design in Stoker's *Dracula*', *Victorian Newsletter*, 72 (1987), 21, 23.

15. Gerard, *The Land Beyond the Forest*, vol. 1, p. 30.

16. See, for example, the opening of Noyes's *Roumania* (1857). Noyes, an American surgeon living in Vienna, ascends 'a lofty mountain' overlooking the city and gazes across the river at the 'Orient': 'There, looking into the purple distance eastward ... I resolved to visit that mysterious Orient whose glowing portals seemed to open just beyond' (p. 1).

17. Wolfgang Iser, *The Implied Reader: Patterns of Communication in Prose Fiction from Bunyan to Beckett* (Baltimore, 1974), p. 34. See also Hans Robert Jauss, *Toward an Aesthetic of Reception*, trans. Timothy Bahti (Minneapolis, 1982).

18. Crosse, *Round About the Carpathians*, p. 342.

19. Rudyard Kipling, 'Miss Youghal's Sais', in *Plain Tales from the Hills* (1886; rpt. Oxford, 1987), p. 24.

20. Gerard, Vol. 1, p. 211. Gerard accepts the idea, common in the nineteenth century, that the Roumanians possessed a Roman heritage. This defuses some of the potential anxiety of her observation, since the Roumanians are thereby reclaimed as a 'Western' race.

21. Christopher Craft, '"Kiss Me with Those Red Lips": Gender and Inversion in Bram Stoker's *Dracula*', *Representations*, 8 (1984), 107). [Reprinted in this volume – Ed.]

22. David Seed, 'The Narrative Method of *Dracula*', *Nineteenth-Century Fiction*, 40:1 (1985), 74.

23. Apart from Franco Moretti's essay, little has been written on Morris. See Franco Moretti, 'The Dialectic of Fear', *New Left Review*, 136 (1982), 67–85. [Book version of this essay excerpted in this volume – Ed.] Burton Hatlen gives the majority view when he says that Morris's function is to become 'an honorary Englishman', whose 'reward' is the 'privilege of dying to protect England'. See 'The Return of the Repressed/Oppressed in Bram Stoker's *Dracula*', *Minnesota Review*, 15 (1980), 83.

24. Moretti extends these speculations by asking why 'Lucy dies – and then turns into a vampire – immediately after receiving a blood transfusion from Morris' ('The Dialectic of Fear', p. 76). I am indebted to his essay for pointing out that Morris is the first to mention the word 'vampire'. Moretti goes on to argue that Morris, like Dracula, is a metaphor for monopoly capitalism.

25. Stoker's ambivalence about America is more visible in his earlier *A Glimpse of America* (London, 1886). Stoker claims a kinship between the two countries, since their citizens spring from the same racial stock, but he also sees America becoming racially different, and he suggests that the countries may become antagonistic in the future. His racial language is drawn straight from late-Victorian evolutionism.

26. In this context, we can note Stoker's apparent confusion over where Van Helsing resides while in London. Van Helsing asks Seward to book him rooms at the Great Eastern Hotel (p. 138), but he apparently never stays there, since Seward later calls for him at the Berkeley (p. 161). The name of the former points clearly enough to the potential for anxiety over the 'Great East'. The name of the latter, however, points in the most indirect way possible to the threat posed by the West, since it was Bishop Berkeley who, after his visit to America, penned the well-known line 'Westward the course of empire takes its way'. While Stoker's concerns about the East are generally on the surface of *Dracula*, it takes some digging before his anxieties over the West appear.

8

Dracula: A Vampire of Our Own

NINA AUERBACH

DRACULA'S NEW ORDER

Dracula is so musty and foul-smelling, so encrusted with the corruption of ages, that it sounds perverse to call him 'new'. The up-to-date young people who hunt him dread his ancientness. To them, Dracula is not simply evil; he is an eruption from an evil antiquity that refuses to rest in its grave. The earnest Jonathan Harker, who visits Castle Dracula to his bane, fears that although his shorthand diary 'is nineteenth century up-to-date with a vengeance', 'the old centuries had, and have powers of their own which mere "modernity" cannot kill'.[1] Ruthven and Carmilla looked as young as their enthralled prey; Dracula flings his weight of ages against the acquired skills of a single generation. Surely this antediluvian leech has no role in their smart new century.

In his novel, Dracula awes because he is old, but within the vampire tradition, his very antiquity makes him new, detaching him from the progressive characters who track him. Ruthven was in some threatening sense a mirror of his schoolfellow Aubrey; Varney reflected his predatory society; Carmilla mirrored Laura's own lonely face. But in our first clue to Dracula's terrible nature, Jonathan Harker looks in his shaving mirror and sees no one beside him. In Jonathan's mirror, the vampire has no more face than does Dickens's Spirit of Christmas Future. In his blankness, his impersonality, his emphasis on sweeping new orders rather than insinuating intimacy, Dracula *is* the twentieth century he still haunts. Not until

145

the twentieth century was he reproduced, fetishised, besequelled, and obsessed over, though many of his descendants deny his lovelessness – and perhaps their own as well. Dracula's disjunction from earlier, friendlier vampires makes him less a spectre of an undead past than a harbinger of a world to come, a world that is our own.[2]

Most critics who bother to study Dracula at all proceed on the lazy assumption that since all vampires are pretty much alike, his origins extend neatly back through the nineteenth century to Lord Ruthven, Varney, and, particularly, Carmilla.[3] Dracula, however, is less the culmination of a tradition than the destroyer of one. His indifference to the sort of intimacy Carmilla offered a lonely daughter is a curt denial of the chief vampire attribute up to his time.

Carmilla aspired to see herself in a friend. Dracula, in one of his few self-definitions, identifies only with a vanished conquering race whose token is not a mortal but an animal: 'We Szekelys have a right to be proud, for in our veins flows the blood of many brave races who fought as the lion fights, for lordship' (p. 28). No human can share the mirror with a lord of lost races whose names Englishmen can't pronounce. Dracula's strangeness hurls to oblivion the Byronic vampire refrain, 'Remember your oath'. Earlier vampires insinuated themselves into a humanity Dracula reshapes, through magic and mesmerism, into his unrecognisable likeness.

Dracula's literary affinities lie less with vampires in earlier prose tales than with Keats's *Lamia* (1820), a poem that insists on the barriers between immortal predator and human prey. Lamia is a gorgeous serpent-woman whose influence flowers in vampire works of the 1890s; before that, she mattered less to vampire writers than did Geraldine, the serpent-woman of Coleridge's *Christabel*, who bequeathed human sympathies to the vampires she engendered.

Geraldine, we remember, diffused herself into Christabel's bleak household, exuding her identity into Christabel herself and half-becoming – as Le Fanu's Carmilla would do – the dead mother of her beloved female prey. Geraldine's potency rested in the breast that transfixed Christabel, a breast the reader never saw: the fountain of her expansive power was 'a sight to dream of, not to tell'.

Lamia dreams and tells; its serpent-woman is less sharer than spectacle. Like Lycius, the innocent young man she seduces, we watch Lamia's transformative gyrations from without. Some of us might have breasts, but none of us has Lamia's exotically endowed body, 'Striped like a zebra, freckled like a pard, / Eyes like a peacock, and all crimson barr'd.'[4] Like Dracula with his Szekelys and lions, Lamia transfixes spectators because she belongs to a world only exotic animals share; no human body can emulate hers. Like Dracula's, Lamia's main vampiric attribute is not interpenetration, but transformation. Keats's poem, like Stoker's novel, is a tale of metamorphoses. Lamia mutates continually (from serpent to goddess to mortal woman to nullity), confirming as she does so the barriers between life forms; over and over, she defines herself by what she is not. The world of Keats's gods, to which she belongs, is as distinct from that of mortals as is the world of Stoker's vampires: 'Into the green-recessed woods they flew; / Nor grew they pale, as mortal lovers do' (ll. 144–5). In Coleridge's poem, Christabel's father understandably mistook Geraldine for his friend's daughter, but Keats's Lycius never thinks Lamia is human, even after her transformation into a maiden: like Stoker's seemingly mad Renfield, Lycius worships another order of being and knows he does. Christabel's household absorbed the vampire, while Lamia is segregated from the society she intoxicates: Lycius abandons his own home for Lamia's 'purple-lined palace of sweet sin', a retreat as distinct from an ordinary residence as Stoker's Castle Dracula.

As with Dracula, to know Lamia is to destroy her. In the spirit of Stoker's interdisciplinary expert Van Helsing, Lycius's tutor Apollonius recognises Lamia for what she is; he eyes her piercingly at her wedding feast, forcing her to vanish. The lore – scientific, superstitious, theological, criminological, legal, and geographic – with which Van Helsing comes equipped similarly allows Dracula to be defined and thus dissipated. For Keats and Stoker, vampires are so distinct from humanity that to know them is to dispel them; they can be catalogued, defined, and destroyed. Scientific expertise supplants the oath with which Polidori bound vampire to mortal.

Expertise had little relevance to Dracula's ancestors in English prose. Weaving in and out of their human prey, mysteriously incorporating their nature into our own, they were not remote spectacles, but congenial fellow travellers who were scarcely separable from their victim or from us, their victim/reader. Dracula is on a journey that is not ours. With his advent, vampires cease to be sharers; instead, they become mesmerists, transforming human consciousness rather than entering it. When he rejected Coleridge's Geraldine for Keats's gorgeous Lamia, Bram Stoker created an uncongenial vampire for an obscure future.

Dracula is defined by repudiations and new beginnings. Conventional wisdom assumes its derivation from *Carmilla*, but

Stoker's most significant revision excised from his manuscript the shadow of Carmilla and everything she represented. In a cancelled, posthumously published opening chapter, frequently anthologised as 'Dracula's Guest', Jonathan Harker is trapped in a blizzard on his way to Castle Dracula. He stumbles into the tomb of

COUNTESS DOLINGEN OF GRATZ
IN STYRIA

Terrorised by her sleeping, then shrieking, spectre, he is trapped until a great wolf, which may be Dracula himself, shelters him from the storm and saves him from this terrible woman.[5]

Since Carmilla is also a female vampire from Gratz, in Styria, scholars take Countess Dolingen as proof of Le Fanu's influence on Stoker.[6] Actually, though, the shadowy Countess personifies an influence rejected: the spectacle of a 'beautiful woman with rounded cheeks and red lips, seemingly sleeping on a bier' (p. 170) has little to do with Le Fanu's insinuating guest, who, infiltrating the dreams of her hostess, is most dangerous when awake. Moreover, if this chapter was ever part of *Dracula*,[7] Stoker wisely deleted it, thereby exorcising an imperial female vampire who drives Dracula into an alliance with Jonathan. The women Stoker retained – Dracula's three lascivious sister-brides; the vampirised Lucy and Mina – may writhe and threaten, but all are finally animated and destroyed by masterful men. A ruling woman has no place in the patriarchal hierarchy *Dracula* affirms, a hierarchy that earlier, more playful and sinuous vampires subverted.

Dracula is in love less with death or sexuality than with hierarchies, erecting barriers hitherto foreign to vampire literature; the gulf between male and female, antiquity and newness, class and class, England and non-England, vampire and mortal, homoerotic and heterosexual love, infuses its genre with a new fear: fear of the hated unknown. Earlier prey knew their vampires and often shared their gender: Carmilla introduces herself to Laura in a childhood dream. But Dracula is barred from the dream of Stoker's hero, which admits only three 'ladies by their dress and manner', one of whose faces Jonathan, like Laura, 'seemed somehow to know ... and to know it in connection with some dreamy fear' (p. 51). Jonathan's flash of recognition remains unresolved, tempting later vampire hunters to identify this fair predator with Lucy or Mina or both.[8] But whichever woman arouses his dreamy fear, Jonathan surely does *not* recognise his own face in the vampire's as Le Fanu's Laura did. Like the empty mirror, the face of the demon cannot reflect its prey, nor can Dracula participate in Jonathan's exclusively heterosexual vision of three laughing chomping women who are not only an alien species, but an alien gender. Stoker austerely expels from his tale of terror the 'intimacy, or friendship' that had, since Byron's time, linked predator to prey.

Like Lord Ruthven, Dracula was a proud servant's offering of friendship to a great man: the actor Henry Irving, whose splendid Lyceum Theatre Stoker managed from its ascendancy in 1878 to its fall out of Irving's control in 1898. Like Byron, Irving became a hero for his age because he played damnation with flair; his celebrated Mephistopheles gave Dracula his contours, just as Byron's sexual predations, in verse and out of it, had flowed into Ruthven. Moreover, Irving, like Byron, could be turned into a vampire by an underling not simply because he posed as a demon, but because both men radiated the hero's simulated transparency. Though they were known by all, they were tantalisingly unattainable in private to the men they lured into fellowship.

But friendship with Irving was a tribute to exalted distance, not a spur to dreams of intimacy. Ellen Terry, Irving's partner at the Lyceum, wrote shrewdly about his almost inhuman remoteness:

> H. I. is odd when he says he hates meeting the company and 'shaking their greasy paws'. I think it is not quite right that he does not care for anybody much. ... Quiet, patient, tolerant, impersonal, gentle, *close*, crafty! Crafty sounds unkind, but it is H. I. 'Crafty' fits him. ... For years he has accepted favours, obligations to, etc., *through* Bram Stoker! Never will he acknowledge them himself, either by business-like receipt or by any word or sign. He 'lays low' like Brer Rabbit better than any one I have ever met.[9]

Accepting with pride the role of Irving's liaison with the outside world, Stoker was no Polidori, fantasising class equality and impossible communion. Stoker knew his place, a mightier one than Polidori's. As Byron's personal physician, Polidori was hired to care for that famous body, but he ministered only to be mocked. Stoker had no access to Irving's body but he did run his empire, where his responsibilities were 'heady and overwhelming. He oversaw the artistic and administrative aspects of the new theatre, and acted as Irving's buffer, goodwill ambassador, and hatchet man. He learned the pleasures of snobbery', admitting only the artistic and social elite to the glamorous openings and even more theatrical banquets over which Irving presided after the performance.[10] Like Jonathan in

Dracula, Stoker deftly manipulated the business of modern empire – particularly the intricacies of money, travel, and human contact – that paralysed his master. Onstage, Irving's power to mesmerise crowds was as superhuman as the vampire's, but he relied, as Byron never did, on the worldly dexterity of the servant who made him immortal.

Byron's dismissal was Polidori's mortal wound, but Irving never betrayed Stoker's faith in his master's protection. Even when Irving's theatrical fortunes began to decline, shortly after *Dracula* was published, Stoker continued to celebrate his master's benevolent omnipotence, writing glowingly about 'the close friendship between us which only terminated with his life – if indeed friendship, like any other form of love, can ever terminate'.[11] One doubts whether the friendship was 'close' in Polidori's sense, but when that life did terminate, Stoker wrote a two-volume official memoir, *Personal Reminiscences of Henry Irving* (1906), that consecrated his subject with a reverence granted only to dignitaries and authors – never, until then, to an actor. The Irving of *Personal Reminiscences* is as marmoreally undead as the more animated Dracula.

Polidori never recovered from the humiliation of his service to Byron, writing truculently that 'I am not accustomed to have a master, & there fore my conduct was not free & easy'; Stoker grew stately in his master's shadow, feeding on hero worship while paying extravagant lip service to heterosexual love.[12] Polidori's 'free & easy' vampire who subsists on mortal affinities yielded at the end of the century to Stoker's master, an impenetrable creature hungering for control.

JONATHAN'S MASTER

Dracula's protracted intercourse with Lucy and Mina, whom he transforms in foreplay so elaborate that few readers notice its narrative incoherence, made him a star in the twentieth century. Jonathan Harker, the only man who is Dracula's potential prey, is overshadowed by bitten women who, in Lord Ruthven's time, were mere shadowy counters in the game between the men. Jonathan, however, is no player. His relation to Dracula is defined solely by power and status, with none of the sympathetic fluctuations that characterised the intercourse between Ruthven and Aubrey.

Polidori's Aubrey was a 'young gentleman' flattered to travel with Lord Ruthven; Stoker's Jonathan Harker is not a gregarious youth on a grand tour, but a lonely tourist on a disorienting business trip who enters Castle Dracula as an employee. Dracula's ritual greeting – 'Welcome to my house. Come freely. Go safely. And leave something of the happiness you bring' (p. 16) – sheds on his plodding solicitor the aura of an earlier age when travellers were gentlemen whose freedom of motion could be assumed. Fussing about his itinerary and his comfort, Jonathan is a coerced and reluctant tourist who is never his own man even before he becomes the vampire's prisoner. Encompassed by wonders and horrors, he relinquishes all responsibility for his journey with the querulous exclamation, 'Was this a customary incident in the life of a solicitor's clerk sent out to explain the purchase of a London estate to a foreigner?' (p. 13).

In fact, as Jonathan goes on to remind himself, he is no longer a clerk, but a full-fledged solicitor. By the same standard, Count Dracula surely would prefer to be referred to by his title, and he is no foreigner in his own country. The edgy civil servant diminishes everything he describes; Dracula inspires in him neither wonder nor curiosity. Because Jonathan withdraws from communion into petty professionalism, employee and employer have nothing in common. Dracula's initial orations about his own heroism are a self-obsessed public presentation far from the intimate confessions of Carmilla, which demanded a response in kind. Like the Irving of Stoker's *Personal Reminiscences*, Dracula requires only an audience onto whom he can exude his construction of himself. Like the Stoker of the *Reminiscences*, Jonathan is merely the intoning man's scribe: 'I wish I could put down all he said exactly as he said it, for to me it was most fascinating' (*Dracula*, p. 28).

Even when Jonathan, spying, realises that since there are no servants in the castle, Dracula has been cooking and serving his meals, making his bed, and driving him in the coach, he feels no affinity with his host in this menial role: the servant's proficiency only reinforces the master's intimidating omnipotence. From the beginning to the end, this vampire monotonously plays the role he has assigned himself – 'I have been so long master that I would be master still' (p. 20) – relinquishing the versatility of his kind.

There are no more companionable journeys, only Jonathan's uncommunicative voyeurism.[13] Instead of sharing with Dracula or feeding him, Jonathan spies on him from distant sites. Critical ingenuity can detect various subtle affinities between the horrified young man and the horrible old vampire[14] – Jonathan, does, for instance, crawl out of the castle in the same lizardlike fashion that appalled him when he watched Dracula do it – but finally, both assume the rigid roles of master and servant, spectacle and spectator, tyrant and victim, monster and human, making no attempt to bridge the distance. Caste, not kinship, determines their relationship. It is impossible to imagine Dracula admonishing Jonathan to remember his oath, for though Jonathan is a scrupulously obedient employee and even, for a while, a courteous guest, he is incapable of the voluntary – and lordly – fealty an oath demands. 'Sent out' to the vampire, he quickly becomes the vampire's possession, though since he is too pure and proper to be possessed, he fittingly remains unbitten.

According to Stoker's working notes, the heart of *Dracula* was not blood, but an assertion of ownership. 'One incident and one alone remained constant [from 1890] right up to publication day [in 1897]': Dracula's occupation of Jonathan. One of Stoker's editors unearths the claim at the heart of his novel:

> In March 1890 Bram Stoker wrote on a piece of scrap paper, in handwriting which he always called 'an extremely bad hand': 'young man goes out – sees girls one tries – to kiss him not on the lips but throat. Old Count interferes – rage and fury diabolical. This man belongs to me I want him.' Again, in February 1892, in one of the many 'structures he scribbled down: "Bistritz – Borgo Pass – Castle – Sortes Virgil – Belongs to me."' And in shorthand, again and again, over the next few years: '& the visitors – is it a dream – women stoop to kiss him, terror of death. Suddenly the Count turns her away – "this man belongs to me"'; 'May 15 Monday Women kissing'; 'Book I Ch 8 Belongs to me.'[15]

Belongs to me. These words define the vampire the twentieth century cannot leave alone. The shared Romantic journey in which nothing impedes two gentlemen's movements but the occult ends with a servant immobilised and imprisoned in a castle he never wanted to enter. Byron's 'journey through countries not hitherto much frequented by travellers' terminates in a monomaniac's refrain: 'Belongs to me.'

JONATHAN'S PROGRESS

Dracula's possession of vampire literature was so unremittingly bleak that his best-known progeny tried not to hear their master's words. Whether they are moviemakers or literary critics, twentieth-century acolytes want to turn this account of appropriation into a love story, as if invoking 'love' and 'sex' would save our culture from seeing its own unresponsive face in the mirror.[16] It goes against the grain to recast Stoker's novel as a love story, but the first (and still the best-known) film adaptations tried to return to a pre-*Dracula* tradition by restoring, even intensifying, the homoerotic bond between predator and prey: both discard Stoker's Jonathan, a loyal employee to his bones, for a self-determined protagonist who wilfully abandons domesticity to embrace undiscovered countries. But restoring the mutuality between victim and vampire does not restore the half-human vampire of an earlier tradition; instead, it forces us to question the possibility of human men.

F. W. Murnau's silent *Nosferatu* (1922) and Tod Browning's stagy *Dracula* (1931) feature the first male mortals in our tradition whom the vampire not only lures, but actually bites.[17] Both choose to go to his country; as penance for voluntarily crossing the border, both belong to the vampire not only in body, but in blood. The young traveller into the unknown is not an infatuated schoolmate, as Polidori's Aubrey was; he is not simply 'sent out', like Stoker's Jonathan; he re-creates himself in his journey toward the vampire. These early cinematic pilgrims are infected by the vampire's hunger before they set off to meet him. Their restless willingness to abandon decorum adds psychological dimension to their relation with the vampire, but it softens Stoker's impersonal vision of dominion. Stoker's Dracula can subjugate the most stolidly reluctant mortal, while these movie Draculas cast their spell only over alienated, even tainted visitors.

Murnau's film features a sick city, not an invaded nation. Renfield,[18] Stoker's lone 'zoophagous' madman who becomes Dracula's acolyte only after incarceration in Dr Seward's asylum, is in *Nosferatu* Jonathan's mad employer, a secret enemy agent who chortles over the vampire's occult messages and gloats over his wish to buy a house 'in our city'.

Jonathan – who now represents only a real estate agency, not the lofty British law – is as receptive to the vampire's infection as is the city itself. Gustav von Wangenheim's performance is all preening and guffawing. He is delighted to abandon the embraces and mystic foreboding of Nina (not 'Mina'; see n. 18 above) – to whom he is already married in Murnau's version – for a stint in the land of the phantoms. Cautionary expertise, here embodied in the *Book of Vampires* he finds at his inn, only makes him guffaw further; with his instinctive respect for authority, Stoker's Jonathan wore the cross the worried peasant gave him, while Murnau's Jonathan tosses the book, and all authorities, aside with a blasphemous self-delighted laugh.

Unlike Stoker's traveller, who waits with impatient helplessness for various and increasingly sinister vehicles, Murnau's *walks* across the border. His coachman refuses to pass over the bridge into the land of phantoms, and so Jonathan crosses it on foot, accompanied by the portentous title: 'And when he had crossed the bridge, the phantoms came to meet him.'

This momentous transition is far from the nervous docility of Stoker's Jonathan: 'I feared to go very far from the station, as we had arrived late and would start as near the correct time as possible. The impression I had was that we were leaving the West and entering the East' (p. 1). In Murnau's film, at the moment of Jonathan's crossing, the world changes: beyond the bridge, the film is photographed in negative, reversing the phantasmal country to black-on-white rather than conventional white-on-black.

Max Schreck's Dracula is closer to the ghostly Ruthven of the Victorian state than to the heavily material creatures of Stoker's novel. Murnau's looking-glass photography and Schreck's luminous makeup, with his radiantly obtruding bald dome, fingers, ears, nose, and ratlike teeth (which, unlike the familiar dripping canines, he never seems to use), function like the Victorian vampire trap to de-materialise the creature's hunger. Like those of the Victorian actor disembodied in the vampire trap, his movements are ostentatiously unnatural: on the ship, he doesn't climb out of his coffin, but is miraculously elevated from it; in Bremen, he dissolves (with his coffin!) through a solid door.

Moreover, while Stoker gets his first big effect by revealing that his corporeal Dracula has no soul and therefore casts no shadow, Schreck *becomes* his shadow in the climactic episodes when he stalks Jonathan and Nina, a shadow even more elongated than his body, its interminable fingers seeming to slide through matter as it glides toward his prey. This vampire is scarcely bounded by matter, expanding into the shadow, or looking-glass image, of the madly chortling community that courted him, of which Jonathan is the representative.

Murnau not only has Dracula bite Jonathan at least once (Nina's somnambulistic powers prevent a second attack); his crosscutting emphasises the parallel rhythms of the vampire's and Jonathan's journeys back to Bremen – a suggestive convergence that Stoker's narrative chronology suppresses – so that when the invasion finally comes, we are never sure whether Dracula or Jonathan (or both in collusion) unleashes the rats that carry the plague that wastes the city.

Like his vulnerable agents (Renfield is lynched for his collaboration with the vampire, and Jonathan is ambiguously debilitated for the rest of the movie), Murnau's Dracula is more carrier than master. His ghostliness makes him as fragile as he is agile. Isolated by his clownlike makeup and by immobilising compositions that confine him within closed spaces or behind bars, he is no more than a shadow of the community he infects. As the first vampire to be destroyed by the sun under which Stoker's Dracula paraded vigorously,[19] he inaugurates an important twentieth-century tradition; but when Nina sacrifices herself to family and community by keeping Dracula with her after daybreak, Schreck merely vanishes. Unlike the more seductive vampires of the 1960s and '70s, he is not fleshly enough to burn.

The final title – 'as the shadow of the vampire vanishes with the morning sun' – presumably heals the stricken community and Jonathan as well, allowing us to forget the ominous fact that the sun usually *creates* shadows rather than dissipating them. But Bremen has already infected itself from within. It was Jonathan's wanton walk across the bridge that desecrated his family and city, thereby fusing the domestic and the foreign, the mortal and the monster, the victim and the tyrant, all of whom Stoker kept carefully apart. By making Dracula a shadow of the good men of Bremen, Murnau also crosses the bridge between men and women that Stoker scrupulously erects: Stoker's Dracula possesses only females, while Murnau's uses no lustful, animalistic women as his agents, but only respectable men. According to the *Book of Vampires* that Jonathan discovers, 'Nosferatu drinks the blood of the young'. Indifferent to gender, Nosferatu unleashes mass death, not individual sexuality. Anyone, under Murnau's rules, will satisfy a vampire.

But only a pure woman can destroy one. Nina accordingly becomes the final, crucial bridge between town and invader, humanity and the monster. By luring the vampire to her bed so that he will vanish with daybreak, Nina both dies for humanity and, more knowingly than her husband, crosses the bridge beyond it. Nina's ambiguous sacrifice abolishes Stoker's polarisation between pure and carnal women, for Nina is less a victim than a link between shadow and substance, life and death, corruption and respectability.

She may dispel Max Schreck, but she also marries him to the civil domesticity she represents.[20]

Murnau's film is, of course, admonitory, not, as Stoker wanted to be, congratulatory: Stoker quarantined his vampire from British civilisation, while Murnau's was a shadow of his own diseased Germany.[21] Thus, *Nosferatu* itself crosses the bridge between classes, genders, and orders of being that *Dracula* erected so carefully. But in bringing Jonathan and Dracula together, as sinister collaborators if not friends (Murnau's Dracula reads with silent disdain as Jonathan wolfs down his meals, while Stoker's declaims about himself at length as Jonathan nibbles delicately), Murnau does not restore the vampire's mortal sympathies; instead, he intensifies Stoker's vision of impersonal power. Max Schreck is dispelled, but he was only the city's shadow. *Nosferatu* seems to begin where *Dracula* might have ended, in a community that has been transformed into something savage and rampant. An image of the picturesque antihuman, Bremen survives its citizens, whether they are mortals or vampires.

Tod Browning's American *Dracula* is famous now only for Bela Lugosi's performance, but in one sense this commercial American movie, inexpertly adapted from a popular if quite un-Stokeresque Broadway play, is more daring than the masterpiece of German Expressionism serious audiences revere. Following Murnau's lead, Browning transforms Jonathan from a dutiful servant with corporate loyalties to an eccentric trespasser who courts transformation, but Browning's defiant explorer, the wild and maddened Renfield, is no prospective husband; he is scarcely even a man of business. Dracula's visitor is no longer Stoker's stolid, if fragile, emissary of Western civilisation; as Dwight Frye plays him, Renfield is so effete and overbred that he is more bizarre than Lugosi's impeccably mannered vampire.[22]

Renfield has nothing of the employee about him: florid and faintly effeminate, he is a Hollywood version of a decadent English gentleman. Stoker's Jonathan was infallibly, if condescendingly, courteous to his Transylvanian hosts; Browning's Renfield orders them around like a stock American tourist, even calling imperiously to his unholy coachman, 'Hi, Driver! What do you mean by going at this —.' His disapproval is squelched only when he sees that his coach is being led by a bat (not, in this version, by Lugosi himself, whose Dracula is too stately to make a good servant). Renfield's white hat and cane make him an oddly dapper figure among the hefty Transylvanians; he floats through his coarse surroundings with a demeanour of dreamy rapture that anticipates Fred Astaire's until, to his horror, the ghostly vampire women swarm around him and he faints, only to be swooped upon by Dracula. This Dracula never affirms 'This man belongs to me', for Dwight Frye's Renfield belongs to nobody. He does claim that his journey is 'a matter of business', later muttering something to Dracula about the lease on Carfax Abbey, but he represents no organisation, nor is he tied to the domestic characters we will meet later. 'I trust you have kept your coming here secret', Dracula intones. Renfield indicates that a secret journey posed no problem, thereby breaking the social web that bound Stoker's Jonathan to the mighty institutions of British law and marriage and implicated Murnau's Jonathan in civic corruption and domestic hypocrisy.

The doomed traveller in the American *Dracula* floats beyond ties, so it is safe for him to become Dracula's servant. Once bitten, he turns extravagantly mad, but unlike the women, he isn't quite a vampire. In the long, dull domestic portion of the film, Dwight Frye's pyrotechnics provide a counterpoint to the stolidity of humans and vampire alike, just as his character – the vampire's servant who can't shake off human sympathies – links human to inhuman by belonging to neither. Renfield is as alien and irritating to Dracula, who finally tosses him down a huge staircase, as he is to his mortal and supposedly sane caretakers. In the American 1930s, the corrupt traveller, not the vampire, is the movie's authentic alien. Sucking blood is less sinful than is Renfield's mercurial desire to leave home.

The Transylvanian beginning, the most compelling portion of the movie, hints at the old Byronic fellowship between dandy and vampire. Renfield is not Dracula's property as Stoker's Jonathan was, but neither is he Dracula's friend. The film establishes an identification between these two overdressed creatures – Lugosi wears cloak, tuxedo, and medals even indoors – that in 1931 America whispered of perversity. Bela Lugosi is not the phantom Max Schreck was; he is corpulent, clothes-conscious, and, in close-up, clearly wearing lipstick and eye makeup, the only male character who does. In the 'dinner' scene that follows Jonathan's arrival, no food is served; this Dracula avoids the indignity of cooking for his guest and the awkwardness of watching him eat.[23] There is no cosiness in this Castle Dracula, only the covertly titillating effect of two baroque men eyeing each other in a grosteque set freighted with cobwebs, candelabra, and suits of armour. Renfield gets only a glass of wine, and that only so Lugosi can intone his deathless 'I never drink – *vine*', an archly self-aware aside that Browning's movie originates: Stoker's growling Count was no ironist.

The wine also allows Renfield to cut himself so that Dracula can eye him hungrily and then shy away from his crucifix. But even before he sees blood, Dracula has been leaning lewdly toward Renfield; when Renfield sucks the blood from his own finger, Dracula grins knowingly, presumably savouring their affinities. When, in a silent, gracefully choreographed sequence, he banishes the vampire women and stretches toward Renfield's throat, he communicates less pride of ownership than the embrace of kinship. Browning's Renfield is so clearly beyond the pale of any human community that the bond between vampire and mortal Stoker did his best to break is, however briefly and perversely, renewed.

But once they leave Transylvania and the domestic story begins, this faint communion of dandies is over: power and mastery prevail.[24] Renfield mutates from fop into madman who is always trying vainly to elude his many keepers; Lugosi also drops his foppishness, becoming so dependent on commanding attitudes and penetrating stares that he practically turns into a monument. His affinities are no longer with the mercurial Renfield, but with Edward Van Sloan's marmoreal Van Helsing, who is even more autocratic than the vampire. Whatever intensity the movie retains comes less from Dracula's predations among sketchily characterised women than from Van Helsing's and Dracula's battle of wills.

Humanity triumphs when Van Helsing becomes a more overbearing patriarch than the vampire. He disposes of the other human men almost as easily as he stakes Dracula, for Seward is a cipher and Jonathan a fool. Unable to imagine a heroic human lover, Browning's adaptation consigns Jonathan to romantic parody, breathing such lines as 'My, what a big bat!' and (to Mina as she is manifesting vampiric tendencies) 'You're so – like a changed girl. You look wonderful!' Such a silly man might become a husband when the vampire is dead, but he is no use to heroes. Browning drops the corporate ethos that makes the vampire hunt possible in Stoker's novel.[25] Van Helsing brooks no collaborators; he saves humanity by barking out the Dracula-like demand, 'I must be master here or I can do nothing.' The affinities of Transylvania fall away; the question of Browning's film is which is to be master. Once the movie concludes that humanity needs a leader, Dracula becomes surprisingly vulnerable, allowing himself to be staked with scarcely an offscreen grunt. Does he refuse to fight for his life because he misses home and Renfield?

Immediate descendants of Stoker's novel, Murnau's *Nosferatu* and Browning's *Dracula* struggle to reunite the vampire to his mortal friend. In both cases, though, apparent affinity yields to that more vulnerable bond, perversity.[26] Finally, both films acquiesce in the emphasis on power they inherit from Stoker: Murnau's stricken Jonathan languishes into the civic corruption both he and the vampire represent; Browning's Dracula abandons Renfield to his keepers to engage in an authoritarian duel with Van Helsing. Both movies finally succumb to the coldness at the heart of Stoker's novel, the requiem of a tradition of intimacy.

Dracula is a desolate inheritance for Murnau's *Nosferatu* and Browning's *Dracula*, which become more joyless as they proceed, concluding in images of ineffable loss. Both are more doleful than the novel they adapt because both banish Stoker's Lucy Westenra, whose kaleidoscopic transformations are Stoker's substitute for the affection that had been the primary vampire endowment. Lucy's transformations, the most memorable spectacles of the novel and of most movies after the 1960s, leaven the heterosexual hierarchies that deform the creatures vampires had been. By relegating Lucy to the role of an incidental off-screen victim, Murnau and Browning cast off Stoker's sadism as well as his spectacle; by focusing instead on a restless man who travels beyond boundaries toward the vampire, both apparently look back with some yearning toward the homoerotic phase of vampire literature. Finally, though, their stories are trapped in the weary decorum with which Stoker made vampires palatable in the 1890s.

VAMPIRE PROPRIETY

Critics unfamiliar with vampire evolution fail to notice the relative respectability of Stoker's predators, especially his women. Bram Dijkstra, for example, deplores *Dracula*'s legacy in terms quite different from mine. Disapproving of vampires in general rather than these particular vampires, he laments that after Stoker, 'Female vampires were now everywhere. ... By 1900 the vampire had come to represent women as the personification of everything negative that linked sex, ownership, and money.'[27] But Stoker cleaned up more than he degraded. Above all, he gentrified female vampires, who, for the first time, are monogamously heterosexual. Van Helsing even seems to doubt whether Lucy can digest female blood, at least from the veins of servants. According to his diagnosis, 'A brave man's blood is the best thing on this earth when a woman is in trouble' (p. 149), and also, presumably, when she needs nourishment.

Not only do Lucy and the sister-brides in Castle Dracula prowl exclusively at men;[28] Lucy, at least, becomes more virtuous after death than she was in life. Far from personifying a reversion to woman-hating in late Victorian men, Lucy raises the tone of female vampirism by avoiding messy entanglements with mortals, directing her 'voluptuous wantonness' to her fiancé alone.

'Come to me, Arthur. Leave those others and come to me. My arms are hungry for you. Come, and we can rest together. Come, my husband, come!' (p. 257). As a vampire, Lucy the flirt is purified into Lucy the wife. The restless pet who had collected marriage proposals and complained, 'Why can't they let a girl marry three men, or as many as want her, and save all this trouble?' (p. 28), the enticing invalid who had 'married', through blood transfusions, those very three men (plus the smitten Van Helsing), ignores, as a vampire, 'those others' who bled into her adoringly: for the first time she wants her prospective husband and no one else.

Vampirism in *Dracula* does not challenge marriage, as it did earlier; it inculcates the restraints of marriage in a reluctant girl. Even before Arthur celebrates their wedding night with hammer and stake, thumping away unfalteringly while her 'body shook and quivered and twisted in wild contortions' (p. 262), Dracula had baptised Lucy into wifely fidelity.

Lucy is more monogamous than the promiscuous vampires she inspired. Two representative vampire women from 1900 have no loyalties left; both are indiscriminate incarnations of female hunger. Hume Nesbit's story 'The Vampire Maid' reduces its Ariadne to a biting thing: 'I had a ghastly dream this night. I thought I saw a monster bat, with the face and tresses of Ariadne, fly into the open window and fasten its white teeth and scarlet lips on my arm. I tried to beat the horror away, but could not, for I seemed chained down and thralled also with drowsy delight as the beast sucked my blood with a gruesome rapture.'[29] When church restorers disinter an ancient demon in F. G. Loring's story 'The Tomb of Sarah', scientific reality is more ghastly than any dream: 'There lay the vampire, but how changed from the starved and shrunken corpse we saw two days ago for the first time! The wrinkles had almost dis-appeared, the flesh was firm and full, the crimson lips grinned horri-bly over the long pointed teeth, and a distinct smear of blood had trickled down one corner of the mouth.'[30]

Lucy's progeny, Ariadne and Sarah, do not, like her, mature through vampirism into true womanhood: they are closer to the will-less killing machines who dominate later twentieth-century vampire literature. These dreadful female mouths that feed on popular culture at the turn of the century do personify unleashed female energy in the fear-mongering way Dijkstra suggests, but this energy is not as anarchic as it looks. Since these indiscriminate biters are heterosexual, their raging desire aggrandises men as well as depleting them.

Moreover, their men are immune from female demonism: Ariadne and Sarah offer not Carmilla's dangerous empathy, but oblivion. Ariadne induces 'drowsy delight'; Sarah lures a young man by murmuring, 'I give sleep and peace – sleep and peace – sleep and peace' (p. 103). These fin-de-siècle vampires do not arouse un-classified sensations; they induce postcoital fatigue. Their horror springs from their propriety. As good women, they want only men; in approved motherly fashion, they do not stimulate, but lull. The vampires Lucy spawned may be more promiscuous than she, but they are, like her, sexually orthodox. A model of wifeliness, as much a true woman as a new one, Lucy infused womanliness into her kind. Her innovative propriety is a testament to the heterosexuality of her twin creators, Dracula and Bram Stoker.

Perhaps because he is so normal, Dracula is the most solitary vampire we have met. He is, as far as we see, the only male vampire in the world: there is no suggestion that the sailors he kills on his voyage to England will join the ranks of the Undead. Moreover, he can anticipate no companionship, for Stoker's rules allow only humans to unite. 'We have on our side power of combination – a power denied to the vampire kind' (p. 238), Van Helsing assures his vigilante community. Ruthven, Varney, Carmilla, and their ilk flour-ished because of their 'power of combination': gregariousness was their lethal talent.

Innovative in his isolation, Dracula can do nothing more than catalyse homoerotic friendship among the humans who hunt him. His story abounds in overwrought protestations of friendship among the men, who testify breathlessly to each other's manhood. In fact, Van Helsing should thank the vampire for introducing him to such lovable companions. Borrowing the idiom of Oscar Wilde's letters to Lord Alfred Douglas, he declares himself to Lucy's former fiancé: 'I have grown to love you – yes, my dear boy, to love you – as Arthur' (p. 169). For Dracula and his acolyte Renfield, blood is the life, but the men who combine against him find life by drinking in each other's 'stalwart manhood' (p. 168).

Dracula forges this male community of passionate mutual admiration, but he cannot join it. Only indirectly, by drinking Lucy's blood after the four men have 'married' her (and each other) in a series of transfusions, can Dracula infiltrate the heroic brotherhood. Turning women into vampires does nothing to mitigate his solitude: his mindless creations have too little in common with him to be friends. Many twentieth-century adaptations soften Dracula's contempt for women by making him fall in love with Mina, aiming to promote her to his co-ruler, but in Stoker's original, Mina is only a pawn in his battle against the men. Stripped of his power of combination, catalysing homoerotic friendships in which he cannot participate, this vampire loses his story, for he has no confidante willing to hear it.

Dracula begins the novel by telling an unresponsive Jonathan Harker his history in almost flawless English, but thereafter he is silent. In the massive, impeccably collated testimony that comprises the long English portion of the novel, Dracula has no voice: he leaps in and out to make occasional florid boasts, but his nature and aspirations are entirely constructed – and diminished – by others, especially Van Helsing.

As Van Helsing gains authority, Dracula's fluency evaporates into the dimensions of a case history. The lordly host who began the novel was, according to Jonathan, a master of civilised skills: 'He would have made a wonderful solicitor, for there was nothing that he did not think of or foresee. For a man who was never in the country, and who did not evidently do much in the way of business, his knowledge and acumen were wonderful' (p. 44). In England, though, Jonathan and the rest turn their judgement over to Van Helsing, whose floundering English somehow confirms his authority, as that of psychiatrists will do in 1930s popular culture. Van Helsing assures his followers that the vampire is still precivilised, 'a great child-brain' growing only slowly into the position of 'the father or furtherer of a new order of beings' (pp. 302–3). Having devolved, under Van Helsing's authority, from magus to embryonic patriarch, Dracula is easily immobilised and trapped. As a presence, he is extinguished so early that at the end, a mere bowie knife kills him: his death requires neither Bible nor stake. Dracula is so easily, even inevitably, obliterated that all concerned forget the elaborate rituals needed to still the writhing Lucy.[31]

Dracula is dissipated less by science or the occult than by the clamour of experts that gave form to his decade. His responsiveness to his enemies' classifications sets him apart from the other great monsters of his century. Frankenstein's creature galvanised his book with an eloquent apologia halfway through. Even monsters who had not read Milton defined themselves with ease: Lord Ruthven in his various incarnations, Varney, Carmilla, all renewed themselves through compelling and compulsive self-presentations. Varney dissociated himself easily from the ignorant mob that pursued him, whose superstitious violence threw the vampire's superior humanity into relief. Dracula has no mob to tower over, but only the constraining categories of professional men. His relative silence has, of course, fed his life in the twentieth century: as we shall see, he is so suggestively amorphous in Stoker's novel that he is free to shift his shape with each new twentieth-century trend.[32] In 1897, though, Dracula was, despite his occult powers, so comparatively docile a vampire, so amenable to others' definitions, that he stifled the tradition that preceded him.

As the first vampire who conforms to social precepts, fading into experts' definitions rather than affirming his unnatural life, Dracula is a consummate creation of the late 1890s, dutifully transmitting its legacy to our own expert-hounded century. The British 1890s were haunted not only by the Undead, but by a monster of its own clinical making, the homosexual.[33] In constructing an absolute category that isolated 'the homosexual' from 'normal' men and women, medical theory confined sexuality as narrowly as Van Helsing does the vampire. More in conformity than in ferocity, Dracula takes definition from a decade shaped by medical experts.

I suspect that Dracula's primary progenitor is not Lord Ruthven, Varney, or Carmilla, but Oscar Wilde in the dock.[34] The Labouchère Amendment of 1885, which criminalised homosexuality among men, not only authorised Wilde's conviction: it restricted sexuality in the next decade 'by shifting emphasis from sexual acts between men, especially sodomy, the traditional focus of legislation, to sexual sentiment or thought, and in this way to an abstract entity soon to be widely referred to as "homosexuality"'.[35] The Wilde trials of 1895 put a judicial seal on the category the Labouchère Amendment had fostered. As a result of the trials, affinity between men lost its fluidity. Its tainted embodiment, the homosexual, was imprisoned

in a fixed nature, re-created as a man alone, like Dracula, and, like
Dracula, one hunted and immobilised by the 'stalwart manliness' of
normal citizens. Now unnatural and illegal, the oath that bound
vampire to mortal was annulled.

Before the Wilde trials, vampires felt free to languish in overtly
homoerotic adoration of their mortal prey: in 'The True Story of
a Vampire' by Eric, Count Stenbock, published the year before
Wilde's incarceration, Count Vardalek madly plays Chopin to a faun-
like young man, kisses him on the lips, and weeps over his 'darling's'
diminishing 'superabundance of life'.[36] Dracula was born in reaction
to Vardalek's devouring love: new rules imposed on his alien kind
forbid him to love anyone on earth. The only music that moves him
is the music of the wolves, and he cannot participate even in that.

Dracula's silence recalls the silence forced on the voluble Wilde
after his trials. The foreigner who had poured out irresistible words
in flawless English tried vainly to speak after the judge had sentenced him to prison. '"And I?" he began. "May I say nothing, my
lord?" But Mr Justice Wills made no reply beyond a wave of the
hand to the warders in attendance, who touched the prisoners on
the shoulder and hurried them out of sight to the cells below.'[37] As
in the London books of *Dracula*, the versatile and florid performer
disappears under institutional regulation.

The ghostliness of earlier vampires had deflected improper intercourse with mortals: when a vampire walked through walls or turned
for life to the moon, audiences remembered that he was another
order of being, one whose body (as opposed to his teeth) could not
quite penetrate a human's. Dracula, fully corporeal, has no sheltering
spirituality, and so he is as vulnerable as Oscar Wilde to opprobrium
and incarceration. Unlike Wilde, however, Dracula is careful.

His intensifying silence, his increasing acquiescence in what
experts say he is, reflect the caution of Stoker's master, Henry
Irving. In 1895, just after the Wilde trials – which subdued English
manhood in general and the English theatre in particular – Stoker
began in earnest to write *Dracula*, which had haunted him for five
years. Irving had spent 1895 lobbying for his knighthood (the first
ever awarded to an actor) by petrifying himself and his Lyceum into
attitudes of patriotic grandeur, although his imperial postures had
been assaulted by two wicked Irishmen: Shaw, whose savage reviews
exposed, in the person of Irving, all British heroes to terrible laughter; and the seductively rude Wilde, whose comedies mocked everything that was supposed to inspire Irving's audiences. Bram Stoker,

a third Irishman but a loyal one, protected Irving against potentially lethal laughter. His *Dracula* was fed by Wilde's fall, but its taboos were those of his master, whose reward came on 24 May 1895: on that day Irving's knighthood and Wilde's conviction were announced, ending the comedy. As a martyr, though, Wilde had won, for he drained the vitality of Stocker's vampire as consummately as he had deflated Irving's heroics in his glory days.

When Irving died ten years later, the *Daily Telegraph* praised him for rescuing England from the 'cult' of Oscar Wilde.[38] But he never rose again. Irving and all heroes were forced to define themselves in opposition to the devastating figure of Wilde, whose fate became an actual vampire that drained the vitality of future theatrical generations.[39] Irving held the stage for a few more years because of what he was not; he turned from player to exemplary façade. Oscar Wilde in prison constricted actors as well as vampires, forcing expansive figures into self-protecting silence. The Wilde trials, and the new taboos that made them possible, drained the generosity from vampires, forcing them to turn away from friendship and to expend their energies on becoming someone else.[40]

From Nina Auerbach, *Our Vampires, Ourselves* (Chicago, 1995), pp. 63–85.

NOTES

[In the book from which this essay is excerpted, *Our Vampires, Ourselves*, Nina Auerbach reads the history of vampires from the early nineteenth century to the present day as the history of social and political change. Drawing upon feminist and cultural criticism, Auerbach offers an analysis of *Dracula* which argues against many of the points which have become accepted tenets of Stoker criticism; considering Dracula in the context of pre-Stoker vampires, for example, she argues against seeing him as transgressive. Auerbach further suggests we need to consider *Dracula* in the context of the twentieth century and our own adaptations and recreations of the vampire, and explore the ways in which historically specific readings are generated. Ed.]

1. Bram Stoker, *The Essential Dracula*, ed. Leonard Wolf (New York, 1993), pp. 49–50. All further references given in text.

2. Recent critics assiduously confine Dracula in his century; New Historicism or blindness to Dracula's role in shaping our present inhumanity inspires ingenious readings that see in him the spirit of 1897,

Victoria's Diamond Jubilee year. Dracula has never been recognised as Stoker's bequest to a future that includes ourselves. [Works subsequently cited are all reproduced in this volume – Ed.] In *Signs Taken for Wonders* Franco Moretti, for instance, sees in *Dracula* an allegory of 1897 capitalism; Christopher Craft, in '"Kiss Me with Those Red Lips": Gender and Inversion in Bram Stoker's *Dracula*', brilliantly exposes its homoerotic undercurrents, 'a pivotal anxiety of late Victorian culture', without acknowledging the more compelling and explicit homoeroticism of a tradition Stoker does his best to purge from *Dracula*; Stephen D. Arata reads *Dracula* as a late-Victorian nightmare of 'reverse colonisation', whereby 'primitive' races supplant enervated Anglo-Saxons in 'The Occidental Tourist: *Dracula* and the Anxiety of Reverse Colonization'; Judith Halberstam's 'Technologies of Monstrosity: Bram Stoker's *Dracula*' analyses Dracula's convergence with late-nineteenth-century anti-Semitic constructions of the smelly, parasitical Jew.

3. See, for instance, Christopher Frayling's tidy genealogy in *Vampyres: Lord Byron to Count Dracula* (London, 1992), pp. 3–84.

4. *The Poems of John Keats* (London, 1961), p. 162, lines 45–50.

5. Bram Stoker, 'Dracula's Guest' (1897; first published 1914), reprinted in *The Penguin Book of Vampire Stories*, ed. Alan Ryan (New York, 1988), pp. 163–74.

6. See, for instance, Robert Tracy, 'Loving You All Ways: Vamps, Vampires, Necrophiles and Necrofilles in Nineteenth-Century Fiction', in *Sex and Death in Victorian Literature*, ed. Regina Barreca (Bloomington, IN, 1990), p. 42. William Veeder assumes that Van Helsing derives from Le Fanu's Dr Hesselius and Baron Vordenburg, but long before Le Fanu's time, the vampire expert was a stock character in the theatre: Planché's helpful chorus of spirits tells us what the vampire is, as does Boucicualt's more accessible Dr Rees. Keats's nasty expert Apollonius in *Lamia* is the most canonical example of the vampire hunter who kills by expertise. See William Veeder, Foreword, *Dracula: The Vampire and the Critics*, ed. Margaret L. Carter (Ann Arbor, MI, 1988), p. xvi.

7. An assumption I, like Christopher Frayling, *Vampyres* (p. 351), find implausible.

8. In Stoker's *Essential Dracula*, editor Leonard Wolf suggests that the blond vampire 'may have something in common with Lucy' (p. 51); Gerold Savory's thoughtful 1977 adaptation, starring Louis Jourdan and directed by Philip Saville, superimposes on the slavering vampire a memory of Mina's face as she demurely brushes her hair.

9. Ellen Terry's 'About H.I.', her diary during the 1890s, which her daughter appended to the final edition of her autobiography. See *Ellen*

Terry's Memoirs, with a preface, notes, and additional biographical material by Edith Craig and Christopher St John (1932; rpt. New York, 1969), pp. 270–1.

10. David J. Skal, *Hollywood Gothic: The Tangled Web of Dracula from Novel to Stage to Screen* (New York, 1990), pp. 26–7. Also see Nina Auerbach, *Ellen Terry, Player in Her Time* (New York, 1987), especially pp. 190–200.

11. Quoted in Phyllis A. Roth, *Bram Stoker* (Boston, 1982), p. 5. Roth goes on to claim 'that Stoker's friendship with Irving was the most important love relationship of his adult life' (p. 136), though she suggests shrewdly (p. 14) that *Dracula* somehow sapped Irving's imperial potency.

12. His great-nephew claims that Stoker died of syphilis caught from the prostitutes to whom he turned when his chilly wife refused further sexual relations after the birth of their son. See Daniel Farson, *The Man Who Wrote Dracula: A Biography of Bram Stoker* (New York, 1975). This rehearsal for Ibsen's *Ghosts* is a suggestive genesis of the most theatrical vampire ever created, but the rigidly polarised roles – frigid wife and contaminating whore – allotted to the women of this biographical script are probably the consequence, not the cause, of Stoker's consuming hero worship of Irving. We should not condescend to Stoker's supposedly 'Victorian' definitions of women without remembering their entanglement in Irving's theatre and Irving's own emotional and imperial magnetism. Many Victorian men reduced their women to labels; few had their imaginations aroused by a compensating Irving.

13. In Fred Saberhagen's wonderfully witty and astute novel *The Dracula Tape*, in which Dracula gets to tell the story Stoker refuses to include, the vampire complains sardonically about his doltish guest: 'He misinterpreted these oddities, but never asked openly for any explanation, whilst I, wisely or unwisely, never volunteered one. ... My little Englishman was tolerant of it all, but he was dull, dull, dull. A brooder, but no dreamer. There was no imagination in him to be fired.' *The Dracula Tape* (1975; rpt. New York, 1980), pp. 16, 31. Saberhagen's Dracula wants to restore the communion with mortals that was the birthright of earlier vampires.

14. Craft, '"Kiss Me with Those Red Lips"' is particularly ingenious in describing, and thereby authorising, the homoerotic contact that does *not* take place in *Dracula*.

15. Stoker's 'original Foundation Notes and Data for his *Dracula*' in the Rosenbach Library in Philadelphia, quoted in Frayling, *Vampyres*, p. 301; reprinted by permission.

16. Two of the most stylised *Dracula* films, directed by Tod Browning (1931) and Francis Ford Coppola (1992), advertised themselves as love

stories; Browning's was billed as 'the strangest love story ever told', while Coppola's ads reassured us that 'love never dies'. In both, though, the vampire performs on a plane so remote from the other characters that one can scarcely imagine vampire and mortal touching or even conversing, much less biting or loving.

17. These Jonathans are presumably uninfected at the redemptive endings of their movies, but later film Jonathans amplify Murnau's suggestive variation by actually becoming vampires. See especially Terence Fisher's *Horror of Dracula* (1957), the first of the brightly coloured Hammer films that illuminated the 1960s, in which Jonathan, here a susceptible vampire-hunter, is easily seduced by a chesty vampire woman who wears a tunic; Dan Curtis's TV movie (*Bram Stoker's Dracula*, 1973), starring Jack Palance, which follows the Hammer tradition by abandoning Jonathan to the three ravenous vampire women so that he can become a snarling monster Van Helsing must stake at the end; and, most dramatically, Werner Herzog's *Nosferatu the Vampyre* (1979), a searing remake of Murnau's film. In Herzog's revision, a grinning, fanged Jonathan ends the movie by galloping off to become king of the vampires after his wife has sacrificed herself in vain. Only Herzog follows Murnau by discarding the three intermediary female vampires, allowing Dracula himself to transform his vulnerable guest.

These later Jonathans are all oafish revisions of Stoker's supposedly heroic civil servant, who obeys a paternalistic employer by bringing to a wild country the light of British law. In the 1960s and 1970s, movie Jonathans, like the imperial mission they represent, are corrupt and vulnerable. Although, unlike Stoker's pure survivor, they become vampires with scarcely a whimper of protest, they resemble Stoker's character, who exists to belong to someone in power, more than they do the passionate friends of the generous Byronic gentry.

18. I use Stoker's names here for the reader's convenience. *Nosferatu* was a pirated adaptation of *Dracula* whose original titles muffle its debt to Stoker by renaming the characters; Dracula, for example, becomes Graf Orlok. Some later prints revert to the Stoker names, though 'Mina' mutates into the more powerful and euponious 'Nina'. Skal, *Hollywood Gothic*, especially pp. 43–63, provides a thorough and witty account of Florence Stoker's Van Helsing-like pursuit of Murnau's elusive film.

19. Stoker's Van Helsing affirms that the vampire's 'power ceases, as does that of all evil things, at the coming of day' (p. 290), but the sun is no threat to Dracula's life: it merely limits his shape-shifting capacity.

20. Gregory A. Waller writes eloquently about the wives in Murnau's original *Nosferatu* and Werner Herzog's remake, whom he sees as solitary warriors, independent of traditional weapons and of the wise directing

father figures who contained Stoker's women. According to Waller, *Nosferatu*'s women are as isolated in bourgeois society as the vampire, sacrificing themselves ironically – and, ultimately, tragically – to institutions that ignore and silence them; see Gregory A. Waller, *The Living and the Undead: From Bram Stoker's Dracula to Romero's Dawn of the Dead* (Urbana, IL, 1986), p. 225.

Waller's excellent account of mutating vampire representations is sometimes sentimental about victimised women, who, in both versions of *Nosferatu*, seem to release through self-sacrifice their own rebellious vampiric allegiance, though they refrain from snarling and growing fangs.

21. Siegfried Kracauer's *From Caligari to Hitler: A Psychological History of German Film* (Princeton, NJ, 1947) reads *Nosferatu* prophetically, as an allegorical warning against the plague of Hitlerism. Kracauer's influential reading is truer, perhaps, to the coldly imperial Dracula than it is to Murnau's ravished ghost.

22. Waller, *The Living and the Undead*, notes astutely that in the American film, Renfield is maddened by Dracula, while in Stoker's novel the vampire manipulates a madness, embodied in Renfield, that lurked in England before his coming (p. 92). This contrast holds if one reads the screenplay alone, but Dwight Frye's performance is so bacchanalian from the beginning that it is difficult to call the pre-Dracula Renfield 'sane'.

23. In the so-called 'Spanish *Dracula*' (1931, dir. George Melford) – a Spanish-language adaptation for Mexican distribution that was filmed at night, on the same set and from the same shooting script as the Hollywood version – Dracula feeds Renfield generously, but Pablo Alvarez Rubio's affable chicken-chewing dispels any erotic tension between himself and Carlos Villarias's vampire. Accordingly, Villarias's Dracula leaves Renfield's prone body to his sister-brides.

    The Spanish *Dracula* is technically superior to the Hollywood original: its photography is more sophisticated, its women are sexier, and its narrative is slightly more logical. It ignores, however, the subterranean attraction between the vampire and his guest that invigorates Browning's version.

24. The jarring shift of rhythm and focus after the movie leaves Transylvania is due in part to the producer's squeamishness; on the final shooting script, Carl Laemmle, Jr, wrote the Van Helsing-like rule, 'Dracula should only go for women and not men!' David Skal, *The Monster Show: A Cultural History of Horror* (New York, 1993), p. 126. Early Hollywood movies allow emotional complexity to spill out in improbable countries like Transylvania or King Kong's Africa or Oz, but it is barred from home.

25. This shift of authority from an egalitarian vampire-hunting community to Van Helsing's autocratic leadership is the thesis of Waller's analysis

of *Dracula*'s immediate descendants in film (Waller, *The Living and the Undead*, pp. 77–109).

26. Jonathan Dollimore writes compellingly about the rise of perversity as a creed in the 1890s, a decade in which the rigid categories erected by new experts in sexology came to restrain the play of affection. Because of Oscar Wilde's imprisonment and its aftermath, the wilful evasion of categories that the creed of perversity proclaims is at best fragile, at worst doomed: 'So in creating a politics of the perverse we should never forget the cost: death, mutilation, and incarceration have been, and remain, the fate of those who are deemed to have perverted nature.' *Sexual Dissidence: Augustine to Wilde, Freud to Foucault* (Oxford, 1991), p. 230.

27. Bram Dijkstra, *Idols of Perversity: Fantasies of Feminine Evil in Fin-de-siècle Culture* (New York, 1986), p. 230.

28. Judith Weissman notes that in *Dracula,* 'the one group of people that [female vampires] never attack is other women'. 'Women and Vampires: *Dracula* as a Victorian Novel' (1977), reprinted in *Dracula: The Vampire and the Critics*, ed. Margaret Carter, p. 75.

29. Hume Nesbit, 'The Vampire Maid' (1900), reprinted in *Dracula's Brood: Rare Vampire Stories by Friends and Contemporaries of Bram Stoker*, ed. Richard Dalby (London, 1987), p. 221.

30. F. G. Loring, 'The Tomb of Sarah' (1900), reprinted in *The Undead: Vampire Masterpieces*, ed. James Dickie (London, 1971), p. 100.

31. Phyllis A. Roth suggests plausibly that since Dracula is not staked, but only stabbed with a bowie knife, he does not die at all: he simply turns himself into mist after sending his captors a last look of triumph. See her 'Suddenly Sexual Women in Bram Stoker's *Dracula*' [reprinted in this volume – Ed.], *Dracula: The Vampire and the Critics*, ed. Margaret Carter, p. 67, note 27. By so flagrantly ignoring his own elaborate rules, Stoker was probably leaving room for a sequel he lacked the heart or energy to write. Dracula's anticlimactic death, if it is a death, reminds the reader that once he has been silenced, even a vampire is easy to kill.

32. Many critics and novelists, even more loyal to the vampire, perhaps, than Renfield, have reconstructed Dracula's suppressed narrative. The most persuasive critic to do so is Carol A. Senf, '*Dracula*: The Unseen Face in the Mirror' (1979), reprinted in *Dracula: The Vampire and the Critics*, ed. Margaret Carter. Senf claims that *Dracula* is dominated by a series of unreliable, even criminal narrators who suppress their vampire/victim: 'Dracula is *never* seen objectively and never permitted to speak for himself while his actions are recorded by people who have determined to destroy him and who, moreover, repeatedly question the sanity of their quest' (p. 95).

Senf's persuasive essay could be a gloss on Saberhagen's *Dracula Tape* (1975), whose urbane Dracula reinserts himself into Stoker's narrative, exposing with relish the incompetent dolts who persecuted him in the 1890s. This Dracula plays Van Helsing by telling Van Helsing's story: 'When I have made you understand the depths of the idiocy of that man, Van Helsing, and confess at the same time that he managed to hound me nearly to my death, you will be forced to agree that among all famous perils to the world I must be ranked as one of the least consequential.' Fred Saberhagen, *The Dracula Tape* (New York, 1980), p. 101. Like Senf, Saberhagen accuses Van Helsing of murdering Lucy with incompetent blood transfusions, then exploiting vampire superstition to cover up his own malpractice. Like most Draculas in the 1970s, Saberhagen's is, emotionally and intellectually, a superior being who genuinely loves Mina. He transforms her to save her from the mortal idiots who bully and adore her.

Saberhagen's iconoclastic Dracula paved the way for garrulous and glamorous vampires like Anne Rice's Armand and Lestat, who not only tell their own stories, but initiate them, thus becoming culture heroes in a manner impossible to Stoker's compliant Count.

33. The word *homosexual* had been part of medical jargon since the 1870s, but it began to infiltrate popular discourse in the 1890s. The first reference to it in the *Oxford English Dictionary* is dated 1897 – *Dracula's* year. – in which Havelock Ellis apologises for using this 'barbarously hybrid word'. There is an abundance of studies exploring the emergence of homosexuality as a new clinical category in the late nineteenth century. All acknowledge their debt to Michel Foucault's pioneering *History of Sexuality*, 2 vols, trans. Robert Hurley (New York, 1980). In writing about nineteenth-century constructions of homosexuality as a clinical monster, I am especially indebted to Lillian Faderman, *Surpassing the Love of Men: Romantic Friendship and Love between Women from the Renaissance to the Present* (New York, 1981), and Richard Dellamora, *Masculine Desire: The Sexual Politics of Victorian Aestheticism* (Chapel Hill, NC, 1990).

34. Eve Sedgwick claims that, in literature, 1891 was a watershed year in the construction of 'a modern homosexual identity and a modern problematic of sexual orientation'. Eve Kosofsky Sedgwick, *Epistemology of the Closet* (Berkeley, CA, 1990), p. 91. For most nonliterary observers, however, 1895 – in which homosexuality was publicly, even theatrically, defined, isolated, and punished in the famous person of Oscar Wilde – was surely the year in which the public learned what writers had sensed four years earlier. Talia Schaffer demonstrates in persuasive detail the association between *Dracula* and the Wilde Trials in '"A Wilde Desire Took Me": The Homerotic History of *Dracula*', *ELH: A Journal of English Literary History*, 61 (1994), 381–415.

35. Dellamora, *Masculine Desire*, p. 200.

36. Eric, Count Seenbock, 'The True Story of a Vampire' (1894), reprinted in *The Undead: Vampire Masterpieces*, p. 169.

37. H. Montgomery Hyde, *Oscar Wilde* (London, 1975), p. 364.

38. Quoted in Skal, *Hollywood Gothic*, p. 36.

39. In the theatre at least, Wilde's disgrace seems to have had, if anything, a freeing impact on the next generation of women, in part because the Labouchère Amendment ignored lesbianism: the new constraints on men freed women to experiment with new theatrical idioms. As they did when they were vampires, women acted uninhibited roles that were taboo for men. See, for instance, Nina Auerbach's account of Edith Craig's unabashed – if admittedly professionally marginal – community of homosocial and homosexual women in *Ellen Terry, Player in Her Time*, especially pp. 364–436.

40. Skal, *Hollywood Gothic*, pp. 34–8, discusses the affinities between Stoker and Wilde, two Irishmen who adored Whitman and loved the same woman: Wilde proposed to Florence Balcombe, whom Stoker later married. Skal does suggest that Wilde's trials motivated the strident anti-sex rhetoric of Stoker's later career, but he ignores the power of the trials over Stoker's imagination of Dracula, a conjunction Schaffer analyses with depth and thoroughness.

9

Technologies of Monstrosity: Bram Stoker's *Dracula*

JUDITH HALBERSTAM

ONCE BITTEN TWICE SHY

By the way of an introduction to Bram Stoker's *Dracula*, I want to tell my own story about being consumed and drained by the vampire. Reading *Dracula* for the first time years ago, I thought I noticed something about vampirism that had been strangely overlooked by critics and readers. Dracula, I thought, with his peculiar physique, his parasitical desires, his aversion to the cross and to all the trappings of Christianity, his blood-sucking attacks, and his avaricious relation to money, resembled stereotypical anti-Semitic nineteenth-century representations of the Jew. Subsequent readings of the novel with attention to the connections in the narrative between blood and gold, race and sex, sexuality and ethnicity confirmed my sense that the anti-Semite's Jew and Stoker's vampire bore more than a family resemblance. The connection I had made began to haunt me. I uncovered biographical material and discovered that Stoker was good friends with, and inspired by, Richard Burton, the author of a tract reviving the blood libel against Jews in Damascus.[1] I read essays by Stoker in which he railed against degenerate writers for not being good Christians.[2] My conclusions seemed sound, the vampire and the Jew were related and monstrosity in the Gothic novel had much to do with the discourse of modern anti-Semitism.

173

Towards the end of my preliminary research, I came across a fantastic contemporary news piece which reported that the General Mills cereal company was being sued by the Anti-Defamation League because Count Chocula, the children's cereal character, was depicted on one of their cereal boxes wearing a Star of David.[3] While I felt that this incident vindicated my comparison between Jew and vampire, doubts began to creep in about stabilising this relationship. By the time my doubts had been fully expressed and confirmed by other readers, I discovered that, rather than revealing a hidden agenda in Stoker's novel, I had unwittingly essentialised Jewishness. By equating Jew and vampire in a linear way, I had simply stabilised the relationship between the two as a mirroring but had left many questions unanswered, indeed unasked, about the production of monstrosity, whether it be monstrous race, monstrous class, monstrous sex.

TECHNOLOGIES OF MONSTROSITY

Attempts to consume Dracula and vampirism within one interpretive model inevitably produce vampirism. They reproduce, in other words, the very model they claim to have discovered. So, an analysis of the vampire as perverse sexuality runs the risk of merely stabilising the identity of perversity, its relation to a particular set of traits. The comparison between Jew and vampire still seems interesting and important to me but for different reasons. I am still fascinated by the occlusion of race or ethnicity in critical interpretations of the novel but I am not simply attempting now to bring those hidden facets to light. Instead, I want to ask how the Gothic novel and Gothic monsters in particular produce monstrosity as never unitary but always an aggregate of race, class, and gender. I also want to suggest that the nineteenth-century discourse of anti-Semitism and the myth of the vampire share a kind of Gothic economy in their ability to condense many monstrous traits into one body. In the context of this novel, Dracula is otherness itself, a distilled version of all others produced by and within fictional texts, sexual science, and psychopathology. He is monster and man, feminine and powerful, parasitical and wealthy; he is repulsive and fascinating, he exerts the consummate gaze but is scrutinised in all things, he lives forever but can be killed. Dracula is indeed not simply a monster but a technology of monstrosity.

Technologies of monstrosity are always also technologies of sex. I want to plug monstrosity and gothicisation into Foucault's 'great surface network' of sexuality 'in which the stimulation of bodies, the intensification of pleasures, the incitement to discourse, the formation of special knowledges, the strengthening of controls and resistances are linked to one another in accordance with a few major strategies of knowledge and power'.[4] Although Foucault does not talk about the novel as one of these 'major strategies of knowledge and power', the Gothic novel in my discussion will represent a privileged field in the network of sexuality. The novel, indeed, is the discursive arena in which identity is constructed as sexual identity; the novel transforms metaphors of otherness into technologies of sex, into machine texts, in other words, that produce perverse identities.[5]

Foucault identifies the figures of 'the hysterical woman, the masturbating child, the Malthusian couple and the perverse adult' as inventions of sex's technology.[6] The vampire Dracula represents all of these figures, he economically condenses their sexual threat into one body, a body that is noticeably feminised, wildly fertile, and seductively perverse. For Dracula is the deviant or the criminal, the other against whom the normal and the lawful, the marriageable and the heterosexual can be known and quantified. Dracula creeps 'facedown' along the wall of the very 'fortress of identity'; he is the boundary, he is the one who crosses (Trans-sylvania = across the woods), and the one who knows the other side.

But the otherness that Dracula embodies is not timeless or universal, not the opposite of some commonly understood meaning of 'the human'. The others that Dracula has absorbed and who live on in him take on the historically specific contours of race, class, gender, and sexuality. They are the other side of a national identity that, in the 1890s, coincided with a hegemonic ideal of bourgeois Victorian womanhood. Mina and Lucy, the dark and the fair heroines of Stoker's novel, make Englishness a function of quiet femininity and maternal domesticity. Dracula, accordingly, threatens the stability and, indeed, the naturalness of this equation between middle-class womanhood and national pride by seducing both women with his particularly foreign sexuality.[7]

To claim that Dracula's sexuality is foreign, however, is to already obscure the specific construction of a native sexuality. Lucy, as many critics have noted, is violently punished for her desire for three men and all three eventually participate in a ritual staking of her vampiric body. Mina represents a maternal sexuality as she nurtures and caters to the brave Englishmen who are fighting for her honour and her body. The foreign sexuality that confronts these women, then, depends upon a burgeoning definition of normal versus pathological sexual function which itself depends upon naturalising the native. It is part of the power of *Dracula* that Stoker merges pathological sexuality with foreign aspect and, as we shall see with reference to the insane Renfield, psychopathology. The vampire Dracula, in other words, is a composite of otherness that manifests as the horror essential to dark, foreign, and perverse bodies.

Dracula the text, like Dracula the monster, is multivalenced and generates myriad interpretive narratives – narratives which attempt to classify the threat of the vampire as sexual or psychological, as class bound or gendered. The technology of the vampire's monstrosity, indeed, is intimately connected to the mode of the novel's production. *Dracula* is a veritable writing machine constructed out of diaries, letters, newspaper clippings, and medical case notes. The process of compilation is similarly complex: Mina Harker, as secretary, makes a narrative of the various documents by chronologically ordering them and, where necessary, transcribing notes from a primitive dictaphone. There is a marked sexual energy to the reading and writing of all the contributions to the narrative. Reading, for instance, unites the men and Mina in a safe and mutual bond of disclosure and confidence. After Mina listens to Dr Seward's phonograph recording of his account of Lucy's death, she assures him: 'I have copied out the words on my typewriter, and none other need now hear your heart beat as I did.'[8] Seward, in his turn, reads Harker's diary and notes, 'after reading his account ... I was prepared to meet a good specimen of manhood' (p. 237). Later, Seward passes by the Harkers' bedroom and on hearing 'the click of the typewriter' he concludes, 'they were hard at it' (p. 237). Writing and reading, on some level, appear to provide a safe textual alternative to the sexuality of the vampire. They also, of course, produce the vampire as the 'truth' of textual labour; he is a threat which must be diffused by discourse.[9]

The novel presents a body of work to which, it is important to note, only certain characters contribute. The narrative episodes are tape recorded, transcribed, added to, edited, and compiled by four characters: Jonathan Harker, Dr Seward, Mina Harker, and Lucy Westenra. The control of the narrative by these characters suggests that the textual body, for Stoker, like the bodies of the women of

England, must be protected from any corrupting or foreign influence. Van Helsing, Lord Godalming, Quincey Morris, Renfield, and Dracula have only recorded voices in the narrative; at no time do we read their own accounts of events. Three of these men, of course, are foreigners: Van Helsing is Dutch, Quincey Morris is American, and Dracula is East European. Lord Godalming, we assume, has English blood but as an aristocrat, he is of a different class than the novel's narrators. Renfield, of course, has been classified as insane and his subjective existence is always a re-presentation by Dr Seward.

The activities of reading and writing, then, are crucial in this novel to the establishment of a kind of middle-class hegemony and they are annexed to the productions of sexual subjectivities. Sexuality, however, is revealed in the novel to be mass produced rather than essential to certain kinds of bodies, a completely controlled production of a group of professionals – doctors, psychiatrists, lawyers. Writing, or at least who writes, must be controlled since it represents the deployment of knowledge and power; similarly, reading may need to be authorised and censored, as indeed it is later in the novel when Mina begins to fall under the vampire's influence. The vampire can read Mina's mind and so Mina is barred from reading the English group's plans. Dracula's reading and Mina's reading are here coded as corrupt and dangerous. Similarly, the English men censor Dracula's contaminated opinions out of the narrative. The vampire, indeed, has no voice, he is read and written by all the other characters in the novel. Dracula's silence in the novel (his only speeches are recorded conversations with Jonathan Harker) is pervasive and almost suffocating and it actually creates the vampire as fetish since, in so much of the narrative, writing takes on a kind of sexual function.

By examining Stoker's novel as a machine-text, then, a text that generates particular subjectivities, we can atomise the totality of the vampire's monstrosity, examine the exact nature of his parasitism, and make an assault upon the naturalness of the sexuality of his enemies. By reading *Dracula* as a technology of monstrosity, I am claiming a kind of productivity for the text, a productivity which leads to numerous avenues of interpretation. But this does not mean that monstrosity in this novel is constantly in motion – every now and then it settles into a distinct form, a proper shape, and in those moments Dracula's features are eminently readable and suggestive. Dracula is likened to 'mist', to a 'red cloud', to a ghost or a shadow until he is invited into the home at which point he becomes solid and fleshly. As flesh and blood the vampire embodies a particular ethnicity and peculiar sexuality.

GOTHIC ANTI-SEMITISM: (1) DEGENERACY

Gothic anti-Semitism makes the Jew a monster with bad blood and it defines monstrosity as a mixture of bad blood, unstable gender identity, sexual and economic parasitism, and degeneracy. In this section I want to flesh out my premise that the vampire, as represented by Bram Stoker, bears some relation to the anti-Semite's Jew. If this is so, it tells us nothing about Jews but everything about anti-Semitic discourse, which seems able to transform all threat into the threat embodied by the Jew. The monster Jew produced by nineteenth-century anti-Semitism represents fears about race, class, gender, sexuality, and empire – this figure is indeed gothicised or transformed into an all-purpose monster.

By making a connection between Stoker's Gothic fiction and late-nineteenth-century anti-Semitism, I am not claiming a deliberate and unitary relation between fictional monster and real Jew, rather I am attempting to make an argument about the process of othering. Othering in Gothic fiction scavenges from many discursive fields and makes monsters out of bits and pieces of science and literature. The reason Gothic monsters are overdetermined – which is to say, open to numerous interpretations – is precisely because monsters transform the fragments of otherness into one body. That body is not female, not Jewish, not homosexual but it bears the marks of the constructions of femininity, race, and sexuality.

Dracula, then, resembles the Jew of anti-Semitic discourse in several ways: his appearance, his relation to money/gold, his parasitism, his degeneracy, his impermanence or lack of allegiance to a fatherland, and his femininity. Dracula's physical aspect, his physiognomy, is a particularly clear cipher for the specificity of his ethnic monstrosity. When Jonathan Harker meets the count on his visit to Castle Dracula in Transylvania, he describes Dracula in terms of a 'very marked physiognomy'. He notes an aquiline nose with 'peculiarly arched nostrils', massive eyebrows and 'bushy hair', a cruel mouth and 'peculiarly sharp white teeth', pale ears which were 'extremely pointed at the top', and a general aspect of 'extraordinary pallor' (p. 18). This description of Dracula, however, changes at various points in the novel. When he is spotted in London by Jonathan and Mina, Dracula is 'a tall thin man with a beaky nose and black moustache and pointed beard' (p. 180). Similarly, the zoo-keeper whose wolf disappears after Dracula's visit to the zoological gardens describes the count as 'a tall thin chap with a 'ook nose and a pointed beard' (p. 145). Most descriptions include Dracula's hard, cold look and his red eyes.

Visually, the connection between Dracula and other fictional Jews is quite strong. For example, George Du Maurier's Svengali, the Jewish hypnotist, is depicted as 'a stick, haunting, long, lean, uncanny, black spider-cat' with brown teeth and matted hair and, of course, incredibly piercing eyes. Fagin, the notorious villain of Charles Dickens's *Oliver Twist*, also has matted hair and a 'villainous-looking and repulsive face'. While Dracula's hands have 'hairs in the centre of the palm' and long, pointed nails, Fagin's hand is 'a withered old claw'. Eduard Drumont, a French National Socialist who, during the 1880s, called for the expulsion of the Jews from France in his newspaper *Libre Parole*, noted the identifying characteristics of the Jew as 'the hooked nose, shifty eyes, protruding ears, elongated body, flat feet and moist hands'.[10]

Faces and bodies, in fact, mark the other as evil so that he can be recognised and ostracised. Furthermore, the face in the nineteenth century which supposedly expressed Jewishness, 'hooked nose, shifty eyes', etc., is also seen to express nineteenth-century criminality and degeneration within the pseudosciences of physiognomy and phrenology.[11] Degeneration and Jewishness, one could therefore conclude (or, indeed, ratify scientifically), were not far apart. Stoker draws upon the relation between degeneration and physiognomy as theorised by Cesare Lombroso and Max Nordau for his portrayal of Dracula.

Towards the end of *Dracula*, as Van Helsing, the Dutch doctor/lawyer, leads Harker, Lord Godalming, Dr Seward, and the American, Quincey Morris, in the final pursuit of the vampire, a discussion of criminal types ensues between Van Helsing, Seward, and Harker's wife, Mina. Van Helsing defines Dracula as a criminal with 'a child-brain ... predestinate to crime' (p. 361). As Van Helsing struggles to articulate his ideas in his broken English, he turns to Mina for help. Mina translates for him succinctly and she even adds sources for the theory Van Helsing has advanced: 'The Count is a criminal and of criminal type. Nordau and Lombroso would so classify him, and qua criminal he is of imperfectly formed mind'

(p. 361). Since Mina, the provincial school teacher, mentions Lombroso and Nordau, we may conclude that their ideas of criminality and degeneracy were familiar to an educated readership rather than specialised medical knowledge. As Mina points out, Lombroso would attribute Dracula's criminal disposition to 'an imperfectly formed mind' or, in other words, to what Van Helsing calls a 'child-brain'. Lombroso noted similarities between the physiognomies of 'criminals, savages and apes' and concluded that degenerates were a biological throwback to primitive man.[12]

Criminal anthropology, quite obviously, as it developed in the nineteenth century, focuses upon the visual aspects of pathology. The attempt to catalogue and demonstrate a propensity for degenerative behaviour by reading bodies and faces demands that, in racial stereotyping, stereotypes be visualisable. And racial degeneracy, with its close ties to a social Darwinist conception of human development, also connects with sexual degeneracy. In describing the medicalisation of sex, Michel Foucault describes a progressive logic in which 'perversion-hereditary-degenerescence'[13] becomes the basis of nineteenth-century scientific claims about the danger of undisciplined sexuality. Sexual perversions, within this chain, arise out of inherited physical weaknesses and they potentially lead to the decline of future generations. Furthermore, theorising degenerescence or degeneration as the result of hereditary perversion takes, he claims, the 'coherent form of a state-directed racism' (p. 119).

Elsewhere, Foucault claims that 'modern antisemitism developed, in socialist milieus, out of the theory of degeneracy'. And this statement, surprisingly, occurs during a discussion of vampire novels of the nineteenth century. Foucault is being interviewed by Alain Grosrichard, Guy Le Gaufey, and Jacques-Alain Miller when the subject of vampires arises out of a discussion of the nobility and what Foucault calls 'the myth of blood'. In relating blood as symbolic object to the development of racial doctrines of degeneracy and heredity, Foucault suggests that the scientific ideology of race was developed by the Left rather than by Right-wing fanatics. Lombroso, for example, he points out, 'was a man of the Left'. The discussion goes as follows:

> **Le Gaufey** Couldn't one see a confirmation of what you are saying in the nineteenth century vogue for vampire novels, in which the aristocracy is always presented as the beast to be destroyed? The vampire is always the aristocrat and the saviour a bourgeois. ...

> Foucault   In the eighteenth century, rumours were already circulat-
> ing that debauched aristocrats abducted little children to slaughter
> them and regenerate themselves by bathing in their blood. The
> rumours even led to riots.

Le Gaufey again emphasises that this theme develops as a bourgeois
myth of that class's overthrow of the aristocracy. Foucault responds,
'Modern antisemitism began in that form'.[14]

I have described this discussion at length to show how one might
begin to theorise the shift within the Gothic novel that transforms
the threat of the aristocrat into the threat of the degenerate foreigner, the threat of money into the threat of blood. The bad blood
of family, in other words, is replaced by the bad blood of race and
the scientific theory of degeneracy produces and explains this transition. While neither Le Gaufey nor Foucault attempts to determine
what the role of the Gothic novel was in producing these new categories of identity, I have been arguing that Gothic fiction creates the
narrative structure for all kinds of gothicisations across disciplinary
and ideological boundaries. Gothic describes a discursive strategy
which produces monsters as a kind of temporary but influential response to social, political, and sexual problems. And yet, Gothic, as
I have noted, always goes both ways. So, even as Gothic style creates
the monster, it calls attention to the plasticity or constructed nature
of the monster and, therefore, calls into question all scientific and
rational attempts to classify and quantify agents of disorder. Such
agents, Gothic literature makes clear, are invented not discovered by
science.

GOTHIC ANTI-SEMITISM: (2) JEWISH
BODIES/JEWISH NEUROSES

I am calling modern anti-Semitism 'Gothic' because, in its various
forms – medical, political, psychological – it, too, unites and therefore produces the threats of capital and revolution, criminality and
impotence, sexual power and gender ambiguity, money and mind
within an identifiable form, the body of the Jew. In *The Jew's Body*,
Sander Gilman demonstrates how nineteenth-century anti-Semitism
replaced religious anti-Judaism with this pseudoscientific construction of the Jewish body as an essentially criminalised and patholo-
gised body. He writes:

The very analysis of the nature of the Jewish body, in the broader culture or within the culture of medicine, has always been linked to establishing the difference (and dangerousness) of the Jew. This scientific vision of parallel and unequal 'races' is part of the poly-genetic argument about the definition of 'race' within the scientific culture of the eighteenth century. In the nineteenth century it is more strongly linked to the idea that some 'races' are inherently weaker, 'degenerate', more at risk for diseases than others.[15]

In *Dracula* vampires are precisely a race and a family that weakens the stock of Englishness by passing on degeneracy and the disease of blood lust. Dracula, as a monster/master parasite, feeds upon English wealth and health. He sucks blood and drains resources, he always eats out. Jonathan Harker describes the horror of finding the vampire sated in his coffin after a good night's feed:

> [T]he cheeks were fuller, and the white skin seemed ruby-red under-neath; the mouth was redder than ever, for on the lips were gouts of fresh blood, which trickled from the corners of the mouth and ran over the chin and neck. Even the deep, burning eyes seemed set amongst the swollen flesh, for the lids and pouches underneath were bloated. It seemed as if the whole awful creature were simply gorged with blood. He lay like a filthy leech, exhausted with his repletion.
>
> (p. 54)

The health of the vampire, of course, his full cheeks and glowing skin, comes at the expense of the women and children he has vamped. Harker is disgusted not simply by the spectacle of the vampire but also by the thought that when the count arrives in England he will want to 'satiate his lust for blood, and create a new and ever-widening circle of semi-demons to batten on the helpless' (p. 54). At this juncture Harker picks up a shovel and attempts to beat the vampire/monster into pulp. The fear of a mob of parasites feeding upon the social body drives Harker to violence because the parasite represents the idle and dependent other, an organism that lives to feed and feeds to live.[16]

Dracula is surrounded by the odour of awful decay as though, as Harker puts it, 'corruption had become itself corrupt' (p. 265). When Harker and his band of friends break into Carfax, Dracula's London home, they are all nauseated by a smell 'composed of all the ills of mortality and with the pungent, acrid smell of blood' (p. 265). Similarly, a worker who delivered Dracula's coffins to Carfax tells Seward: 'That 'ere 'ouse guvnor is the rummiest I ever was in. Blyme! ... the place was that neglected that yer might 'ave smelled ole Jerusalem in it' (p. 240). The worker is quite specific here, to him the smell is a Jewish smell. Like the diseases attributed to the Jews as a race, bodily odours, people assumed, just clung to them and marked them out as different and, indeed, repugnant objects of pollution.[17]

Parasitism was linked specifically to Jewishness in the 1890s via a number of discourses. In business practices in London's East End, Jews were vilified as 'middlemen' who lived off the physical labour of English working-class bodies.[18] Jews were also linked to the spread of syphilis, to the pseudoscientific discourse of degeneration, and to an inherent criminality that could be verified by phrenological experiments. The Jewish body, in other words, was constructed as parasite, as the difference within, as unhealthy dependence, as a corruption of spirit that reveals itself upon the flesh. Obviously, the repugnant, horror-generating disease-riddled body of the vampire bears great resemblance to the anti-Semite's 'Jewish body' described by Gilman as a construction of the nineteenth-century culture of medicine. But the Jewish body does not only bear the burden of a scientific discussion of 'race'. In his incarnations as vampire and madman, the Jew also produces race as a psychological category. Race, in other words, may manifest itself as an inherent tendency towards neurosis, hysteria, or other so-called psychological disturbances. While this may seem completely in keeping with the larger motives of nineteenth-century race ideology – the division of humanity into distinct groups – the psychologisation of race has, in fact, particularly insidious effects. It obscures the political agenda of racism by masquerading as objective description and by essentialising Jewishness in relation to particular kinds of bodies, behaviours, and sexualities.

Dracula's blood bond with the insane Renfield provides a particularly powerful link between his character, the racial and psychological stereotypes of Jews, and Gothic anti-Semitism. Seward's interactions with the insane Renfield fulfil a strange function in the novel; while, one assumes, Renfield should further demarcate the distance between normal and pathological, in fact, Seward constantly compares himself to his patient. 'Am I to take it', ponders Seward, 'that I have anything in common with him, so that we are, as it were, to stand together?' (p. 114). Renfield's frequent violent outbursts and his habit of eating insects convince Seward, temporarily at least, that Renfield's insanity resembles rationality only by chance. Renfield's obsessive behaviour involves trapping flies to feed to spiders and spiders to feed to birds. Renfield then consumes the birds. Having observed the development of this activity, Seward decides: 'I shall have to invent a new classification for him, and call him a zoophagous (life-eating) maniac; what he desires is to absorb as many lives as he can, and he has laid himself out to achieve it in a cumulative way' (p. 75). 'Zoophagous', of course, is a term that may just as easily be applied to Dracula and so, the diagnosis made by Seward on Renfield connects the pathology of one to the other.

In 'The Mad Man as Artist: Medicine, History and Degenerate Art', Sander Gilman shows how nineteenth-century sexologists marked the Jews as particularly prone to insanity. Arguing that the race was inherently degenerate and that degeneration was perpetuated by inbreeding, Krafft-Ebing and Charcot, among others, suggested that, in Gilman's words, 'Jews go crazy because they act like Jews'.[19] We may apply this dictum to *Dracula* with interesting results; Renfield is viewed as crazy when he acts like Dracula (when he feeds upon other lives) and Dracula is implicitly insane because his actions are identical to those that keep Renfield in the asylum. Vampirism and its psychotic form of zoophagy, in Stoker's novel, both make a pathology out of threats to rationality made by means of excessive consumption and its relation to particular social and sexual habits. The asylum and Carfax, therefore, the homes of madman and vampire, sit in the heart of London as disciplinary icons – reminders to the reader of the consequences of over-consumption.

In several of his famous Tuesday lessons at Salpêtrière, Dr Jean-Martin Charcot commented upon the hereditary disposition of the Jews to certain nervous diseases like hysteria. 'Jewish families', he remarked during a study of facial paralysis, 'furnish us with the finest subjects for the study of hereditary nervous disease.'[20] In an article on psychiatric anti-Semitism in France at the turn of the century, Jan Goldstein analyses interpretations of the Jews within the human sciences to show how supposedly disinterested and objective studies fed upon and into anti-Semitism. Charcot's pronouncements on the Jews and hereditary nervous disease, for example, were often used by anti-Semites to prove the degeneracy of that race. Similarly, Charcot's work on 'ambulatory automatism' was used by his student Henry Meige to connect the Jews, via the myth of the wandering Jew, with a particular form of epilepsy which induced prolonged somnambulism in the subject. Goldstein writes: 'The restless wanderings of the Jew, [Meige] seemed to say, had not been caused supernaturally, as punishment for their role as Christ-killers, but rather naturally, by their strong propensity to nervous illness. The Jews were not so much an impious people as a constitutionally defective one.'[21] The pathology of the Jews, according to anti-Semitism, involved an absence of allegiance to a Fatherland, a propensity for economic opportunism, and therefore, a lack of social morality and, in general, a kind of morbid narcissism or selfishness.

Dracula's need to 'consume as many lives as he can', his feminised because non-phallic sexuality, and his ambulism that causes him to wander far from home in search of new blood mark him with all the signs of a Jewish neurosis. Dracula, as the prototype of the wanderer, the 'stranger in a strange land', also reflects the way that homelessness or rootlessness was seen to undermine nation. The threat posed by the wanderer within the novel, furthermore, is clearly identified by Stoker as a sexual threat. The nosferatu is not simply a standard reincarnation of Gothic's wandering Jew but rather an undead body, a body that will not rest until it has feasted upon the vital fluids of women and children, drained them of health, and seduced them into a growing legion of perverts and parasites.

In his essay 'The Uncanny', Freud writes about the roots of the uncanny in the lack of place.[22] He goes on to reveal the mother's genitalia as a primal uncanny place, a place of lack, a site that generates fear and familiarity. Being buried alive, Freud suggests, appears in fiction as 'the most uncanny thing of all' but this fear simply transforms a more pleasurable and familiar fantasy, that of 'intrauterine existence' (p. 151). The uncanny aspect of the vampire, however, is not reducible to an oedipal scene because 'home' in the 1890s was precisely an issue resonating with cultural and political implications. Coming or going home, finding a home, was not simply a compulsive return to the womb, it involved nationalist, imperialist, and colonialist enterprises.[23] Dracula, of course, has no home and wants no home; he carries his coffins (his only permanent resting place) with him and nests briefly but fruitfully in populated areas. Home, with its connotations of marriage, monogamy, and community, is precisely what Dracula is in exile from and precisely what would and does kill him in the end.

His enemies seek to entrap and confine him, to keep him in one place separate from the native population. Mina Harker, the epitome, in the novel, of all that is good in woman, tells Seward that they must 'rid the earth of this terrible monster' (p. 235) and Van Helsing pronounces Dracula 'abhorred by all, a blot in the face of God's sunshine; an arrow in the side of Him who died for man' (p. 251).

Dracula, like the Jew – and the Jew, like the vampire – is not only parasitical upon the community's health and wealth, he is sick, nervous, a representation of the way that an unbalanced mind was supposed to produce behaviour at cross-purposes with nation, home, and healthful reproduction. The relation between Renfield and the vampire suggests that vampirism is, itself, a psychological disorder, an addictive activity which, in Renfield's case, can be corrected in the asylum but which, in Dracula's case, requires permanent exile or the permanent confinement of the grave. The equation of vampirism with insanity implies an essential connection between progressive degeneracy, hereditary perversion, and a Gothic science fiction of race.

GOTHIC SEXUALITY: THE VAMPIRE SEX

Dracula's racial markings are difficult to distinguish from his sexual markings. Critics, indeed, have repeatedly discussed vampiric sexuality to the exclusion of race or the vampire's foreignness as merely a function of his strange sexuality.[24] One critic, Sue-Ellen Case, has attempted to locate the vampire within the tangle of race and sexuality. She is interested in the vampire in the nineteenth century as a lesbian vampire and as a markedly queer and outlawed body. She also connects the blood lust of the vampire to the history of anti-Semitism and she opposes both lesbian and Jew within the vampiric form to a reproductive or maternal sexuality. Case describes the vampire as 'the double "she" in combination with the queer fanged creature. ... The vampire is the queer in its lesbian mode.'[25]

Of course, vampiric sexuality as it appears in *Dracula* has also been described as homoerotic[26] and as heterosexual exogamy.[27] So which is it? Of course it is all of these and more. The vampire is not lesbian, homosexual, or heterosexual; the vampire represents the productions of sexuality itself. The vampire, after all, creates more vampires by engaging in a sexual relation with his victims and he produces vampires who share his specific sexual predilections. So the point really is not to figure out which so-called perverse sexuality Dracula or the vampire in general embodies, rather we should identify the mechanism by which the consuming monster who reproduces his own image comes to represent the construction of sexuality itself.

Vampiric sexuality blends power and femininity within the same body and then marks that body as distinctly alien. Dracula is a perverse and multiple figure because he transforms pure and virginal women into seductresses; he produces sexuality through their willing bodies. Lucy and Mina's transformations stress an urgent sexual appetite; the three women who ambush Harker in the Castle Dracula display similar voracity. Both Lucy and Dracula's women feed upon children. As 'nosferatu', buried and yet undead, Lucy walks the heath as the 'Bloofer Lady' who lures children to her and then sucks their blood. This act represents the exact reversal of a mother's nurturance. Crouching outside her tomb, Harker and his friends watch horrified as Lucy arrives fresh from the hunt. 'With a careless motion', notes Seward, 'she flung to the ground, callous as a devil, the child that up to now she had clutched strenuously to her breast, growling over it as a dog growls over a bone' (p. 223). Lucy is now no longer recognisable as the virginal English woman engaged to marry Lord Godalming and the group takes a certain sexual delight in staking her body, decapitating her, and stuffing her mouth with garlic.[28]

When Mina Harker falls under Dracula's spell, he inverts her maternal impulse, and the woman who, by day, nurtures all the men around her, by night, drinks blood from the bosom of the King Vampire himself: 'Her white nightdress was smeared with blood and a thin stream trickled down the man's bare breast which was shown by his torn-open dress' (p. 298). Apart from the obvious reversal of Mina's maternal role, this powerful image feminises Dracula in relation to his sexuality. It is eminently notable, then, that male, not female, vampires reproduce. Lucy and the three female vampires in Transylvania feed from children but do not create vampire children. Dracula alone reproduces his form.

Dracula, of course, also produces male sexuality in this novel as a composite of virility, good blood, and the desire to reproduce one's own kind. Male sexuality in this respect is a vampiric sexuality (and here I diverge from Case's claim for vampirism as lesbianism). As critics have noted, the birth of an heir at the novel's conclusion, a baby boy named after all the men who fought for his mother's virtue, signifies a culmination of the transfusion scene when all the men give blood to Lucy's depleted body. Dracula has drunk from Lucy and Mina has drunk from Dracula, so paternity by implication is shared and multiple. Little Quincey's many fathers are the happy alternative to the threat of many mothers, all the Bloofer Ladies who might descend upon children at night and suck from them instead of suckling them. Men, not women, within this system reproduce; the female body is rendered nonproductive by its sexuality and the vampiric body is distinguished from the English male bodies by its femininity.

Blood circulates throughout vampiric sexuality as a substitute or metaphor for other bodily fluids (milk, semen) and once again, the leap between bad blood and perverse sexuality, as Case points out, is not hard to make. Dracula's sexuality makes sexuality itself a construction within a signifying chain of class, race, and gender. Gothic sexuality, furthermore, manifests itself as a kind of technology, a productive force which transforms the blood of the native into the lust of the other, and as an economy which unites the threat of the foreign and perverse within a single, monstrous body.

GOTHIC ECONOMIES

A Gothic economy may be described in terms of a thrifty metaphoricity, one which, rather than simply scapegoating, constructs a monster out of the traits which ideologies of race, class, gender, sexuality, and capital want to disavow. A Gothic economy also complies with what we might call the logic of capitalism, a logic which rationalises even the most supernatural of images into material images of capitalism itself. To take a remarkable image from *Dracula* as an example, readers may recall the scene in Transylvania at Castle Dracula when Jonathan Harker, searching for a way out, stumbles upon a pile of gold: 'The only thing I found was a great heap of gold in one corner – gold of all kinds, Roman, and British, and Austrian, and Hungarian, and Greek and Turkish money, covered with a film of dust, as though it had lain long in the ground. None of it that I noticed was less than three hundred years old. There were also chains and ornaments, some jewelled, but all of them old and stained' (p. 49). This image of the dusty and unused gold, coins from many nations, and old unworn jewels immediately connects Dracula to the old money of a corrupt class, to a kind of piracy of nations, and to the worst excesses of the aristocracy. Dracula lets his plundered wealth rot, he does not circulate his capital, he only takes and never spends. Of course, this is exactly the method of his vampirism – Dracula drains but it is the band of English men and Van Helsing who must restore. I call this an instance of Gothic economy because the pile of gold both makes Dracula monstrous in his relation to money and produces an image of monstrous anticapitalism, one distinctly associated with vampirism. Money, the novel suggests, should be used and circulated and vampirism somehow interferes with the natural ebb and flow of currency just as it literally intervenes in the ebbing and flowing of blood.

Marx himself emphasised the Gothic nature of capitalism, its investment in Gothic economies of signification, by deploying the metaphor of the vampire to characterise the capitalist. In *The First International*, Marx writes: 'British industry ... vampire-like, could but live by sucking blood, and children's blood too.' The modern world for Marx is peopled with the undead; it is indeed a Gothic world haunted by spectres and ruled by the mystical nature of capital. He writes in *Grundrisse:* 'Capital posits the permanence of value (to a certain degree) by incarnating itself in fleeting commodities and taking on their form, but at the same time changing them just as constantly. ... But capital obtains this ability only by constantly sucking in living labour as its soul, vampire-like.'[29] While it is fascinating to note the coincidence here between Marx's description of capital and the power of the vampire, it is not enough to say that Marx uses Gothic metaphors. Marx, in fact, is describing an economic system, capitalism, which is positively Gothic in its ability to transform matter into commodity, commodity into value, and value into capitalism. And Gothic capitalism, like the vampire, functions through many different, even contradictory, technologies. Indeed, as Terry Lovell points out in *Consuming Fiction*, capitalism demands contradiction and it predicates a radically split, self-contradictory subject. The capitalist subject is both 'a unified subject who inhabits a sober, predictable world and has a stable self-identity' and a self 'open to infatuation with the wares of the capitalist market place'.[30] The nineteenth-century novel, Lovell claims, 'is deeply implicated in this fracture within capitalism's imaginary selves'.[31] Obviously, the 'imaginary selves' of the vampire and his victims exemplify fractured and contradictory subjectivities. Both vampire and victim are figured repeatedly in desiring relations to both production (as writers and breeders) and consumption (as readers and prey).

Vampirism, Franco Moretti claims, is 'an excellent example of the identity of fear and desire'.[32] He, too, points to the radical ambivalence embodied within the Gothic novel and to the economy of metaphoricity within Gothic monstrosity. For Moretti, Frankenstein's monster and Dracula are 'totalising' monsters who embody the worker and capital respectively. Dracula is gold brought to life and animated within monopoly capitalism. He is, as we have discussed, dead labour as described by Marx. While Moretti finds Dracula's metaphoric force to be inextricably bound to capital, he acknowledges that desire unravels and then confuses the neat analogy. The vampire represents money, old and new, but he also releases a sexual response that threatens bourgeois culture precisely from below.

As with Frankenstein's monster, Dracula's designs upon civilisation are read by his enemies as the desire to father a new race. Harker fears that Dracula will 'create a new and ever-widening circle of semi-demons to batten on the helpless' (p. 54). More than simply an economic threat, then, Dracula's attack seems to come from all sides, from above and below; he is money, he is vermin, he is the triumph of capital and the threat of revolution. Harker and his cronies create in Dracula an image of aristocratic tyranny, of corrupt power and privilege, of foreign threat in order to characterise their own cause as just, patriotic, and even revolutionary.

In one interaction between Harker's band of men and the vampire, the Gothic economy that Dracula embodies is forcefully literalised. Having broken into Dracula's house, the men are surprised by Dracula's return. In the interaction that follows, the vampire is turned into the criminal or interloper in his own home. Harker slashes at him with a knife: 'A second less and the blade had shorn through his heart. As it was, the point just cut the cloth of his coat, making a wide gap whence a bundle of bank-notes and a stream of gold fell out' (pp. 323–4). Dracula is then driven back by Harker, who holds up a crucifix, and forced out of the window but not before 'he swept under Harker's arm' in order to grasp 'a handful of the money from the floor'. Dracula now makes his escape: 'Amid the crash and glitter of the falling glass, he tumbled into the flagged area below. Through the sound of the shivering glass I could hear the "ting" of the gold, as some of the sovereigns fell on the flagging' (p. 324).

This incident is overdetermined to say the least. The creature who lives on a diet of blood bleeds gold when wounded; at a time of critical danger, the vampire grovels upon the floor for money; and then his departure is tracked by the 'ting' of the coins that he drops during his flight. Obviously, the metaphoric import of this incident is to make literal the connection between blood and money and to identify Harker's band with a different and more mediated relation to gold. Harker and his cronies *use* money and they use it to protect their women and their country; Dracula hoards gold and he uses it only to attack and seduce.

But there is still more at stake in this scene. A Gothic economy, I suggested, may be identified by the thriftiness of metaphor. So, the image of the vampire bleeding gold connects not only to Dracula's abuses of capital, his avarice with money, and his excessive sexuality, it also identifies Dracula within the racial chain of signification that, as I have shown, links vampirism to anti-Semitic representations of Jewishness. The scene vividly resonates with Shylock's famous speech in *The Merchant of Venice*: 'I am a Jew. Hath not a Jew eyes? Hath not a Jew hands, organs, dimensions, senses, affections, passions? fed with the same food, hurt with the same weapons, subject to the same diseases ... if you prick us do we not bleed? if you tickle us do we not laugh? if you poison us do we not die? and if you wrong us shall we not revenge?' (III.i). Bram Stoker was stage manager for the 250 performances of *The Merchant of Venice* in which Henry Irving, his employer, played Shylock and so it is not so strange to find echoes of Shakespeare's quintessential outsider in Stoker's Dracula. But Stoker epitomises the differences between Dracula and his persecutors in the very terms that Shylock claims as common ground. Dracula's eyes and hands, his sense and passions are patently alien; he does not eat the same food; he is not hurt by the same weapons or infected by the same diseases; and when he is wounded, 'pricked', he does not bleed, he sheds gold. In the character of Dracula, Stoker has inverted the Jew's defence into a damning testimony of otherness.[33] The traditional portrayal of the Jew as usurer or banker, as a parasite who uses money to make money, suggests the economic base of anti-Semitism and the relation between the anti-Semite's monster Jew and Dracula. I have shown that the Jew and the vampire, within a certain politics of monstrosity, are both degenerate – they both represent parasitical sexuality and economy, they both unite blood and gold in what is feared to be a conspiracy against nationhood.

We might interpret Moretti's claim that the vampire is 'a totalising monster' in light of the Gothic economy which allows Dracula to literalise an anticapitalist, an exemplary consumer, and the anti-Semite's Jew. With regard to the latter category, Dracula is foreignness itself. Like the Jew, his function within a Gothic economy is to be all difference to all people, his horror cannot and must not be pinned down exactly.

Marx's equation of vampire and capital and Moretti's analysis of Dracula and gold must be questioned in terms of the metaphoricity of the monster. As Moretti rightly points out, in the literature of terror 'the metaphor is no longer a metaphor: it is a character as real as the others'.[34] Gothic, indeed, charts the transformation of metaphor into body, of fear into form, of narrative into currency. Dracula is (rather than represents) gold – his body bleeds gold, it stinks of corruption, and it circulates within many discourses as a currency of monstrosity. The vampire's sexuality and his power, his erotic and economic attraction, are Gothic in their ability to transform multiple modes of signification into one image, one body, one monster – a totality of horror.

BITING BACK

The technology of *Dracula* gothicises certain bodies by making monstrosity an essential component of a race, a class, or a gender or some hybrid of all of these. I have tried to show that gothicisation, while it emerges in its most multiple and overt form in the Gothic novel, is a generic feature of many nineteenth-century human sciences and ideologies. Gothic economies produce monstrous capitalist practice; gothic anti-Semitism fixes all difference in the body of the Jew; and Gothic fiction produces monstrosity as a technology of sexuality, identity, and narrative. But I have also tried to make the case for the productivity of the Gothic fiction. Rather than simply demonising and making monstrous a unitary other, Gothic is constantly in motion. The appeal of the Gothic text, then, partly lies in its uncanny power to reveal the mechanisms of monster production. The monster, in its otherworldly form, its supernatural shape, wears the traces of its own construction. Like the bolt through the neck of Frankenstein's monster in the modern horror film, the technology of monstrosity is written upon the body. And the artificiality of the monster denaturalises in turn the humanness of its enemies.[35]

Dracula, in particular, concerns itself with modes of production and consumption, with the proximity of the normal and the pathological, the native and the foreign. Even though, by the end of the novel, the vampire is finally staked, the monster is driven out of England and laid to rest; even though monogamous heterosexuality appears to triumph in the birth of Quincey Harker, the body is as much the son of Dracula as he is of the 'little band of men' (p. 400) after whom he is named. Blood has been mixed after all and, like the 'mass of material' which tells the story of the vampire but contains 'hardly one authentic document', Quincey is hardly the authentic reproduction of his parents. Monster, in fact, merges with man by the novel's end and the boy reincarnates the dead American, Quincey Morris, and the dead vampire, Dracula, as if to ensure that, from now on, Englishness will become, rather than a purity of heritage and lineage or a symbol for national power, nothing more than a lost moment in Gothic history.

From Judith Halberstam, *Skin Shows: Gothic Horror and the Technology of Monsters* (Durham, NC, 1995), pp. 86–106.

NOTES

[In the book from which this essay comes, *Skin Shows: Gothic Horror and the Technology of Monsters*, Judith Halberstam examines monsters from Mary Shelley's *Frankenstein* to Jonathan Demme's *The Silence of the Lambs*. Suggesting that purely psychoanalytic readings tend to erase components of race and class, Halberstam shows how the Gothic novel produces monstrosity as an aggregate of race, class, and gender, in order to demonstrate their cultural position as 'meaning machines'. These 'meaning machines' can represent varying social, political, and sexual threats and become the perfect figure for negative identity against which the human as white, male, middle class and heterosexual can be constructed. In this poststructuralist reading of *Dracula*, she identifies the vampire as analogous to the nineteenth-century construction of the monstrous Jew; what is important for Halberstam is not what they represent as 'other' – which is, anyway, infinitely interpretable – but the way in which they expose the actual process of othering. All quotations from Bram Stoker's *Dracula* in this essay are taken from the Bantam 1981 edition. Ed.]

1. Sir Richard Burton, *The Jew, the Gypsy and El Islam*, ed. and with preface and notes by W. H. Wilkins (London, 1898). In *The Devil Drives: A Life of Sir Richard Burton* (New York, 1967), a generally sympathetic biography of Burton, Fawn Brodies notes that Burton backed up his accusations against the Jewish population of Damascus with no historical evidence whatsoever and he simply 'listed a score or so of such murders attributed to Jews from 1010 to 1840' (p. 266)! Burton was unable to find a publisher for his book because the subject matter was considered too inflammatory and libellous. When the book did finally appear (posthumously) in 1898, thanks to the efforts of Burton's biographer and friend W. H. Wilkins, an appendix entitled 'Human Sacrifice amongst the Sephardim or Eastern Jews' had been edited out.

W. H. Wilkins, in addition to editing Burton's work, was very involved in the debate about Jewish immigration to England in the 1890s. See W. H. Wilkins, 'The Immigration of Destitute Foreigners', *National Review*, 16 (1890–91), 114–24; 'Immigration Troubles of the United States', *Nineteenth Century*, 30 (1891), 583–95; 'The Italian Aspect', in *The Destitute Alien in Great Britain*, ed. Arnold White (London, 1892), pp. 146–67; *The Alien Invasion* (London, 1892).

2. See Bram Stoker, 'The Censorship of Fiction', *The Nineteenth Century*, 47 (September 1908). Degenerate writers, he claims, have 'in their selfish greed tried to deprave where others had striven to elevate. In the language of the pulpit, they have 'crucified Christ afresh' (p. 485).

3. AP, 'General Mills Puts Bite on Dracula's Neckpiece', *Minneapolis Star and Tribune* (October 17, 1987), sec. B, p. 5. The caption notes that the offensive picture of Dracula on the cereal box came from Bela Lugosi's 1931 portrayal of him in *The House of Dracula*. General Mills responded to the protest by saying that 'it had no intention of being antisemitic and would redesign the covers immediately'.

4. Michel Foucault, *The History of Sexuality, Volume 1, An Introduction*, trans. Robert Hurley (New York, 1980), pp. 105–6.

5. See Nancy Armstrong, *Desire and Domestic Fiction: A Political History of the Novel* (New York, 1987). Armstrong argues convincingly in this book that 'the history of the novel cannot be understood apart from the history of sexuality' (p. 9).

6. Foucault, *History of Sexuality*, p. 105.

7. In an excellent essay on the way in which 'foreignness merges with monstrosity' in *Dracula*, John Allen Stevenson claims that the threat of the vampire is the threat of exogamy, the threat of interracial competition. See 'A Vampire in the Mirror: The Sexuality of *Dracula*', *PMLA*, 103:2 (March 1988), 139–49.

8. Bram Stoker, *Dracula* (New York, 1981), p. 235. All further references appear in the text.

9. A wonderfully clever and witty discussion of the technology and modernity of *Dracula* and its participation in the production of mass culture can be found in Jennifer Wicke, 'Vampiric Typewriting: *Dracula* and its Media', *ELH*, 59 (1992), 469–93. Wicke claims that the vampire Dracula 'comprises the techniques of consumption'. I am much indebted, as is obvious, to her reading.

10. As quoted in George L. Mosse, *Toward the Final Solution: A History of European Racism* (New York, 1978), p. 156.

11. See Sander L. Gilman, 'Sexology, Psychoanalysis, and Degeneration: From a Theory of Race to a Race of Theory', in *Degeneration: The*

Dark Side of Progress, ed. J. Edward Chamberlain and Sander L. Gilman (New York, 1985). Gilman writes: 'Nineteenth-century science tried to explain the special quality of the Jew, as perceived by the dominant European society, in terms of a medicalisation of the Jew' (p. 87).

12. Cesare Lombroso, introduction to Gina Lombroso Ferrero, *Criminal Man Acccording to the Classifications of Cesare Lombroso* (New York, 1911), p. xv.

13. Foucault, *History of Sexuality*, Vol. 1, p. 118.

14. Michel Foucault, 'The Confession of the Flesh', in *Power/Knowledge: Selected Interviews and Other Writings 1972–1977*, ed. Colin Gordon, trans. Colin Gordon, Leo Marshall, John Mepham, and Kate Soper (New York, 1980), pp. 222–4.

15. Sander L. Gilman, *The Jew's Body* (New York, 1991), p. 39.

16. In an anti-Semitic tract called *England Under the Jews* (1907), Joseph Banister, a journalist, voiced some of the most paranoid fears directed against an immigrant Jewish population, a population steadily growing in the 1880s and 1890s due to an exodus from Eastern Europe. Banister feared that the Jews would spread 'blood and skin diseases' among the general population and he likened them to 'rodents, reptiles and insects'. Banister, whose book went through several editions, made pointed reference to Jews as parasites, calling them 'Yiddish bloodsuckers', as quoted in Colin Holmes, *Anti-Semitism in British Society, 1876–1939* (New York, 1979).

17. These beliefs are linked to what is commonly known as the blood libel and have a long history in England. See C. Roth (ed.), *The Ritual Murder, Libel and the Jew* (London, 1935).

18. See, for example, Henry Arthur Jones, 'Middlemen and Parasites', *The New Review*, 8 (June 1893), 645–54; and 'The Dread of the Jew', *The Spectator*, 83 (9 September 1899), 338–9, where the author discusses contemporary references to Jews as 'a parasitical race with no ideals beyond the precious metals'.

19. Sander L. Gilman, 'The Mad Man as Artist: Medicine, History and Degenerate Art', *Journal of Contemporary History*, 20 (1985), 590.

20. Jean-Martin Charcot, *Leçons du Mardi a la Salpêtrière* (Paris, 1889), as quoted in Jan Goldstein, 'The Wandering Jew and the Problem of Psychiatric Anti-Semitism in Fin-de-Siècle France', *Journal of Contemporary History*, 20 (1985), 521–52.

21. Goldstein, 'The Wandering Jew', 543.

22. Sigmund Freud, 'The Uncanny' (1919), reprinted in *On Creativity and the Unconscious: Papers on the Psychology of Art, Literature, Love, Religion*, trans. Joan Riviere (New York, 1958), p. 148.

23. 'Homelessness' in relation to the Jews became an issue with particular resonance in England in the 1890s when approximately 10,000 Eastern European Jews fled the Tsar's violence and arrived in England. See Holmes, *Anti-Semitism in British Society*.

24. On vampiric sexuality see Carol A. Senf, '*Dracula*: Stoker's Response to the New Woman', *Victorian Studies*, 26 (1982); but also Stephanie Demetrakopoulos, 'Feminism, Sex Role Exchanges, and Other Subliminal Fantasies in Bram Stoker's *Dracula*', *Frontiers: A Journal of Women's Studies*, 2 (1977); Phyllis Roth, 'Suddenly Sexual Women in Bram Stoker's *Dracula*', *Literature and Psychology*, 17 (1977) [reprinted in this volume – Ed.]; Judith Wasserman, 'Women and Vampires: *Dracula* as a Victorian Novel', *Midwest Quarterly*, 18 (1977).

25. Sue-Ellen Case, 'Tracking the Vampire', *differences*, 3:2 (Summer 1991), 9.

26. Christopher Craft, '"Kiss Me with Those Red Lips": Gender and Inversion in Bram Stoker's *Dracula*', in *Speaking of Gender*, ed. Elaine Showalter (New York, 1989) [reprinted in this volume – Ed.].

27. See Stevenson, 'A Vampire in the Mirror'.

28. It is worth noting a resemblance between the Bloofer lady and the terms of the blood libel against the Jews.

29. Karl Marx, *Grundrisse: Foundations of the Critique of Political Economy*, trans. Martin Nicolaus (Harmondsworth, 1973), p. 646.

30. Terry Lovell, *Consuming Fiction* (London, 1987), pp. 15–16.

31. Ibid., p. 16.

32. Franco Moretti, *Signs Taken For Wonders: Essays in the Sociology of Literary Forms*, trans. Susan Fischer, David Forgacs, and David Miller (London, 1983), p. 100. [Excerpted in this collection – Ed.]

33. The 'pound of flesh' scene in *The Merchant of Venice* also connects suggestively with Stoker's *Dracula*. Shylock, after all, is denied his pound of flesh by Portia's stipulation that 'in the cutting it, if thou dost shed / One drop of Christian blood, thy lands and goods / Are (by the laws of Venice) confiscate / Unto the state of Venice' (IV.i.305–8).

34. Moretti, *Signs Taken For Wonders*, p. 106.

35. In the recent film by Francis Ford Coppola, *Bram Stoker's Dracula*, it must be observed that this Dracula was precisely not Stoker's, not the nineteenth-century vampire, because Coppola turned this equation of humanness and monstrosity around. While I am claiming that Dracula's monstrosity challenges the naturalness of the 'human', Coppola tried to illustrate how Dracula's 'humanity' (his ability to love and to grieve) always outweighs his monstrous propensities.

10

Travels in Romania – Myths of Origins, Myths of Blood

DAVID GLOVER

> Thus does the régime, in vampire-like fashion, feed off blood spilt in
> the past, while proceeding to spill fresh blood.
>
> (Branka Magas)[1]

Vampires, according to a recent essay in *Le Monde*, are currently
making a big comeback. 'With the crisis of rationalist thought,'
wrote Edgar Reichmann, 'Dracula and his rivals are returning in
force.' Thanks to the retreat in Enlightenment philosophy and
the failure of utopian politics ('l'échec des utopies matérialistes')
'a certain romanticism' has reappeared and with it all manner of
'creatures of the night' – 'gnomes, goules, striges et vampires'.[2]
Reichmann's bestiary has its familiar human counterparts, running
from Vlad the Impaler to Nicolae Ceauşescu and ending with references to the Balkan killing fields, so that his article becomes an extension of his own thesis in which real and imaginary monsters are
indistinguishable. In spite of its rarefied cultural generalities,
Reichmann's staunchly Cartesian perspective is certainly correct in
pointing to the vampire's increasingly frequent incursions into political discourse, and I would suggest that it is this feature which provides a bridge between Stoker's work and contemporary vampire
myths. Where a nineteenth-century image like 'the Irish vampire'
was once unusual enough to cause comment, today we find its descendants are well-nigh ubiquitous, invading our quotidian dream-
scapes and demonologies at every turn. 'Bush and Reagan. Took
your money. Drank your blood' was one graffito added to the

posters for Francis Ford Coppola's film of *Bram Stoker's Dracula* in the New York subway during the final run-up to the 1992 election.[3]

At the same time, one of the most striking aspects of the current vogue for vampire stories in popular culture has been its enduring fascination with ethnic difference, a preoccupation it shares with the previous *fin-de-siècle*. Throughout this study I have argued that Stoker's writing was driven by a many-sided bio-politics whose racialised fears and desires preyed upon every aspect of his work from its hesitant nationalist yearnings to its theories of sexual fulfilment. In this coda, however, I want to consider the cultural legacy of Stoker's work in our own era, the parallels and adaptations that return us conceptually to the continuing dilemmas faced by the liberal tradition. For just as the bio-political questions with which Stoker grappled were seen as a stumbling block for the type of liberal individualism he espoused, so today's 'tribal' solidarities and interethnic conflicts are often conceived as archaic obstacles to the advance of liberal modernity, the terrifying obverse of civility and rational choice. This is because, in liberalism's narrative of progress, human biological and cultural differences have tended to be regarded as ephemeral and inessential modes of variation destined to be superseded by 'a single form of life, a universal civilisation' in which intractable rivalries and divisions would fade before the spread of humane and rational political principles.[4] But, as Jean Baudrillard has observed, the corollary of this extraordinary faith in the future has been a widening system of exclusions in which 'the progress of Humanity and Culture are simply the chain of discriminations with which to brand "Others" with inhumanity'. Those who fall outside 'the sign of a universal Reason' find themselves 'pushed to the fringes of normality' or consigned to a zone of refractory, but ultimately malleable, entities that includes 'inanimate nature, animals and inferior races'.[5]

The vampire stands at the threshold between the human and the subhuman and it is entirely appropriate that Dracula and his kind make their mark through their shifting affinities with a variety of nonhuman forms: wolves, lizards, bats, and dogs. 'There is much to be learned from beasts', the Count tells Mina Harker, his victim-lover in Coppola's recent film adaptation.[6] And there *is* a lesson here. For while the vampire's peculiarly perverse polymorphousness is the source of its resistance to representation, making it notoriously difficult to pin down – throwing no shadow on the floor, leaving no footprints in the dust, casting no reflection in the mirror – its polymorphous perversity is what allows it to proliferate. Though, in Stoker's imagination at least, Dracula's likeness cannot be captured either by painting or photography, the vampire continues to reproduce itself in a seemingly endless series of copies, always resourcefully different from previous incarnations, often revising the rules of the game in order to secure a new lease on life, without ever finally being laid to rest.[7] This protean durability of the Undead is undoubtedly what confers true immortality upon them and it is also what qualifies their incessant returns as *myths*, those potent cultural stories we listen to again and again and never tire of retelling. 'Love never dies', announced the slogan for Coppola's movie, and because vampires never simply fade away, we need to ask why, to explore the links between myth, representation, and repetition that explain this busy cultural traffic.

Before looking in detail at what is at stake in some of our contemporary vampire narratives, real and unreal, I want to begin by reexamining the concept of myth's usefulness for questions of popular culture. If popular culture is, as Stuart Hall has recently reminded us, 'an arena that is *profoundly mythic* ... a theatre of popular desires, a theatre of popular fantasies', then one way in which a myth may be defined is as a structure of repetitions, as a story whose essential features are always already known by its audience.[8] Part of the appeal of a novel like *Dracula* lies not only in its spectacular depiction of the return from the dead, but also in its deathlessness *as* narrative, a story that never seems to come to an end, that never quite drops out of circulation.[9] Moreover, this very persistence of myth is echoed by its static or recursive mode of construction, making it tempting to see myth as a virtual negation of history and, more strongly still, as an impediment to social change. So, for example, in the work of Roland Barthes and Claude Lévi-Strauss, two of the most influential analysts of myth, their otherwise divergent accounts concur in seeing myths as 'machines for the suppression of time', whose codes are 'constituted by the loss of the historical quality of things'.[10] Nevertheless, to view this opposition between myth and history as an irreconcilable split would be to overlook their complex interdependence. Myths need to 'ripen', Barthes conceded: the extent to which they dehistoricise our grasp of things is really a matter of degree, their largely conservative political function notwithstanding. And Lévi-Strauss, who strongly believes that the recurrence of the same mythic elements over and over again can be traced to universal structures of the human mind, once argued that since most myths clearly do 'tell a story, they are in a temporality'. What matters, then, is that 'this history' is 'closed in on itself, locked up by the myth' rather than 'left open as a door into the future'.[11]

A history 'closed in on itself': for a mythic narrative as claustrophobic as *Dracula* with its profusion of locked or sealed interiors – castles, asylums, chapels, mausoleums, coffins– this phrase sounds peculiarly apt. But what history? And how is it secured? A partial answer can be found in a new definition of myth advanced by Jean-Jacques Lecercle which realigns history and myth, using Stoker's novel as one of its key examples. Lecercle follows Barthes and Lévi-Strauss in suggesting that myth should be read as a species of ideology which provides an imaginary solution to real and insoluble contradictions. But, unlike these earlier writers, he argues that this phantasmatic solution is accomplished not so much by occluding or minimising history as by drastically altering its form.[12] History is compacted into myth through a kind of chiasmus, a double movement of ideological inscription in which, just as the historical conjuncture is sexualised (or 'familialised'), so conflicts within the family structure are projected out onto the wider public sphere. That is to say, for Lecercle, *Dracula* (like *Frankenstein*) is simultaneously a sort of historical romance and a family romance 'au sens freudien', and it is as a mythic fusion of 'the personal and the historical that it is able to persist and to feed into new conjunctures'.[13]

Schematically, Lecercle argues that *Dracula* belonged to ('il reflétait) a difficult historical moment in which the beginning of Britain's decline was signalled politically by setbacks during the First Boer War (1880–81), economically by the Great Depression between 1873 and 1896, and culturally by a pervasive sense that the high point of the Victorian era was now past and the signs of decadence were plainly visible for anyone to see. These anxieties are condensed in the threat the vampire poses to London, the heart of the empire and centre of the civilised world. Yet, at the same time, the novel's topicality is displaced onto an external struggle between good and evil, repeatedly embodied in fears of sexual possession through the flagrantly sexualised motivations that give the vampire's actions their bite. In *Dracula* scenes of seductions are just a breath away from rape, and defencelessness is a precondition of pleasure, whether in the vampirisation of Victorian children, young women, or eligible bachelors. However dated Stoker's book may appear, the undying appeal of his nosferatu depends upon a confusion of temporalities in which ancient folktales, medieval legends, and modern obsessions may all be instantaneously present, coalescing with horrifying effect. Reaching back through time in order to immure us in a mythological past, *Dracula* appears as the very paradigm of what Lecercle calls a 'mythe réactionnaire', a narrative that immobilises history.[14]

What makes *Dracula* a reactionary myth in Lecercle's eyes is precisely its pull back into the past, 'vers l'origine', insisting on the primeval thirst for blood that is imagined always to be lurking just below the civilised surfaces of the psyche and the social fabric. But, as I have suggested throughout this book, the contrast between civility and barbarity takes many forms in Stoker's work, depending upon the kinds of knowledges that are being invoked. Nevertheless, Stoker's various attempts to promote a science of origins invariably place the liberal citizen, the ideal of the rational, fully autonomous agent, on one side of the equation and everything that is excluded by it on the other. One might say that Stoker's project is to settle the question of origins scientifically, to transcend the limitations of a traditional or mythic past by bringing it within the scope of rational comprehension. Stoker's heroes and heroines come to know their own rationality – and even seek to achieve a revitalised sense of reason – through their immersion in a kind of mythical prehistory, an encounter which provides the raw materials for a vigorous counter-myth. To the extent that this counter-myth triumphs over and displaces its primitive substructure, *Dracula* may be a somewhat less reactionary species of myth than Lecercle supposes. Yet insofar as this vision of liberal reason depends upon or is constituted through an excluded other, it inevitably risks becoming ensnared in the logic of its own construction. And Lecercle is surely right to stress the ways in which historical and sexual discourses are inextricably intermingled and intertwined through the endless work of mythic signification.

The complications that arise from the two-way street between history and sexuality so neatly articulated by Lecercle's theoretical definition become clearer when we consider two recent versions of the *Dracula* myth which appeared in 1992: Francis Ford Coppola's film *Bram Stoker's Dracula* and Dan Simmons's novel *Children of the Night*.[15] Each of them invokes the 1897 *Dracula* only to rewrite it by returning to the mythologised history that formed Stoker's original starting point. It is as if the Dracula myth can only be renewed by disinterring more of its folkloric past, an extended movement perfectly captured by the subtitle given to the published script for Coppola's film: *Bram Stoker's Dracula: The Film and the Legend*. As the director observed in one of his postproduction interviews, 'You could make a movie on Dracula even without the Stoker, it would still be fascinating'.[16] And Dracula-without-Stoker exactly describes Dan Simmons's project – except, as might be expected and as his novel's title duly indicates, shades of Stoker are never very far away.

Paradoxically, while Coppola and scriptwriter James V. Hart expand and enhance *Dracula*'s mythic content, the net result of their innovation is thoroughly to demystify the narrative, reducing the vampire's pure unmotivated evil to rational proportions from the very beginning. In Stoker's story vampirism figured as an unknowable given, a challenge to established scientific modes of thought – 'there are always mysteries in life', says the scientist and metaphysician Professor Van Helsing (p. 230) – and it is not until fairly late in the novel, when Dracula is finally on the run, that the vampire can be dismissed as a mere criminoloid aberration 'of imperfectly formed mind' (p. 406). By contrast, not only does Coppola use his opening shots to reveal the historical source of vampirism, by revamping the life of Vlad the Impaler, but the few loose ends and misconceptions that still remain are diegetically dispatched almost as soon as they arise. 'The vampire, like any other night creature, can move about by day', Van Helsing helpfully instructs the unenlightened viewer, but 'it is not his natural time and his powers are weak'. Where the central device of Stoker's novel was the slow accumulation of evidence and testimony as the characters struggled to make sense of experiences that pushed them to the limits of their reason, Coppola's *Dracula* substitutes fast cutting, abrupt transitions, and shifts of style to create a dazzling tangle of scenes and surfaces that tends to conceal the film's underlying narrative order, whose meanings are only overtly spelled out in the omniscient voiceover.

This is perhaps clearer in James Hart's screenplay, which begins and concludes with Van Helsing's offscreen commentary, considerably reduced in the final cut. Fully unpacked, the film's metanarrative most resembles a kind of rational theology, for it reveals the origin of Dracula's condition in the tragic alienation of this fifteenth-century warrior-king from God, following the suicide of his bride who mistakenly believed him to have died in battle defending his church against the 'Moslem Turks'. It is therefore the vampire's redemption that is at issue here, not his exorcism. At root, Coppola's *Dracula* is a tale of spiritual exile, of an apostate prince who is given a second chance by the reincarnation of his lost princess in a circular story of sacrifice and salvation through undying human love, hinting at 'a definite Christ parallel, oddly enough'.[17] From a generic point of view, the film's achievement is to transform Gothic horror into religious melodrama; in short, to prefer *The Robe* over *The Fly*, however much our sympathy with the devil may be engaged.

Dracula's erotic power is given a new genealogy, but one which renders him curiously innocent, a monster who has been wronged, a victim without redress. By providing him with a traumatic personal history, Coppola not only romanticises the vampire, he also sentimentalises him and, as a corollary to this, effectively removes him from the realm of sexual polymorphousness so insistently evoked by the novel – where, in a strangely prescient moment, the endangered Jonathan Harker complains of 'all sorts of queer dreams' (p. 10).[18] Dracula's sartorial outrageousness merely adds a camp veneer that is directly proportional to the normalisation of his desires, now stabilised inside a firmly heterosexual frame. Indeed, one sign of just how solid the vampire's heterosexuality has become is his adherence to an all-too-conventional double standard, remorselessly pursuing the sexually precocious and 'positively indecent' Lucy Westenra with her 'free way of speaking', while devotedly and conscientiously withholding his full vampire nature from the straitlaced Mina Harker, who has failed to realise that she is a reincarnation of his former bride. Yet, before his entry onto the streets of London in the romantic guise of a young and somewhat eccentric Continental gentleman, the Dracula who welcomes Mina's fiancé Jonathan to his Transylvanian castle seems to epitomise the sexual and cultural uncanny: an unsettling otherness which is hauntingly familiar, insinuatingly intimate but always somehow deeply foreign.

'The impression I had was that we were leaving the West and entering the East.' Jonathan Harker's journal, quoted directly from the 1897 *Dracula*, is superimposed over the lower part of a wide shot of the Orient Express travelling into the sunset and simultaneously added as a voiceover by actor Keanu Reeves. Preceded by a train's-eye shot of the railway tracks emerging from a tunnel in the Carpathians, moving toward a fading red sun, this juxtaposition of colours and images establishes Transylvania as a nightmare land of mists and shadows, unrelievedly nocturnal and ill-lit. Where the foundational Christian narrative prologue suggested a world at once feudal and Byzantine, in which stone crucifixes and religious iconography dominate the visual field, this return to Transylvania radically expands the orientalist elements of the earlier *mise-en-scène* to create an effect of alterity and menace. Dracula becomes a bizarre figure of indeterminate age and sexuality, with high-coiffed Kabuki hair and dressed in a long red silk tunic embossed with golden Chinese dragons and trailed by an enormous cloak 'designed to undulate like a sea of blood'.[19] And, though the elongated fingers with their sharp pointed nails are staple vampire fare, in this newly orientalised context Dracula's hands and costume conjure up another popular Eastern villain, the ageless Dr Fu Manchu.

Symptomatically, the film's designer Ishioka Eiko refers to both Dracula's 'aura of transsexuality' and 'the androgynous quality of his character', confusing these terms as if they were synonymous – but the real point here is that the film provides no basis for telling one from the other.[20] Gary Oldman's performance teasingly alternates between belligerence and camp, his dandyish swishiness of gesture suddenly giving way to the hiss of his sword. However, these nods toward vampiric transgression only serve as a temporary screen and are rapidly resolved into an avowedly heterosexual object choice once Dracula catches sight of Jonathan's pocket daguerreotype of Mina/Elizabeta. As if to underscore this sexual closure, Jonathan's subsequent seduction by the Count's three 'brides' becomes an occasion to display the unbridled nature of vampire eroticism which also allows Dracula to answer their reproach against his interference ('you yourself never loved') with the softly introspective reply 'Yes – I too can love. And I shall love again'. At the same time, by leaning heavily toward orientalist fantasy, this scene reinforces Dracula's identification with the mysterious East, for it is modelled on the conceit that the influence of Turkish culture on Vlad the Impaler, following his youthful days in Istanbul, would have led him to keep a harem. Hence the Turkish cymbals on the soundtrack, the diaphanous gauzy dresses partly copied from Bombay shrouds, and the attempt to cast the 'brides' as identifiably 'ethnic types'.[21]

The sense that sexuality is being produced through race, that the function of racial difference is to key in and give definition to the fear and fascination of sexual excess gains added impetus from the scenes at the country house at Hillingham, which are intercut with the Castle Dracula episodes, providing a chiaroscuro of English daylight and Transylvanian night. Hillingham too is an unmistakably orientalised milieu: from Mina's tightly buttoned high-collared silk tunic, to the turbaned servant who accompanies the arrival of Lucy's suitor 'Lord Arthur', to the Byzantine influences on the decor of the conservatory and drawing room, the house and its occupants are steeped in the plush acquisitions of a well-developed imperialist culture. The linchpin of this anxious infatuation with the East occurs in the first scene at Hillingham when Lucy discovers a shocked Mina looking at an erotic illustration to Sir Richard Burton's *Arabian Nights*. Mina's question 'Oh, can a man and a woman really do – that?' implies that desire is constituted *as* desire by first being staged as an exotic aberration that needs to be policed. From this perspective, the afflictions of those who have returned from Transylvania – Jonathan's male hysteria and his predecessor Renfield's madness – serve as warnings of cultural contamination, the risks of 'going native', especially evident in Renfield's case, for since his return he 'is now obsessed with some bloodlust, and with an insatiable hunger for life in any form'. He remains confined to an asylum cell throughout the film.

Here the ghostly traces of an earlier Coppola film begin to intrude. As the script slyly suggests, the journey 'through the magnificent Carpathian Mountains' takes 'us into the heart of Transylvanian darkness', and, if this is so, then Dracula's struggle to defend the West against the 'sensual Orient' has turned him into a kind of Kurtz.[22] At the same time, we can also begin to see some of the ways in which Coppola's Dracula blurs into other (post)modern vampire stories, helping to nourish a different but related type of cultural myth, and one which goes right to the heart of Dan Simmons's gory Romanian thriller *Children of the Night*. One of the legendary depictions of horror for our own era can be found in those popular and journalistic histories of Romania which deploy Nicolae Ceauşescu as a dead ringer for the vampire himself, 'the communist Dracula'.[23] According to London's *Sunday Times*, Ceauşescu was 'like a character from a Transylvanian fairy tale': 'the demon cobbler' became 'the evil emperor who cast a seductive spell on the Western world while he violated his own people'.[24] Yet such narratives often reveal a certain ambiguity, an equivocation around the intentionality of evil: 'was it the monster, or was it the swamp?'[25] Thus in his book *The Life and Evil Times of Nicolae Ceauşescu*, cheek by jowl with folk rumours that Ceauşescu sucked the blood of infants in order to gain strength, John Sweeney portrays Romanian political culture as a tight combination of submissiveness and authoritarianism explained by the country's history of incorporation into the Ottoman empire, symbolically clinching his argument with the observation that Turkish style coffee is the preferred drink in Bucharest: 'dark, impossibly sweet and disgustingly gritty'.[26] As one critic has noted, underlying this sort of account is a 'concept of "Europeanness"' which forms 'the dividing line' between the civilised and the primitive, a racialised separation that is reduplicated through the region, pitting Serbs against Croats, Czechs against Slovaks, or Bulgarians against Pomaks.[27] Small wonder, then, that Jonathan Harker has an acute sense that Western rationality is slipping away from him as he crosses the Danube and moves 'among the traditions of Turkish rule' (p. 9). In his Transylvanian journal he records his dismay at having 'to sit in the carriage for more than an hour before we began to move', complaining 'that the further East you go the more unpunctual are the trains'. 'What ought they to be in China?' he asks, not altogether rhetorically (pp. 10–11).

The amplification and primitivisation of difference by local prejudices and sensationalised reportage can also be found in more serious-minded analyses of East European ethnic politics, and it reaches a peak in the rival myths of ethnogenesis which stake out official nationalist claims to particular territories or provinces. Transylvania is a stark example of just such a 'contested terrain', the subject of competing histories of autochthonous peoples that also offer models of racial purity and continuity. In the Romanian state myth evidence of indigenous Daco-Roman tribes has been used to assert that Transylvania was 'the original homeland of the Romanian people for more than two thousand years', and the rival mythology of a Hungarian Transylvania based upon claims that such ethnic groups as the Szekelys should be recognised as true Hungarians has been hotly disputed.[28]

Moreover, the promulgation of this nationalist myth of origin was closely linked to the Ceauşescu regime's bio-politics, since its programmes of community resettlement, ethnic dispersal, and sweeping demolition of the traditional built environment sought to undermine local ways of life that were held to impede the 'true' unity of the Romanian people. One fear, for example, was that 'the "pure" Romanian birthrate' was falling behind that of the country's ethnic minorities, putting 'the "special" character of the Romanian genetic pool' at risk.[29] When Ceauşescu took over the leadership of the

Romanian Communist Party in 1965 he committed the nation to raising its population from nineteen to thirty million by the year 2000. Since giving birth was designated 'a patriotic duty', abortion was banned for women under forty-five and with fewer than five children, monthly pregnancy tests were required of women under thirty as a condition for receiving free state medical or dental care, special taxes were imposed on couples who remained childless after two years of marriage, and, in 1985, contraception was outlawed.[30] Ruthlessly enforced, Ceauşescu's policy had succeeded in raising the Romanian population to twenty-three million by 1977, but the additional strain it placed on ordinary families already suffering considerable economic hardships led to large numbers of dangerous illegal abortions and the dumping of tens of thousands of unwanted and abandoned children into state orphanages. More gruesome still, the archaic practice of giving micro-transfusions of blood to these malnourished orphans in the belief that this would boost their immune system created an AIDS epidemic resulting from the use of unscreened blood banks and recycled syringes. But the idea that the nation's stock could be in any way polluted was unthinkable within the Romanian myths of racial purity, and until Ceauşescu was deposed in 1989, AIDS officially did not exist. It was a disease belonging only in the non-Communist West.

Since, both at home and abroad, Ceauşescu has popularly been coded as a political monstrosity of vampiric dimensions, preying upon and perpetuating a backward nation, it was but a further twist of the cultural myth to use the enormities of Romanian bio-politics as raw material for a new Transylvanian Gothic. Dan Simmons's *Children of the Night* is a novel that maps the linked crises of AIDS, abandoned children, and Romanian autocracy onto more traditional vampire themes, crossing Bram Stoker with the kind of ultracontemporary post-Communist thriller associated with Martin Cruz Smith. The book posits an inbred vampire strain with a weakness in their immune systems which can only be offset by ingesting human blood, since an inherited retrovirus allows them to rebuild damaged tissue even to the point of 'cannibalising' their own blood cells when 'host blood' is inconveniently out of reach.[31] This physiological mutation confers extraordinary powers of recuperation and longevity, releasing the vampire from the phantom space beyond the mirror and turning its thirst for blood into a genetic peculiarity. This peculiarity permits an eternalised Vlad the Impaler to figure as one of the novel's central characters, just as he does in Coppola's film.

Historically and scientifically, then, 'the myth has its origins in reality' (*CN*, p. 136). And so, 'reality' turns out to be another variant of the vampire myth.

As I noted earlier, part of the work that myth performs upon narrative is to make its component actions conform to some timeless design, classically the battle between good and evil, which transcends immediate historical interests and dilemmas. In Coppola's *Dracula* this opposition is mediated by race, using orientalism as a visual repertoire for marking out the exotic and alluring thresholds of transgression. *Children of the Night* shares this use of race as the primary means by which evil is made tangible, but the vampire's distinguishing traits are remarkably unexotic, its ethnic hallmarks 'secrecy, solidarity, inbreeding', and a strategic desire to pass unnoticed and unremarked (*CN*, p. 136). Ethnicity here is unostentatiously clannish and insular, as furtive, conspiratorial, and patriarchal as a Mafia family. Nor is it too far-fetched to see traces of a *Godfather*-type narrative through the Romanian Gothic haze, since the clash between good and evil manifests itself in the book as a battle over the custody of a child, none other than Vlad Dracula's successor. When Kate Neuman, an American doctor – and possibly the first haematologist heroine in the history of the vampire novel – discovers an 'abandoned, nameless, helpless' baby boy in a Romanian isolation ward 'who responded to transfusions but who soon began wasting away again' from some undiagnosable immune disorder, her decision to adopt him brings her up against the *strigoi*, the legendary vampire caste that has dominated the country for generations (*CN*, p. 53). Symbolically the stakes are extraordinarily high: for Kate's experimenting with the child's unusual retrovirus offers hope of 'a cure for cancer, for AIDS' because of its similarity and resistance to HIV, while, for the *strigoi*, restoring this boy she calls Joshua to the bosom of the clan promises to preserve the original Dracula lineage intact (*CN*, p. 337). The clinical and genetic rarity of the virus makes this a zero-sum game of survival on both sides. Unlike traditional vampires, the *strigoi* are only able to reproduce themselves infrequently because of the unusual double recessive nature of the virus, and they typically produce normal human offspring. True-born *strigoi* are therefore highly prized and their more commonplace brothers and sisters are treated with contempt and abandoned. This disregard toward ordinary human life is closely related to the *strigoi*'s chronic craving for power and, although they need human blood in order to live, it is their callousness that makes them so wholly pernicious. In the lore that passes among their potential victims Gothic imagery and political rhetoric combine in a single register, feeding on each other like the parasites they name: 'these animals bleed my people dry and lead our nation into ruin' (CN, p. 223).

Behind the novel's detailed evocation of a troubled post-Ceauşescu Romania is a view of history as an immense conspiracy stretching back through Communist and Fascist regimes to at least the fifteenth century, depicting 'a nation which has never taken a breath outside of totalitarian madness' (CN, p. 336). The *strigoi*'s pure will-to-power has no time for those features which make some systems of rule more tolerable than others, interesting itself in political institutions solely to exploit them for their tactical advantage. In contemporary Romania 'we've got the government versus the protestors versus the miners versus the intellectuals, and the *strigoi* seem to be pulling most of the strings on each side' (CN, pp. 301–2). Part of the paranoid logic of conspiracies is that it is impossible to fathom how far they stretch, and in *Children of the Night* this impenetrability is compounded by Vlad the Impaler's own mysteriously elided history. He appears in the novel as an aged and decaying tyrant who has survived for over five centuries, and whose bloodcurdling memories dwell on his younger days, on the uncompromising sadism of his military exploits, which are interspersed throughout the narrative as sinister 'dreams of blood and iron', warnings of the terror that may still be to come. This is a figure who despises 'Stoker's idiot, opera-cloaked vampire' for having done 'nothing but blacken and trivalise the noble name of Dracula', but who confesses to being irresistibly drawn to one of Stoker's own phrases when boasting of his own achievements: 'I have bred and led a race of children of the night' (CN, pp. 227–8). The significant addition to Stoker's original phraseology here is the word 'race'.

Curiously, however, he is first introduced to us in the persona of 'the Western billionaire, Mr Vernor Deacon Trent', a corporate magnate whose transnational commercial operations give his work a global reach and influence, though we never learn how he managed to fabricate this impressive new identity (CN, p. 10). When he and Kate finally meet on the evening before Joshua is to be initiated into the practice of drinking human blood, Vlad tells her that 'the vast and varied affairs of the Family' are dispersed across 'a hundred-some cities in twenty-some nations' and that he plans to take advantage of the AIDS epidemic to move into the 'market for safe transfusions', estimating its worth at over two billion dollars per year. Far from the *strigoi* being mere Eastern European revenants who 'keep orphanages stocked for our needs', Vlad makes clear that for his kind 'it is not the addiction of blood that is so hard to break', but rather 'the addiction to power' (*CN*, pp. 318–19). In this he is our most ancient contemporary: hypocrite vampire – mon semblable – mon frère.

Despite disclaimers to the contrary, *Children of the Night* does actually parallel 'Stoker's abominable, awkwardly written melodrama' – at least, up to a point (*CN*, p. 277). The expeditionary journey into Transylvania, the vampire invasion of the West (here substituting Boulder, Colorado for imperial London), the kidnapping of babies, the role of contemporary medicine in the power-knowledge standoff against the 'Family of Night', the cathartic narrative finale at the Castle Dracula – all recognisably transpose key elements from the original story into a modern idiom. Similarly, at a more episodic level, Kate's desperate climb *up* the walls of the castle to rescue her adopted child at the novel's climax is a neat textual inversion (a mirror image, one might say) of the Count's sinister climb *down* them in one of *Dracula*'s opening chapters, a climb also motivated by the pursuit of babies. Yet, in common with Coppola, Simmons's rewriting of Stoker is also heavily rationalised, straining toward a verisimilitude that almost makes too much sense for a tale of 'nature's eccentricities and possible impossibilities' (p. 231). In the end, Vlad the Impaler is a monster whose aspirations turn out to be entirely rational (or, as he says, 'more progressive'), the calculative ambitions of the corporate entrepreneur (*CN*, p. 319). Conniving at the destruction of the majority of his diseased blood relations, he converts to a newly manufactured 'haemoglobin substitute' and plans to return to 'the States, or at least the civilised part of Europe'. But, perhaps remembering his oriental past, his thoughts also turn East and he contemplates a visit to Japan, 'an intriguing place, filled with the energy and business that is the lifeblood I feed on now' (*CN*, p. 379). Soon he is imagining once more that he might live forever.

In this eerily happy ending one can see what is perhaps the most distinctive feature of the modern vampire myth, at least as currently narrated: the tormented humanisation of the nosferatu, which reverses the emphasis on the monstrous in texts like the original *Dracula* and brings them closer to us.[32] Indeed, in Stoker's work the vampire is essentially mysterious and much of the novel's psychological interest stems from the struggle within the victims between their good and demonic selves. Here, however, it is the vampire himself who is torn between conflicting forces, who is looking for a way out. And clinically this turns him into something of a borderline case.

If Simmons and Coppola offer us *Dracula*'s doubles, these are doubles with a difference. Less concerned with containing and destroying the vampire, they pose – often in the vampire's own words – the pressing question of his cure, the remedial treatment that would expel his worst self while still allowing him to remain unmistakably Other.[33] What a cure might mean in such a context is always ambiguous and liminal, sliding uncertainly between moral and medical metaphors. Hence in Coppola's film, the sympathy engendered by Dracula's plight produces a demand that he receive absolution ('give me peace'), that his condition be ameliorated. This is accomplished by Mina Harker in the movie's final frames when she cuts into her lover's heart and then cuts off his head, simultaneously purging herself of her adultery and laying Dracula's soul to rest in a renunciation of her deepest, most contradictory desires. In so doing she is ensuring that her 'prince' dies as a human being.[34] Similarly, in *Children of the Night* the *strigoi* baby Joshua, who is physiologically identical to the other members of the 'Family', is saved from exposure to the corrupting practice of drinking human blood by Kate's intrepid efforts, a victory that is echoed by Dracula's own more questionable conversion to the virtues of private enterprise. But in each case, the part played by female agency in forcing the narrative to a conclusion should not blind us to the way their own actions restore them to conventional family life as wives and mothers, Mina returning to Jonathan Harker, Kate to a new romance with Mike O'Rourke, the ex-priest who has been her companion in these adventures. After all, when Jonathan Harker announces at the end of the film that 'Our work is finished here ... hers is just begun', he is publicly underlining his wife's duties. In a sense, at least in these two texts, the ambivalence we feel toward the familiar, the homely, and the intimate, an ambivalence which Freud locates at the sexual heart of those fearsome Gothic fictions he calls 'the uncanny' (*das Unheimliche*), seems to be dissolving back into the cosiness of hearth and home, of kith and kin, even if home is no longer quite what it once was.

I began by drawing attention to the fabled insubstantiality of vampires, but the trouble with these more recent specimens is that they are altogether too real, their reality a little too easily explained.

They come to us saturated in a history whose living presence is encoded in the racialised markings they bear, signs which lend these vampires substance, whether as oriental despots or members of ethnic clans. It is precisely this stain of particularity that torments the vampire and that his opponents must evade or disavow if they are to prevail in the struggle against him. Thus Mina Harker's moral imperative compels her upright Victorian persona to slough off her ethnic past, forcing her to part company forever from her reincarnated Romanian forebear, Princess Elizabeta. And in a revealing passage in *Children of the Night*, Kate, escaping with Mike O'Rourke and the vampire child from the ruined Castle Dracula, looks down from a stolen helicopter at the country below and experiences a moment of freedom and relief from the ties of blood and birthright, the glimpse of an escape from the messy contingencies of history: 'There was no sense now of national boundaries, or of nations, of the darkness that lay below those clouds' (*CN*, p. 375). These words recall the 'internationalist' expedition against Count Dracula in Coppola's film, with its Dutch scientist, English aristocrat, and American adventurer, in which Stoker's Western imperial alliance is supplemented by Japanese corporate backing and global distribution. So it might seem as if the new myth that is on view holds out the promise of a transcendence of petty historical and ethnic differences, subsuming them into a new liberal cosmopolitanism, a universalistic identity in which everyone can find their place. But before accepting this promise too quickly, it is worth stressing the dangers to which this humanism, its eyes upon the ever-improvable future, is sometimes blind.

In an important essay on racism and nationalism, Etienne Balibar has drawn attention to the way in which 'the classical myths of race, in particular the myth of Aryanism' imagine purity or superiority to reside in a phantasmatic collectivity 'which transcends frontiers and is, by definition, transnational'. There is, he suggests, 'a racist "internationalism" or "supranationalism" which tends to idealise timeless or transhistorical communities such as the "Indo-Europeans", "the West", "Judaeo-Christian civilisation" and therefore communities which are at the same time both closed and open, which have no frontiers or whose only frontiers are ... inseparable from the individuals themselves or, more precisely, from their "essence" (what was once called their "soul").'[35] The ideological operation that chiefly constructs these myths is that of separation, the sifting of an ideal humanity from the detritus of history, safeguarding it from an animal or tribal or degenerate past. Vlad's conspiracy to destroy the bulk of his *strigoi* entourage in *Children of the Night* perfectly exemplifies this process of ethnic cleansing, 'purifying the Family of its decadent branches' (*CN*, p. 378). That this narrative aggression is sexualised through and through, not merely in the virility of its heroes and heroines but in the preoccupation with heredity, inter-breeding, and the erotic bestiality of the Other, is entirely in keeping with the racist metatext to which these vampire tales are closely ar-ticulated. Hence the profusion of animalistic representations around and within Coppola's vampire, the mark of the beast that must be purged, are of a piece with one of the cornerstones of racist doc-trine, the 'discovery of which it endlessly rehearses, ... that of a humanity eternally leaving behind and eternally threatened with falling into the grasp of animality'.[36]

Of course this is very much Stoker's own paranoid rhetoric too. For him it is axiomatic that even the most evil white European shows 'traces of the softening civilisation of ages', whereas the top-hatted African factotum Oolanga in *The Lair of the White Worm* (looking 'like a horrible distortion of a gentleman's servant') is without doubt 'the lowest and most loathsome of all created things which were in some form ostensibly human ... in fact, so brutal as to be hardly human' (*LWW*, pp. 35–6). It used to be said that the fantastic tropes of nineteenth-century Gothic fiction were 'nothing but the bad conscience' of a 'positivist era'.[37] If, as Coppola's Count Dracula suggests, there really is a lesson 'to be learned from beasts', perhaps it is that the compassion for the vampire that many of today's texts elicit has its roots in the bad conscience of a racialised humanism.

From David Glover, *Vampires, Mummies, and Liberals: Bram Stoker and the Politics of Popular Fiction* (Durham, NC, 1996), pp. 136–51.

NOTES

[David Glover's essay forms the concluding chapter to his *Vampires, Mummies, and Liberals. Bram Stoker and the Politics of Popular Fiction*. In this book he considers Stoker's literary career, examining both his fictional and non-fictional writings as they engage with the moral, political and scientific discourses of late-Victorian Britain. Drawing upon the methods of cultural studies, Glover focuses in particular upon the interconnections between cultural practices and questions of power. In this coda, he analyses two key examples of the many recent attempts to retell *Dracula* for a late-twentieth-century audience, Francis Ford Coppola's *Bram Stoker's Dracula* and Dan Simmons's *Children of the Night*, and draws upon this analysis to reconsider the nature of myth and its relationship with popular culture. All quotations from Stoker's *Dracula* in this essay are taken from the Penguin 1979 edition. Ed.]

1. Branka Magas, *The Destruction of Yugoslavia: Tracking the Break-Up, 1980–92* (London, 1993), p. 320.

2. Edgar Reichmann, 'Le retour des vampires', *Le Monde* (27 May 1994), viii. My translation.

3. For a different political spin, consider the opening lines of Martin Walker's article 'Spectre of Cold War Returns', *Manchester Guardian Weekly* (25 August 1991), 7: 'If the corpse of the Cold War is clambering from its grave, the West's timorous and complacent leaders must agonise whether they failed to drive a stake through its heart when they had the chance.' Of course, such examples are legion.

4. See John Gray, 'Agonistic Liberalism', *Social Philosophy and Policy*, 12 (Winter 1995), 111.

5. Jean Baudrillard, *Symbolic Exchange and Death*, trans. Iain Hamilton Grant (London, 1993), pp. 125–6.

6. Unless otherwise indicated, all quotations are taken directly from the film of *Bram Stoker's Dracula* (Columbia Pictures, 1992), which differs in detail from the published screenplay.

7. See Bram Stoker, *Original Foundation Notes and Data for Dracula*, Rosenbach Museum and Library, Philadelphia.

8. Stuart Hall, 'What Is This "Black" in Black Popular Culture?', in *Black Popular Culture*, a Project by Michèle Wallace, ed. Gina Dent (Seattle, 1992), p. 32.

9. Since it is both a myth of uncanny return and a myth which is itself forever returning, one might almost see *Dracula* as the most quintessential of myths, the myth of myths. I owe this point to Rachel Bowlby.

10. Claude Lévi-Strauss, *Mythologiques: Le Cru et le Cuit* (Paris, 1964), p. 26, and Roland Barthes, *Mythologies*, trans. Annette Lavers (St Albans, 1973), p. 142.

11. Claude Lévi-Strauss, 'A Confrontation', *New Left Review*, 62 (July–August 1970), 63.

12. Lecercle sees a convergence in this formula between Hegelian-Marxist analyses of myth and Lévi-Strauss's early view that myth provides 'a logical model capable of overcoming a contradiction (an impossible achievement if, as it happens, the contradiction is real)' (Claude Lévi-

Strauss, *Structural Anthropology*, trans. Claire Jacobson and Brooke Schoepf [Harmondsworth, 1977], p. 229). But it is clear that there is a debt to Althusserian Marxism here too: ideology as the imaginary relation of subjects to their real condition of existence.

13. Jean Jacques Lecercle, *Frankenstein: Mythe et Philosophie* (Paris, 1988), pp. 75–7. My translation. Lecercle's brief remarks on *Dracula* are introduced by way of illustrative contrast to his analysis of *Frankenstein*. *Dracula* is precisely 'l'autre grand mythe fantastique'. Reichmann makes a similar point about the sexualisation of the vampire when he notes that writers and artists gave the history of Vlad the Impaler 'une connotation érotique' ('Le retour des vampires', p. viii).

14. Lecercle, *Frankenstein: Mythe et Philosophie*, p. 122. At this point it becomes necessary to separate out two somewhat different aspects of Lecercle's argument. For if his analysis of myth remains theoretically indebted to earlier models that have increasingly been viewed as resting upon highly questionable foundations – reflectionism, structuralism, and the like – in practice, Lecercle's reading of myth as a process of articulation suggests an unstable mix of structurally heterogeneous elements that ultimately evades any fixed order of causality. See Jacques Derrida, 'Structure, Sign, and Play in the Discourse of the Human Sciences', in *Writing and Difference*, trans. Alan Bass (London, 1978).

15. When *Children of the Night* recently appeared as a mass market paperback from Warner Books it was hyped as 'the brilliant vampire novel by America's new prince of horror', and featured an encomium by Stephen King on its cover.

16. 'His Bloody Valentine', Francis Ford Coppola in interview with Manohla Dargis, *Village Voice* (24 November 1992), 66.

17. According to Coppola: 'I made a big point about when Dracula dies he just becomes a man, I found that very Christ-like somehow. There are those figures in our lives, and maybe that's what Christ really means, who are the ones that must die or the ones who must court evil, they do it for us. In the end, it's the sacrificial role Christ plays – he who must die' (Dargis, 'His Bloody Valentine', 66).

18. For analyses of the homosexual subtext in *Dracula*, see Christopher Craft's classic essay '"Kiss Me with Those Red Lips": Gender and Inversion in Bram Stoker's *Dracula*', *Representations*, 8 (1984), 107–33 [reprinted in this volume – Ed.], and also Marjorie Howes, 'The Mediation of the Feminine: Bisexuality, Homoerotic Desire, and Self-Expression in Bram Stoker's *Dracula*', *Texas Studies in Language and Literature*, 30:1 (1988), 104–19.

19. Ishioka Eiko quoted in Francis Ford Coppola, Ishioka Eiko, and David Seidner, *Coppola and Eiko on 'Bram Stoker's Dracula'*, ed. Susan Dworkin (San Francisco, 1992), p. 41.

20. Ibid.

21. Francis Ford Coppola, quoted in Francis Ford Coppola and James V. Hart, *Bram Stoker's Dracula: The Film and the Legend* (New York, 1992), p. 64.

22. Coppola and Hart, *Bram Stoker's Dracula*, pp. 30, 47.

23. Ryszard Kapuscinski, foreword to Edward Behr, *Kiss the Hand You Cannot Bite: The Rise and Fall of the Ceauşescus* (New York, 1991), p. xi.

24. Peter Millar, 'The Family a Nation Learned to Loathe', *Sunday Times* (24 December 1989), A13.

25. John Sweeney, *The Life and Evil Times of Nicolae* Ceauşescu (London, 1991), p. 20.

26. Ibid., p. 24. Readers curious as to how Sweeney's political sociology of Romania can find space for the 1989 revolution will be reassured to learn that the least orientalised parts of the country were the first to rebel. For an alternative view, see Sam Beck, 'What Brought Romanians to Revolt', *Critique of Anthropology*, 11:1 (1991), 7–31.

27. David Edgar, 'Whirlpools on the Danube', *Manchester Guardian Weekly* (13 March 1991), 26. For a recent survey of East European ethnic politics, see Stephen R. Bowers, 'Ethnic Politics in Eastern Europe', *Conflict Studies*, 248 (London, 1992), 1–25.

28. Laszlo Kurti, 'Transylvania, Land Beyond Reason: Towards an Anthropological Analysis of a Contested Terrain', *Dialectical Anthropology*, 14:1 (1989), 21–3. Note that Count Dracula tells Jonathan Harker that he belongs to the Szekely, thereby proudly asserting what are entirely uncertain origins (Stoker, *Dracula*, p. 40).

29. George Galloway and Bob Wylie, *Downfall: The Ceauşescus and the Romanian Revolution* (London, 1991), p. 54.

30. Jill Neimark, 'Romanian Roulette', *Village Voice* (1 October 1991), 28.

31. Dan Simmons, *Children of the Night* (New York, 1992), p. 221. Subsequent references to *CN* are given in parenthesis.

32. Vampires are at their most human in Anne Rice's trend-setting *Interview with the Vampire* (1976). But note the opposed tendency for humans (at least *female* humans) to turn into monsters in contemporary thrillers like *Fatal Attraction* and *Single White Female*. See Judith Williamson, 'Nightmare on Madison Avenue', *New Statesman* (15 January 1988), 28–9.

33. While both texts gingerly flirt with the theme of AIDS, neither lets it dominate the narrative. Of the two, the relation of Coppola's film to AIDS is the most vague, the most puzzling, and possibly the most

cynical. Despite an assortment of references to the disease in the movie's publicity and in published extracts from the director's production diary, Coppola is on record as saying that 'the only direct connection between *Bram Stoker's Dracula* and AIDS is that if his film succeeds, he'll go on to make "a real film about AIDS", tentatively titled *The Cure*' (Laurie Winer, 'Death Becomes Him', *Harper's Bazaar*, 3370 [October 1992], 172.)

34. In Stoker's novel, though Dracula dies with 'a look of peace' on his face, it is his extinction at the hands of the book's male heroes (not Mina's) that is important, for he does not die as a man as he does in the film, but immediately crumbles to dust (Stoker, *Dracula*, p. 447).

35. Etienne Balibar, 'Racism and Nationalism', in *Race, Nation, Class: Ambiguous Identities*, Etienne Balibar and Immanuel Wallerstein (London, 1991), p. 61. As Balibar's examples suggest, transnational racisms are typically reinscribed in nationalist ideologies, part of what he terms 'the cycle of historical reciprocity of nationalism and racism' in which each can emerge out of the other. See Balibar, p. 53.

36. Ibid., p. 57. Importantly, Balibar's argument is not antihumanist *per se*; rather, he distinguishes between different *humanisms* in terms of their compatibility/incompatibility with racism. In practical terms, humanism can serve as 'a politics and an ethics of the defence of civil rights without limitations or exceptions'. However, when humanism is conceived theoretically as 'a doctrine which makes man as a species the origin and end of declared and established rights', then the way is open for any number of racist exclusions. See Balibar, pp. 62–4.

37. Tzvetan Todorov, *The Fantastic: A Structural Approach to a Literary Genre*, trans. Richard Howard (Ithaca, NY, 1975), p. 168.

Further Reading

The best place to begin further reading is with the three books excerpted in this collection which contextualise *Dracula* in various ways: David Punter's *The Literature of Terror* for an introduction to the Gothic, Nina Auerbach's *Our Vampires, Ourselves* for a history of vampires in relation to culture, and David Glover's *Vampires, Mummies, and Liberals* for an analysis of Stoker's literary career. The other works listed below offer readings of *Dracula* from various theoretical positions. These positions often overlap; the section headings should be taken as broad guidelines to critical approaches, most of which engage in some sense with poststructuralism. Works are listed chronologically.

EDITIONS

Bram Stoker, *Dracula*, ed. Maurice Hindle (Harmondsworth: Penguin, 1993). Includes biographically focused introduction, notes, brief selections from Stoker's correspondence with Walt Whitman, and Charlotte Stoker's account of 'The Cholera Horror'.

——, *Dracula*, ed. Leonard Wolf (New York: Plume, 1993). Provides highly detailed annotations and brief excerpts of commentary from contemporary horror writers on the legacy of *Dracula*.

——, *Dracula*, ed. Nina Auerbach and David J. Skal (London: Norton, 1997). Includes brief preface, contextual information, reviews, and recent essays on both book and films.

——, *Dracula*, ed. Maud Ellmann (Oxford: Oxford University Press, 1997). Includes introduction and notes.

——, *Dracula*, ed. Glennis Byron (Peterborough: Broadview, 1998). Includes introduction and appendices containing contextual material: reviews, other writings by Stoker, contemporary documents on social and cultural topics.

BIBLIOGRAPHIES

William Hughes, *Bram Stoker: A Bibliography* (Brisbane: University of Queensland, 1997).

BIOGRAPHIES

Harry Ludlam, *A Biography of Dracula: The Life Story of Bram Stoker* (London: Foulsham, 1962). Written in cooperation with Stoker's son, Noel Thornley Stoker. Rather anecdotal, and no documentation.

Daniel Farson, *The Man Who Wrote Dracula: A Biography of Bram Stoker* (London: Michael Joseph, 1975). Written by Stoker's great-nephew, highly readable if a little sensational, and no documentation.

Barbara Belford, *Bram Stoker: A Biography of the Author of Dracula* (London: Weidenfeld and Nicolson, 1996). Best documented biography to date.

GENERIC STUDIES: THE GOTHIC

Fred Botting, *Gothic* (London: Routledge, 1996). Essential introduction which demonstrates the variety of ways in which criticism has engaged with the Gothic.

GENERIC STUDIES: THE VAMPIRE

James Twitchell, *The Living Dead: A Study of the Vampire in Romantic Literature* (Durham, NC: Duke University Press, 1981).

Carol Senf, *The Vampire in Nineteenth-Century English Literature* (Bowling Green, OH: Bowling Green State University Press, 1988).

David J. Skal, *Hollywood Gothic: The Tangled Web of Dracula from Novel to Stage to Screen* (London: Norton, 1990).

Ken Gelder, *Reading the Vampire* (London: Routledge, 1994).

COLLECTIONS

Margaret L. Carter (ed.), *Dracula: The Novel and the Critics* (Ann Arbor: University of Michigan, 1988). Useful collection of *Dracula* criticism.

FORMALIST

Carol Senf, '*Dracula*: The Unseen Face in the Mirror', *Journal of Narrative Technique*, 9:3 (1979), 160–78.

David Seed, 'The Narrative Method in *Dracula*', *Nineteenth-Century Fiction*, 40:1 (1985), 61–75.

Alan Johnson, 'Bent and Broken Necks: Signs of Design in Stoker's *Dracula*', *Victorian Newsletter*, 72 (1987), 17–24.

PSYCHOANALYTICAL

Maurice Richardson, 'The Psychoanalysis of Ghost Stories', *The Twentieth Century*, 166 (1959), 419–31.

C. F. Bentley, 'The Monster in the Bedroom', *Literature and Psychology*, 22 (1972), 27–34.

Stephanie Demetrakopoulos, 'Feminism, Sex Role Exchanges, and Other Subliminal Fantasies in Bram Stoker's *Dracula*', *Frontiers* 2:3 (1977), 104–13.

Richard Astle, 'Dracula as Totemic Monster: Lacan, Freud, Oedipus, and History', *Sub-Stance*, 25 (1980), 98–105.

Gail Griffin, '"Your Girls That You All Love Are Mine": Dracula and the Victorian Male Sexual Imagination', *International Journal of Women's Studies*, 3 (1980), 454–65.

Geoffrey Wall, '"Different from Writing": Dracula in 1897', *Literature and History*, 10:1 (1984), 15–23.

Philip Martin, 'The Vampire in the Looking-Glass: Reflection and Projection in Bram Stoker's *Dracula*', in *Nineteenth-Century Suspense: From Poe to Conan Doyle*, ed. Clive Bloom et al. (Basingstoke: Macmillan, 1988), pp. 80–92.

Friedrich Kittler, 'Dracula's Legacy', trans. William Stephen Davis, *Stanford Humanities Review*, 1 (1989), 143–73.

MARXIST AND HISTORICIST

Burton Hatlen, 'The Return of the Repressed/Oppressed in Bram Stoker's *Dracula*', *Minnesota Review*, 15 (1980), 80–97.

John L. Greenway, 'Seward's Folly: Dracula as a Critique of 'Normal Science', *Stanford Literature Review*, 3:2(1986), 213–30.

Rosemary Jann, 'Saved by Science? The Mixed Messages of Stoker's *Dracula*', *Texas Studies in Literature and Language*, 31:2 (1989), 273–87.

Kathleen L. Spencer, 'Purity and Danger: Dracula, the Urban Gothic, and the Late Victorian Degeneracy Crisis', *ELH*, 59:1 (1992), 197–25.

Daniel Pick, '"Terrors of the night": Dracula and "Degeneration" in the Late Nineteenth Century', *Critical Quarterly*, 30:4 (1988), 71–87.

Jennifer Wicke, 'Vampiric Typewriting: Dracula and Its Media', *ELH*, 59 (1992), 467–93.

FEMINIST AND GENDER CRITICISM

Carol A. Senf, '*Dracula*: Stoker's Response to the New Woman', *Victorian Studies*, 26:1 (1982), 33–49.

Anne Cranny-Francis, 'Sexual Politics and Political Repression in Bram Stoker's *Dracula*', in *Nineteenth-Century Suspense: From Poe to Conan Doyle*, ed. Clive Bloom et al. (Basingstoke: Macmillan, 1988), pp. 64–79.

Marjorie Howes, 'The Mediation of the Feminine: Bisexuality, Homoerotic Desire, and Self-Expression in Bram Stoker's *Dracula*', *Texas Studies in Language and Literature*, 30:1 (1988), 104–19.

Alison Case, 'Tasting the Original Apple: Gender and the Struggle for Narrative Authority in *Dracula*', *Narrative* 1:3 (1993), 223–43.

Talia Schaffer, '"A Wilde Desire Took Me": The Homoerotic History of *Dracula*', *ELH*, 61 (1994), 381–425.

Notes on Contributors

Stephen Arata is Associate Professor of English at the University of Virginia. He is the author of *Fictions of Loss in the Victorian Fin-de-Siècle* (Cambridge, MA, 1996) and of a number of essays on late Victorian and early Modern fiction and culture.

Nina Auerbach is Professor of English at the University of Pennsylvania. Her publications include *Our Vampires, Ourselves* (Chicago, 1995); *Private Theatricals: The Lives of the Victorians* (1990); *Romantic Imprisonment: Women and Other Glorified Outcasts* (New York, 1985); and *Women and the Demon: The Life of a Victorian Myth* (Cambridge, MA, 1982). With David J. Skal, she has recently edited Bram Stoker's *Dracula* (New York, 1997).

Elisabeth Bronfen is Professor of English and American Studies at the University of Zurich. A specialist in nineteenth- and twentieth-century literature, she has also written articles in the areas of gender studies, psychoanalysis, film, cultural theory, and art. Her recent book publications include *Over Her Dead Body: Death, Femininity and the Aesthetic* (Manchester, 1992) and a collection of essays entitled *Death and Representation*, co-edited with Sarah W. Goodwin (Baltimore, 1993). She is currently editing the German edition of Anne Sexton's poetry and letters, and writing a short monograph on Sylvia Plath for the Writers and their Work series. Her forthcoming book is entitled *The Knotted Subject: Hysteria and its Discontents*.

Christopher Craft is Assistant Professor of English at the University of California, Santa Barbara. He is the author of *Another Kind of Love: Male Homosexual Desire in English Discourse, 1850–1920* (Berkeley, CA, 1994); his essays on literature and sexuality have appeared in *Representations*, *Genders*, and various anthologies.

David Glover teaches English at the University of Southampton. His most recent book is *Vampires, Mummies, and Liberals: Bram Stoker and the Politics of Popular Fiction* (Durham, NC, 1996). He has published widely on cultural theory and popular fiction and is currently the editor of the journal *New Formations*.

Judith Halberstam is Associate Professor of Literature at the University of California, San Diego. She is the author of *Skin Shows: Gothic Horror and the Technology of Monsters* (Durham, NC, 1995) and co-editor with Ira Livingston of an anthology called *Posthuman Bodies* (Bloomington, IN, 1995). She has just completed a book called *Female Masculinity* forthcoming 1998 from Duke University Press and has written the text for a book of photographs of drag kings by Della Grace called *Drag Kings: Queer Masculinities in Focus.*

Franco Moretti teaches Comparative Literature at Columbia University. He is the author of *Signs Taken For Wonders* (London, 1983), *The Way of the World* (London, 1987), and *Modern Epic* (London, 1996).

Rebecca A. Pope teaches English and Cultural Studies at Georgetown University. Her publications include *The Diva's Mouth: Body, Voice, Prima Donna Politics*, co-authored with Susan J. Leonardi, and many essays on a wide variety of topics, ranging from detective and Gothic fiction, to the cultural narratives of AIDS, to the erotics of teaching.

David Punter is Professor of English Studies at the University of Stirling. His publications include *The Hidden Script: Writing and the Unconscious* (London, 1985), *The Romantic Unconscious: A Study in Narcissism and Patriarchy* (New York, 1989), *The Literature of Terror: A History of Gothic Fictions from 1765 to the Present* (Longman, 1980; revised 2 vol. edition, 1996), and *Gothic Pathologies* (Macmillan, forthcoming 1998).

Phyllis A. Roth is Professor of English and Dean of the Faculty at Skidmore College. Her publications include *Bram Stoker* (Boston, 1982), *The Writer's Mind: Writing as a Mode of Thinking* (Urbana, IL, 1983), and *Critical Essays on Vladimir Nabokov* (Boston, 1984).

Index